Modern Book of the Black Bass

Modern Book

OF THE

Black Bass

by Byron Dalrymple

STOEGER PUBLISHING COMPANY

Published by Stoeger Publishing Company
55 Ruta Court
South Hackensack, New Jersey 07606

First Stoeger paperback edition, December 1975

This Stoeger Sportsman's Library edition is published by
arrangement with Winchester Press.

Distributed to the book trade by Follett Publishing
Company and to the sporting goods trade by Stoeger
Industries. In Canada, distributed to the book trade by
Nelson, Foster & Scott, Ltd. and to the sporting goods
trade by Stoeger Trading Company.

Printed in the United States of America

ISBN: 0-88317-060-4

To the THREE Ms and other Ms to come.
Now I can start over, teaching another
generation about fishing!

Contents

Modern Book of the Black Bass

CHAPTER ONE

The Unchanging Basics

BASS WILL BE BASS

It's doubtful that a reader can even imagine what it is like for a writer to sit down at a white piece of paper and actually begin a book. Having written a number of them, I know quite well the awestruck feeling of it. I know that after that first word becomes black on white I will have to live with and anguish over the contents for many months, and be responsible for it forever. Yet there is great satisfaction after a while in watching its growth, and in seeing facts and words shape up into some reasonable order and sequence that a writer hopes will be useful.

In this book I have set as my task an attempt to show readers in some detail what *modern* bass fishing is all about. It is a far cry from what it was even a decade ago. No other fishing sport has come of age so swiftly, none has grown to such national recreational importance, nor has any other reached the heights of scientific approach and techniques. There are logical reasons why all this has occurred, and we will examine these as we progress. But I will say that this is one book about which I had no puzzlement as to how and where to begin.

There have been so many changes in bass fishing, in the waters, the equipment, yes, even in the bass and their food and their habits. All are changes that have come about because of man's imprint upon the environment, and because of the thrust of scientific curiosity. But in the face of all the changes, certain fundamentals have stood like sturdy pilings around which the new currents have swirled. If we are to understand modern bass fishing, we have to be absolutely sure we first are thoroughly familiar with the unchanging fundamentals, the basics of bass personality, species, and life histories.

To some advanced bass fishermen that material is old hat. To beginners it is a mandatory elementary course, like required college or high school English or math. And so this first chapter is a compact rundown on our subjects, the fish themselves, how one species differs from and is similar to the other, where each ranges, which habitats each prefers, how bass spend their time "around the year."

Even the old hand might well review the fundamentals. To be sure, there is nothing new in them. *But that is the whole point.* Once a fisherman knows thoroughly what I have called in the title of this chapter, the "Unchanging Basics," then he is well equipped to let new knowledge, facts gathered from recent experimentation and research, wash like dockside waves or the swirl of stream current around those sedate, timeless pillars. Hopefully the combination will bring to him, like bits of interesting driftwood gathered over many years and finally, triumphantly fashioned into an abode housing his display of art, a whole new approach to bass-angling success.

A good place to begin bass basics is with the fact that technically these fish are not bass at all. They are *sunfishes.* This of course is simply a matter of nomenclature. Tht true basses belong to the family *Serranidae.* These are the sea basses, groupers and several other species of salt water, plus the white perch of salt, brackish, and fresh water, and the white bass and yellow bass of fresh water. The sunfish family, *Centrarchidae,* encompasses all of the freshwater sunfishes plus the subjects of this book, the freshwater black basses. Possibly it would have been better long ago to establish another common name for them, but it is too late now. These largest members of the sunfish family do superficially resemble the sea basses and no doubt the common name originated because of that.

Our several basses have acquired over the years dozens of colloquial names. As examples, a largemouth has been dubbed a bayou bass in some southern areas, a chub, a gray bass, a green trout, a lineside, several kinds of perch, and even a white salmon. The smallmouth has received the same regional treatment, with bronzeback a common name, and brownie prominent in parts of the Ozarks. It has been a river bass, several varieties of trout, and so on. While all such names are pleasant reflections of local admiration and have their place in angling history, I dislike the confusion of them. However, bass fishermen should realize that numerous local names exist, so that they may avoid being misled by them. Fortunately, most fishermen today are fairly well informed about the identity of these fish.

Occasionally a bass enthusiast may be confused, however, by scientific names, and by a modest amount of indecision among ichthyologists about how many species and subspecies there are. Fisheries experts are constantly revising and learning, and not infrequently they decide to change a scientific name of a fish, or to place one in a new genus (grouping within a family). Now and then a bass that has evolved characteristics slightly different from others because it has long been isolated in a specific habitat has been given status as a species or subspecies. This occurs only when the physical characteristics seem different enough to demand such recognition. However, scientists don't always agree among themselves, and some stick to the belief that a certain fish is a distinct subspecies, while others say it is not.

If you happen to read some older books about the black basses, you may see a puzzling scientific name such as *Huro salmoides* attached to the largemouth. Over the past fifty years the scientific name of this fish has had several changes. The *"Huro"* genus is no longer valid. Or, you may hear of the Coosa bass and be puzzled when someone tells you it is the redeye bass. Or, you'll hear the spotted bass referred to as the Kentucky bass, a reasonable reference since this fish was first discovered in Kentucky. Subspecies will also be confusing at times. The "splitters" among scientists have a horrible habit of trying diligently to discover differences among fish from every watershed, and to give them individual subspecies status. It *is* important to science continually to investigate changes that occur through evolution. But most laymen do not need to bother the' brains unduly about subspecies designations, and especially so far as fishing techniques are concerned.

For instance, there is the Florida largemouth subspecies. A good many ichthyologists believe the outsize Florida bass are truly a subspecies, a product of environment different enough to be recognized not as a full-fledged species but as a subspecies. Others disagree. The spotted bass has given all kinds of trouble, mostly because so little knowledge has accrued concerning it over the years. Some fisheries people have named a spotted bass subspecies from a single stream of Oklahoma's Wichita Mountains. Another subspecies—presumably authentic because its scale size differs from that of the species—is the Alabama spotted bass, a fish of the Alabama River system. In fact, this is the fish that presently holds the spotted-bass size record.

No doubt new subspecies or perhaps even species of bass will find their way onto the list in coming years, one or more now recognized generally may be deleted. The American Fisheries Society, the organization that attempts to keep tabs on such matters, presently recognizes *six* full-fledged bass *species*. For easy reference these are listed below, with their present scientific names. All, please note, are currently placed in the same genus of the sunfish family.

Largemouth Bass	*Micropterus salmoides*
Smallmouth Bass	*Micropterus dolomieui*
Spotted Bass	*Micropterus punctulatus*
Redeye Bass	*Micropterus coosae*
Suwannee Bass	*Micropterus notius*
Guadalupe Bass	*Micropterus treculi*

THE LARGEMOUTH

I've always admired the earthy practicality of the name "largemouth." It not only identifies the species rather well, but also says much about its personality. The largemouth bass is America's all-out favorite sport fish. It is the most adaptable of all. It lives happily in climates from the subzero winters of southern Canada to deep into Mexico's deserts. Originally native to the Great Lakes and Mississippi system, east to New England, south throughout Florida and westward into eastern Texas, it is now found, by transplant and successful establishment, border to border and coast to coast.

The largemouth is fundamentally a lake fish. It occurs in scores of streams, too, but does not do well in cold, swift streams. Large, slow rivers sustain it, and in faster, smaller streams it is able to get along nicely in the pools where the current is only moderate. But the lakes are where it colonizes best. And these include waters of infinite variety, from farm ponds to the largest impoundments, from much of the Great Lakes waters to the brackish waters of East Coast marshes. Over such an enormous expanse, and variety of abodes, forage is just as varied. Into that huge maw goes every conceivable living item the fish is able to grab. This fish is not selective. But the largemouth—indeed all the basses—are strictly predaceous. They are not scavengers, seldom take dead items unless in error. Insects, aquatic and terrestrial, small fish, frogs, crayfish, snakes, snails, small birds—the largemouth is not fussy. "If it moves, eat it," is a kind of motto of the species.

This bass prefers weedy habitats, and those with submerged debris such as logs, stumps, drowned timber. It can and does make do very well in rocky situations, but not by preference. Clear waters, murky waters—the largemouth thrives in both. I've taken them from northern lakes so clear one could see bottom at fifteen feet, and I've also caught hundreds from ranch tanks so fertile I wondered how the fish could find the lure or bait.

Probably the average adult largemouth that northern fishermen catch runs around one and one-half to two pounds. The average trophy fish in the North, where growth is slow because of short growing seasons, is a bass of five or six pounds. Some, to be sure, grow larger, up to ten. In the South the largemouth has longer growing seasons and average fish and trophy fish both are larger. Bass of two and three pounds are everyday fare, and "mounting" fish of ten and twelve are not uncommon, particularly in Florida. The maximum reaches up above twenty, although largemouths of fifteen and eighteen pounds are already exceptional.

It is interesting to note that in parts of Florida the largemouth grows around the year, with the result that in some cases its age cannot be determined because there are no annual growth rings on the scales. Also, while the largemouth ordinarily spawns only once a year over most of its range, Florida bass may be found spawning here and there at any time of year. The subspecies recognized as the Florida largemouth bass, *Micropterus salmoides floridanus,* is the only presently recognized subspecies, and differs only in scale counts along the lateral line, on the cheek, and the number or rows of scales above and below the lateral line. Its size is clearly a matter of environment, and fisheries people believe there are intergrades of this subspecies with the type species as one moves north into Georgia.

The largemouth is of course the bass 90 percent or more of bass fishermen catch nowadays, and so it is important to be informed technically how to make positive identification, and also to realize how widely color may differ. Ordinarily only largemouths will be caught in a given water. But there are exceptions, where both smallmouth and largemouth, or even spotted bass as well, may be found inhabiting the same lake or stream.

The mouth of the largemouth is a chief point of identification. Close the mouth and you will note that the rear of the upper jaw extends back to a point well past the eye. That is, a straight line drawn down from the rear edge of the eye will intersect the rear portion of the fish's upper jaw. Another good point of identification is the dorsal fin. The forward spiny portion and the rear soft, or rayed, portion are very nearly separate fins. Only a barely noticeable bit of tissue connects them. In other basses the dorsal is either continuous or more nearly so. There are other points of positive identification, but the two above are all one really needs.

Color of the average largemouth is greenish above, white below. But in some waters specimens are almost black above, and in very murky waters extremely pale and silvery. A dark lateral line is evident along the sides of younger fish but in old bass it sometimes disappears. Individual fish show varied blotchy dark markings along the side, and the patterns frequently change when bass are fighting on a hook, or when taken from the water.

The largemouth spawns at somewhere between 62 and 65 degrees of water temperature. It may spawn at higher temperatures, but not usually below 60 degrees. This bass has, however, a wide temperature tolerance, which makes possible its establishment in shallow, extrawarm waters and in others where water temperature seldom gets above that needed for spawning. A most striking attribute of the largemouth from the angler's viewpoint is that the species is not only exceedingly predaceous, but also greedy, and what may be termed "irascible." When feeding it tends occasionally toward gluttony and can be tempted sometimes even when fed full. The smallmouth seldom shows such tendency. The largemouth can also be "pestered" occasionally into striking, apparently out of annoyance. Conversely, the smallmouth seems to have better self-control.

THE SMALLMOUTH

The smallmouth bass is a quite different fish personality. It is much more highly specialized, less adaptable. Although some anglers visualize the smallmouth as a hardy species because it accepts cold waters, this is not the case. The smallmouth is difficult to handle and manage, and its requirements are so specific as compared to those of its relative that its range and numbers are restricted. In addition, minor degrading of any smallmouth habitat usually has a drastic effect. The largemouth is vastly more tolerant of less than optimum situations.

Although anglers may argue the point, it is generally acknowledged that the smallmouth is a more spirited fighter than the largemouth. It is built somewhat deeper and more chunky and muscular. Oddly, the shape of smallmouth bass varies widely from place to place, whereas that of the largemouth seldom does. I have seen hundreds of smallmouths from Lake Michigan that were so short and deep they appeared almost hump-shoul- dered. I recall a lake in Wisconsin from which I've seen a number of smallmouths that were close to the "saucer" shape of old bluegills.

Basically the smallmouth is a stream fish. But studies show that its requirements are so strict that only a modest number of streams, compared to the total, are suitable. Swift flow is required, but within strict limits. One noteworthy study that tells much about where to locate smallmouths determined that the gradient, or "pitch," of a stream where this bass is able to colonize most successfully runs from not less than four feet per mile to no more than twenty-five feet per mile. Note well that many trout streams exceed that swiftness. Of course some stretches of well-rated small- mouth streams do, too, but the streams renowned for stable smallmouth populations fall chiefly within that category. Moreover, in streams, a sub- stantial percentage of riffles in any given stretch is demanded.

There are scores of smallmouth lakes, too. But here also this bass is restricted because it is intolerant of murky waters, and too-soft soil bot- toms, and extensive weed beds. It is a fish of clear, only moderately fertile lakes at least twenty-five feet or more deep, mostly with rocky shores, and gravel shoals. I remember a north Michigan lake that contains both species, where I have fished scores of times. It had some gravel, but expanses of weed-bed shoreline also and a rather soft bottom. Of a hundred bass caught here, not more than one or two would be smallmouths. This illustrates that the habitat was marginal.

The water temperature must reach at least 60 degrees before small- mouths can spawn. But the smallmouth is much inhibited by extremely high temperatures. It finds the high seventies difficult, whereas largemouths can tolerate water temperature in the eighties. Thus, the smallmouth is "boxed in" by its preferences. For example, many streams that are slipping as trout streams will not suffice for establishment of smallmouths because the bass, though it can live well in cold water, cannot spawn below 60 degrees. On the other end of the scale, it cannot colonize in southern waters because they are too warm and the streams mostly too slow.

Originally the smallmouth had a far smaller range than most fishermen realize. It was a fish of the lower Great Lakes, on down into the Ozarks and portions of the mountainous mid-South. It was not a native, for example, in New England, but was introduced there and over large areas of southern and eastern Canada. Today it can be said to range across the northern half of the U.S. because it has been stocked in the West. But the "range" everywhere is spotty because the fish insists on several noted features of habitat.

The food list of the smallmouth does not match in length that of its relative. The fact is, its habitat does not produce as wide a variety. Minnows, crayfish, aquatic nymphs, leeches are staples of its diet. It does take surface insects, but is by no means as avid a surface feeder as the largemouth. Nor is the smallmouth gluttonous. It feeds full and then stops. It is a product in all ways of its sparse and spartan habitat. Smallmouths at maximum seldom run over six pounds, even though the record is almost twelve. Most average stream fishing produces fish to a pound or a bit better. Locations—lake or stream—where fish of three and four are caught are great finds, and uncommon.

Because of smallmouth habitat preferences, fishing for it is more specialized, too. As one example, largemouths often spawn in water only a couple of feet deep. But smallmouths, because they prefer extremely clear water, frequently spawn in lakes anywhere from six down to fifteen feet or more. Obviously a fish on a bed that deep pays little or no attention to a surface lure, whereas largemouths can be taken with deadly effect from spawning beds by using surface lures.

The rear point of the smallmouth's upper jaw does not reach back past a vertical line drawn about through the middle of the eye. And both spiny and rayed dorsal-fin portions are one, with only a slight dip between them. The general smallmouth color is a bronze-green or brassy above and white below. There are darker blotches in irregular pattern along the sides, often all over the upper two-thirds of the body, and there is no distinct dark lateral line. General color differs, just as in the largemouth, in different waters. Some smallmouths are yellowish to clay colored, others very dark. There are three more or less distinct dark stripes fanning out rearward from the snout to the rear of the gill cover. The impression the smallmouth invariably gives is of a close-coupled, chunky fish compared to the more elongate, head-heavy appearance of the largemouth.

Because the smallmouth was somewhat indiscriminately transplanted, often by rail, in early years and with more specific purpose more recently, it has turned up in a number of watersheds where it is isolated and far removed from its original habitat. This of course has evolved strains of smallmouths which appear at least superficially different from the type species. Whether they should be given subspecies status is questionable. At least one such has been named, however, the Neosho smallmouth, *M. dolomieui velox,* a subspecies found in the Neosho River and streams emptying into the Arkansas from Missouri, Arkansas, and Oklahoma.

THE SPOTTED BASS

At one time some fishermen believed they had caught crosses between largemouth and smallmouth when they pulled in spotted bass. This bass was presumed by others to be a true species, but it was not properly identified until the late 1920s. It was called the Kentucky bass, but "spotted" bass is a much better name, for it helps to distinguish the species.

This fish is important to anglers over a fairly large range of the mid-South and South. It is in the Mississippi drainage from the Ohio on south, and covers the Deep South from parts of northwest Georgia and western Florida across into northeastern Texas, parts of eastern Oklahoma, and southeastern Kansas. So far little interest in transplants has been shown.

On the average it is not a large fish. I have caught spotted bass in Texas that were mostly in the half-pound to one-pound category, and in Alabama never more than that, at least where I fished. But it has been well authenticated that spotted bass in some habitats do grow much larger, and a good many bass addicts nowadays are desirous of taking a trophy fish for mounting. Lewis Smith Lake in Alabama has been a hot spot for the past few years, with numerous spotted bass of four and five pounds taken and one of eight pounds.

The spotted bass is not always easy to identify. The vertical line projected from the rear of the upper jaw through the eye usually falls a bit to the rear off center of the eye, whereas this line on the smallmouth is centered, and on the largemouth projects across behind the eye. That, however, is tricky. One apparently infallible checkpoint is the tongue, which has a little spot of teeth on it. Other basses lack these. The "spotted" name arose from the scale coloring below the lateral line. Scale bases are dark, forming longitudinal rows of small spots. On most specimens there are dark markings on the sides that show a distinct diamond shape. The lateral line is made up of dark blotches. The upper general color is green to olive, with the underparts of course whitish. The rear of the gill cover may have a dark spot.

In habits and habitat preferences this fish really does seem to stand midway between largemouth and smallmouth, but leans more toward the smallmouth. It is most often found in streams, but of less pitch than those preferred by smallmouths, a gradient of three feet or less for each mile. Some of the rivers where spotted bass are found in the northern part of the range are large, like the Ohio, others are medium sized, and the bass appear to spend most of their lives in the long pools, not the swifter waters. However, in the South they are found in numerous lively clear streams with gravel bottoms. I recall riding on an old mule-drawn wagon several miles back into the forest in central Alabama to a stream where my host assured me I'd catch smallmouth bass. We didn't. We caught spotted bass, and the stream was sprightly, handsomely clear, and with gravel riffles.

This bass requires clear, deep lakes, too. It has been taken, in lakes where smallmouth and largemouth also occur, much deeper than the others, down in fact to seventy-five and one hundred feet. However, this is unusual. While the lake fishing will turn up larger specimens, the modest-sized clear streams of the South that offer this active, hard-fighting little bass are a great pleasure for an angler who is after classic enjoyment, and not necessarily trophies. Many dedicated bass anglers will want to catch this fish simply to fill out their bassing experience.

Feeding habits are much like those of the smallmouth, but in a warmer clime. At least two subspecies have so far been acknowledged, the Wichita spotted bass, *M. punctulatus wichitae,* from the Wichita Mountains in Oklahoma, and the Alabama spotted bass, *M. p. henshalli,* found in the Alabama River system. It is this last-named subspecies that holds the eight-pound record from Lewis Smith Lake in Alabama.

THE OTHER BASSES

The three remaining bass species all have extremely restricted ranges. Of most interest to sport fishermen probably is the redeye bass. This bass is without doubt a close relative of the smallmouth. It did not receive recognition as a species until 1940. It is found in several southern river systems, usually in the upland tributary streams, among which are the

Alabama, the Savannah, Florida's Chipola, and the Chattahoochee. Although it is found in ponds along the tributary streams, it is predominantly a stream species, and indeed requires stream environment in which to spawn. Thus it is certain to remain range-restricted. There is at least one recognized subspecies, from Georgia's Flint River.

Local fishermen have often confused this fish with the smallmouth. It is not easy to identify by markings. The sides usually have faint bars, but the jaw joint in relation to eye is about the same as in the spotted bass. The red eyes—just as the name states—are probably the best point of identification. Also, until these fish grow old they are ordinarily brightly colored, with the tail and the anal and dorsal fins distinctly reddish. Later the color is less prominent. Vertical dark bars show also on younger fish but become less distinct with age.

What keeps anglers within range of the redeye bass incessantly mesmerized is that specimens of large size are known to exist. The average is small, less than a pound. But some waters produce a good many up to two pounds, and occasional catches up to above four pounds have been made. No official record is known, but the Flint River subspecies has turned up fish to six pounds. Thus, this bass, like the spotted variety, is a challenge to the bass fisherman who desires to round out his experience and put a trophy of each on his wall. A most intriguing trait of the redeye is that it feeds heavily on surface insects, which gives it an attribute highly esteemed by fly fishermen.

The Suwannee bass is a most unusual little fish and inordinately handsome for a bass. But it hardly draws much weight as a sportster, because it seldom weighs over half to three-fourths of a pound and averages from ten to twelve inches long. It was discovered about thirty years ago in a Florida spring-fed stream and since then has been noted in several Florida rivers, including the famed Suwannee for which it is named.

Some years ago, I regret to recall, I was fishing for weeks on the Withlacoochee River in Florida and caught several small bass I could not properly identify. They were reminiscent of the spotted basses and the redeye, with hints of the smallmouth, but an added feature was what I'd call a bright baby-blue coloring underneath and along the lower jaw and the throat and extending less brilliantly rearward along the belly. They were unquestionably specimens of the Suwannee bass, now known to inhabit that river. Right now I wish mightily I had been able to identify them, and had had one mounted for a bass collection. At that time the species had been recognized less than ten years and not in that river. Readers may wish to try to collect one.

The Guadalupe bass is a Texas species, practically on my doorstep, since it is named for the Guadalupe River which flows near my home. However, I have never to my knowledge caught one. It is a difficult fish to identify, presumably a relative of the spotted bass, which it resembles and with which it is confused. It is a small species of the Guadalupe, (Texas) Colorado, and San Antonio river drainages. To laymen it presents identification problems because differences are based on spine and ray counts in the various fins. It is certainly not even remotely important as a sport fish but only noteworthy from a collector's viewpoint, if one wishes to run up a record of having taken each species.

BASS AROUND THE YEAR

Although food and living conditions differ widely from habitat to habitat, the general routine of bass around the seasons remains similar everywhere. These habits are among the unchanging basics, and it is important that anglers know them. Because the spawning season is the most important event in the year of a bass, let us begin with it to launch this brief tour around the seasons.

As we have seen in our discussions of the several species, when the water temperature rises to the proper point the spawning urge is triggered. Roe-heavy females have been growing bulkier over the preceding weeks, and have in fact carried the undeveloped and finally developing roe for months. The males have been feeding heavily during the warming spring months, and are in their best physical condition of the year. The deeper water where all are living before their inshore movement may not have risen to spawning temperature. But the upward temperature trend has set off the restlessness that will end with the migration to the shallows.

It is obvious that activity is tied to latitude also. In the North the spawning season will come later than in the South. In the upper Great Lakes region June will usually be the spawning month, given a normal season. In Florida spawning may be in full swing during April. As noted earlier, some bass in the warmer climes, such as south Florida or Mexico, may be spawning during any month. But the majority, everywhere, will spawn in spring, even though "spring" means a different time depending on latitude.

Some of the year's finest action can be had during spawning. In a few states the opening of the season is set to avoid having bass pressured by anglers during spawning. Traditionally some northern states have used such management tools, but in most states nowadays spring spawning-time fishing is permitted, and except in a few specific cases it does no harm.

The males move into the shallows first. It is the male that fans out the bed. What too many fishermen overlook is that bottom soils and clarity of water and protection of spawning sites from the elements all have total bearing on *where* the fish will be. As mentioned in the section about the smallmouth, it may be found spawning in deeper water than the largemouth simply because the water is so clear. This is a protective urge. Largemouths also will spawn somewhat deeper in direct relation to water clarity. Normally on almost any lake numerous bass beds will be found in given locations fairly close together—that is, scattered over a shoreline area without noticeable pattern—not because the fish are showing gregariousness, but because only a limited number of suitable expanses of shoreline are available.

These selected sites will be in coves and bays, and invariably along shores not buffeted by prevailing spring winds. The fish know instinctively that severe wave action will wash debris and silt into nests, covering the eggs. The most important consideration, however, is *soil*—and few fishermen realize that. Mud shallows won't do, unless nothing else is available. Obviously a fish's choice must be made from whatever its particular habitat offers. Small gravel or hard sand will be selected for bed sites if the fish can find it. Reeds often grow in such bottom soils. This makes reed beds a good bet for spawning bass. Lily pads ordinarily will be over muck bottoms and bass will avoid these, or else in desperation attempt to fan a bed out deep enough to get to firm soil. A well-informed angler can, by checking a lake shore, determine almost exactly where the most beds will be located.

When the males begin to congregate in bedding locations, they first pick and choose for sites, and each will want to have its individual territory, although when bedding locations are few, the nests may be closer together, but seldom closer than twenty to twenty-five feet. While the males are concentrated in these specific areas in the shallows, fishing is excellent, for the competition for food is severe. Presently, with the water temperature no lower than the low sixties, the males begin to fan out the beds.

In a lake of medium or average clarity, largemouth beds will be only a few feet from shore and in anywhere from one and one-half to three feet of water. But in a flat-bottomed cove with good soil, they may be spread out well away from shore. I have seen largemouth beds in Florida along a weedy but firm-bottomed reef fifty yards or more from shore, and I have waded for smallmouths in spring in the Great Lakes when a whole protected bay would have beds all over it. If scattered individual clumps of reeds were present, there was almost certain to be a bed at the foot of each, and in that clear water sometimes too deep to reach even with chest-high waders. The average bass bed is from one and one-half to two feet across, and possibly six inches deep. From above the beds show plainly, invariably lighter colored than the rest of the bottom because of the cleaning the fish have given them.

When water temperature has remained at spawning level or above for several days, the females begin to appear. Each male attempts to herd a female to the nest. Some are skittish, and males may nip at them or bunt them. When the female is convinced and deposits eggs over the nest, the male fertilizes them. But the female deposits only part of her eggs at one time. No very accurate formula has ever been designed to show how many eggs an "average" female bass will carry. But a five-pound female, it is estimated, will have somewhere from 10,000 to 35,000. The female may return to deposit more eggs in the same nest, or she may utilize other nests. Several female bass frequently deposit eggs in the same nest and all are fertilized by the same male.

The male bass, somewhat worn from nest fanning and fertilization of the eggs, stays with the nest to guard it. He swims round and round over it, fanning silt away and making dashes to chase off interlopers bent on eating the spawn. The fish will strike viciously at this time, but with the purpose as a rule not of eating but of doing away with anything that approaches the nest. Depending on water temperature, the eggs hatch within a few days. Largemouth eggs will incubate in less than a week at high water temperature, and smallmouth eggs are known to hatch as quickly as two days after fertilization. The average is probably from five to ten days for both. Male bass may gobble up some of their own fry. But fortunately the male does not stay long with the newly hatched young, usually not more than a week.

Habits differ, however, between largemouth and smallmouth. The former will stay for several days after the young hatch, and the fry remain in the nest while absorbing the yolk sac. Smallmouth males leave the newly hatched young much sooner, and the young fry scatter quickly. They do not remain together, whereas largemouth fry and even young up to an inch or more in length may remain for some time in a family school.

Because smallmouths in so many cases are stream fish, they tend to move up into tributaries where possible in spring to spawn. For them, in moving water, spawning is also somewhat more precarious. In addition, male smallmouths are not always the most dedicated parents, as they are inclined to abandon nests. Temperature drops will cause them to leave, and small predaceous species quickly finish off the eggs, or else silt settles on them and they do not hatch.

In fact, cold snaps will ruin spawning for largemouths, too. Occasionally nests will be prepared, then a cold snap sends the males back to deeper water. If the routine is repeated, it may be that few females get to spawn that year, for they will not deposit eggs if the water is too cold. They hold the eggs and absorb them and a "poor hatch" for that year means a debacle for what would have been that age group of fish. It should be noted that a sharp angler who has the opportunity to study a given lake intimately can observe spawning each spring and can quite accurately predict, by success or lack of a hatch, the effect several years hence when the fry of that year were slated to become adults.

The knowledgeable angler also has at least a general idea about growth rates. This depends primarily on latitude, that is, length of the growing season. But water fertility and abundant or sparse food also influence it. In the North, either the largemouth or the smallmouth, given average to good conditions, will probably be at least seven years old by the time it is one and one-half feet in length—a big bass. In a stream that is of poor quality, a smallmouth may be as much as four years old and still only ten inches or less in length, but in a quality stream habitat a two-year-old smallmouth will be ten inches long. In some optimum lakes smallmouths will grow faster. Southern largemouths grow much faster than their northern kin, particularly the south Florida bass. Feeding experiments in Texas have shown that what may be termed "forced growth" can be obtained in largemouths so that a fish two years old weighs as much as two and one-half pounds.

In one of my lakes, unstocked, I tried stocking an exact number of fish caught from another pond. The bass had been placed in that lake at three inches, but the lake had been far overstocked in error. They grew to an average seven inches, however, the first year. I caught thirty with small flies to avoid injury, and rushed them upstream to the unstocked lake. The next year those fish weighed an average of two and one-half pounds, but the fish in the crowded lake had grown only another two inches!

After spawning, bass scatter out over the lake bottom, again taking up selected abodes. In a later chapter we will discuss in detail their likes and dislikes. The postspawning period is one of eager foraging, and the fish rather quickly gain back their lost weight. But immediately after spawning, the spawned-out and frazzled bass are in poor condition. By a month after spawning it is believed that the summer hangouts and patterns have been well established. The fish are now spending most of their time on or near bottom, and making daily foraging movements into their "hunting grounds."

In streams, smallmouths (and other bass species) will drift down from the tributaries or from their spawning locations and take up regular stations again. In especially warm waters, and during the hottest months, there is apparently a "shuffle" of fish again. This will always be to still deeper water, or to places where currents cool surrounding water to the comfort level. In Chapter 8 we will have a look at precisely what those temperature levels are.

In the southernmost bass ranges, summer and winter lairs may differ little if at all. But wherever water temperature cools appreciably in fall, there will be another shuffle of fish to establish living and feeding quarters. Most of these movements, bear in mind, are not vast cruising expeditions. They are vertical movements, and if suitable quarters are discovered within a few feet up, or down, the bass will settle for those rather than make any long treks. There may be exceptions. Great Lakes smallmouths supposedly range widely during the year. But the Great Lakes, as habitats, are themselves exceptions.

During winter anglers can be misled. Comfort will be the usual desire of a bass, and it may find this in the deepest water rather than in shallower spots. The colder the clime, the more the metabolism of the fish slows and the less food it requires. But bass do not "disappear mysteriously" in winter, as many an old hand used to believe, nor do they become totally inactive. Their habits, in fact, are the same as before, except the comfort factor may become more critical and their food needs less. Winter, remember, also brings similar influences to bear upon bass forage, and so the summer feeding grounds may now become less productive, and the bass less attentive.

In streams, smallmouths will move down, seeking the deep pools for comfort, and will quite often be ganged up in the holes. Concentrations will be found in lakes, too. The angler must search diligently, but when he finds the fish he can have just as good sport as at any other time of year, and sometimes better. These facts, then, are the unchanging basics. Modern bass fishermen have little influence upon them—but, as we shall see, they certainly have caused just about everything else about bass fishing to change!

CHAPTER TWO

Modern Bass Fishing is Different

HOW IT WAS

The memory is as vital and full of drama today as it was on that soft spring afternoon years ago when it occurred. I still can see the dilapidated, flat-bottomed green rowboat that I had rented for fifty cents. One oar was split and the oarlocks were rickety. A tin can in the bottom beckoned every few moments because of the incessant seep that swiftly grew to a slosh of water around my feet.

The place was a small lake outside Ann Arbor, Michigan. Lily pads rimmed its shores, hay fields of the local farms surrounded it, and one farmer had had the sharp business sense to fix up a rental dock of ancient planks and poles to which three scruffy, homemade rowboats were tied. You stopped at his nearby house where a scrawled sign proclaimed this convenience, paid your half dollar for a half-day use of a boat, complete with oars and an anchor contrived from stone and rope.

I was alone, and so eager to be after the bass that I despised having to man the bailing can every few minutes to avoid sinking. I was outfitted with an extralong cane pole to which was tied a length of braided salt-and-pepper line about the same length as the pole. This of course was standard

18

equipment for an average fisherman in those days. But the remainder of the rig was not. Missing was the small bolt nut so commonly used by still fishermen at that time as a sinker. And tied to the end of the line was the most unorthodox attraction possible to imagine. It was a bass bug—a deer-hair bass bug, natural tan in color but with the addition of a brief length of red-dyed chicken feather sticking out the rear end.

I had bought the lure in a small hardware store in Ann Arbor that sold odds and ends of fishing supplies, which were at that time meager and sparse and by today's standards ridiculously crude. It was the first deerhair bass "fly" I had ever seen. And now, with awesome anticipation, I jockeyed the old tub of a craft broadside to the lily pads, stood up well spraddled to keep the tippy boat from dumping me over the side. I swung the line around behind me and with a powerful heave and whoosh flailed ahead, attempting to lay the deerhair lure upon the water.

The line, unlike a fly line with weight designed to carry the fly, had little influence upon the bug, particularly because the newfangled lure itself stubbornly resisted the air. But after some exasperation and many determined attempts, I managed with help of a breeze behind me to get the bug out away from the boat and beside a lily pad.

The breeze was pushing me shoreward. The heavy pole made twitching the bug an exercise chiefly in coincidence. Anyway, I had not the faintest idea what action to give the lure. Fortunately—or maybe unfortunately as it turned out, what with the influence of the occurrence fascinating me with such power that I have been addicted all these years—a bass of possibly a pound took matters out of my hands. There was a swirl and a splash into which the bug disappeared. I reared back, jerking the pole and barely staying in the boat. The bass shot out of the water in a handsome flower of spray, and was etched right there, indelibly, upon memory.

Without regard for ceremony or sportsmanship, I stuck the pole butt into my stomach, bent it as I lifted and swung the hapless bass. I reached forward to seize the line and flop the fish into the boat. I sat down, the pole dropped aimlessly half into the water. I stared at the fish and a glow of immense satisfaction spilled over me. I had just caught my first large-mouth black bass on a fly.

I relate the incident because no other in my long years of fishing experience could better establish the fantastic changes that have come to fishing, and to bass fishing specifically, over what is really an astonishingly brief span of years.

THE OLD AND THE NEW

You see, the incident occurred in 1931, as I write this almost exactly forty years ago. It may seem almost unbelievable to younger readers that the black bass, though fished for by a substantial number of early day anglers throughout the South and over much of the eastern U.S., was not considered through the early part of the 1900s any especially great shakes as a sport fish. It simply was common, and catchable. Cane-pole fishing was the rule, with bait, which usually meant worms, minnows, or crayfish. To be sure, Dr. Henshall had much earlier proclaimed the smallmouth the greatest of sport fishes, and he had even developed deerhair bugs to use for them. But he was one of the few specialists. Even up toward the 1930s the development of *sport* fishing tackle on a mass basis and at prices average anglers could afford was barely getting off the ground.

In fact, the bass plug that we know today in its endless variety of design had not even come into existence until early in the 1900s when James Heddon whittled out the first one at Dowagiac, Michigan, and finally set up a shop to build them. Late in the last century the so-called "bait casting" reels, named because they were intended to cast minnows or other bait (lures castable with such a reel were not then even in popular existence) were individually hand-made gems that cost anywhere from fifty dollars to more than one hundred dollars, a tremendous amount at that time. And it was not until well toward the end of the last century that the first braided silk casting lines were developed.

Rods were of course crude and heavy and stiff even well into this century. The so-called "fly fishing" outfits I remember seeing in the twenties and the early thirties were by today's standards horribly unwieldly contraptions, especially those used for bass. The bass flies of the day—until the advent of the deerhair bug mostly sinking flies—were abominable to cast, too. A book of my own issued in the late forties well illustrates the swiftly changing times. In it I proclaimed as the great advance the new tubular metal rods for both fly and bait casting. Today they are long gone. But at that time glass was considered experimental. Spinning had at that late date barely been introduced to U.S. anglers and only the few knew of it or practiced it.

It is interesting to note that as I cast that bug with the cane pole and still-fishing line, though cork-bodied bass bugs had been invented about 1906, the *popping* bug with its concave face was not even on the scene.

It did not appear until 1934. Meanwhile, however, Heddon had created a stir with his bass plugs. Nevertheless, using "bait casting" tackle to cast artificial lures was actually just getting nicely launched during the twenties, and spurting a bit in the thirties so that it had slowly become a common method for catching bass.

The leap from there to today is one that would confuse the expert of the early years of the century. Keep in mind my first experiment with that bug, and remember that prior to then I had caught bass only with bait—and then take a quick look at today's all-out bass addict. He runs a boat specially designed not only for fishing, but for *bass* fishing. He uses a powerful motor at the rear because he must move over large expanses of water swiftly. But up front he has mounted a small auxiliary electric motor on a folding bracket, for quiet use when he shuts off the big job and begins casting.

The boat is carpeted to avoid noise inside. There is a depth sounder mounted somewhere in the craft. There's an electronic water-temperature gauge handy. He carries hydrographic maps so he can read the lake bottom, which if he is super-hep he speaks of as "structured." On a bracket there are at least three or four rods, selected and set up for varied specialized purposes. The main tackle box is huge, containing dozens of lures, and there is another set aside for nothing but heaps of varicolored plastic worms.

These amazing developments are of course far more recent than the ones I have noted during earlier years. The pace has been swift of late. Fishing for black bass has, indeed, become to some extent more a science than a sport. Or, to put it another way, the new science of bass fishing *is* the new sport. Whether this is good or bad is debatable but to no worthwhile end, for this is how it is, today.

It is all a result, of course, of endless technological progress in this country and of endless study by those scientists all but unknown in earlier years, the "fisheries biologists." By comparison with what was known about bass in the first few decades of this century, today's angler has massive, almost limitless, stores of solid information ready at hand, if he will but seek it.

But there is more than that. It is not the imprint of scientific achievement alone, nor the development of better tackle and other equipment that has made bass fishing what it is today, bringing the largemouth to nationwide prominence as the Number One Freshwater Game Fish—yes, the

Number One, period, fresh or salt—far and away. Consider in addition the curious fact that today there are *more* bass than there have been at any time before or since the Indians had this continent to themselves. Not just a few more—*billions* more. And, they are not range-restricted as they once were. They are virtually everywhere within the contiguous U.S. and well outside those borders. Further, there are literally millions of acres of bass water that were not even in existence thirty or forty years ago, and these have been growing phenomenally over the past several decades and are continuing to do so.

BASS WATERS THEN AND NOW

Perhaps one may more easily visualize what has happened by coming back with me once more to my early days of bass fishing, back even a bit farther than those early-thirties days when I flung the first deerhair lure. When I was a boy we lived in the Thumb area of Michigan, about thirty-five miles from what is now the sprawling industrial city of Flint. Small towns were truly small towns then, and country was truly country. The first bass I ever saw came out of the Flint River. In those years this lovely, slow stream meandered ox-bow by ox-bow through the shady hardwood bottoms of this rolling countryside. Its waters were clear and gentle. Logs and varied natural debris crisscrossed it here and there, forming perfect hides for fish. Today, like many another once-fine though not necessarily famous stream, the Flint is a filthy ditch and dwellings in masses have obliterated the peace and pastoral quality it once had.

The bass were what we called "green bass" or "river bass." Actually some of these were smallmouths, though as a kid I didn't know it. We never caught many, just an occasional one, and invariably on a small frog or minnow, using cane pole and bobber. I mention this small river because at that time it was truly a prominent piece of fishing water in that area and the old hands who were expert enough caught many bass from it. It was typical of stream bass water almost anywhere.

Occasionally as I grew up through grade school and on into high school, someone took me lake fishing. A "bass lake," as anglers then knew them throughout all of the Great Lakes region, was a small lake such as the tens of thousands that still exist in that area, and in others. Many lakes that I came to know should have qualified only as ponds, weedy, with boggy

shorelines and a border of reeds and lily pads. A lake that covered a section—640 acres—was considered a fair piece of water and might be
thought of as a "typical" bass lake.

Oddly, the Great Lakes, which were stiff with smallmouths in certain
areas, were not even fished for bass to any extent. Only a few shoreline
residents knew the bass were there, until years later. So, if you were going
bass fishing, you went to a stream like the Flint, or to one of the many
small lakes that were scattered everywhere. No one caught many large
bass—I mean bass of five to seven or more pounds. The fact was, few
fished properly for big bass, as they would realize now if the experts of
that day were still around. When a bass of three pounds was brought in,
everybody had to have a look at it or at least retell the tale and embellish
it. Nor were many large strings of bass caught. A fellow who wound up
with five or six had, we all were sure, some "secrets" nobody else knew.
Compare that to the present-day science-oriented tournaments where a
single boat may bring in sixty pounds or more of bass in a single afternoon!

Much the same general types of bass waters existed and were fished by
bass enthusiasts of the day over most of the northern half of the bass range.
But bear in mind, now, that the black bass—and I'm speaking now chiefly
of the largemouth, which is and undoubtedly always will be the most
abundant of the species—had by no means the large geographic range it
enjoys today. Very generally, it was found in moderate to warm waters
only over most of the eastern half of the U.S. The Mississippi Valley was
roughly the cutoff point westward, with the range extending of course
somewhat past that and down into eastern Mexico. Southern Canada also
had some largemouths in the same longitudes, north a short distance, that
is, as far as water temperature and other water conditions would allow.

Some of the great bass waters of the Mississippi Valley in those early
days were the old "river chutes" or cutoffs—small lakes and bayous formed
from flooding that remained more or less permanently. They're still good
today. In the Deep South, where largemouths were locally called "green
trout," the natural waters were certainly much as they are today, and teeming. But a lot of the lakes and sluggish streams were not accessible to any
but local fishermen, and the bass, though impressively abundant, was considered far below the catfish for table use. Except via the cane pole, sport
fishing as such in fresh waters of the Deep South was not pursued at all
extensively. As I've said earlier, bass were simply common and catchable.
Old-timey southerners were in fact occasionally puzzled by northern fancy-

tackle "sports" who invaded the swamps seeking bass for fun. In the early decades of the century, it didn't make much sense.

An event that occurred only a couple of years after I caught that first bass on a fly was to have, eventually, vast influence upon U.S. bass fishing, in fact to change it completely, although few bass fishermen of today recognize it. Congress in 1933 established the Tennessee Valley Authority —TVA. One of the early dams was Norris, completed in 1936, and forming a lake larger than local fishermen had ever seen. All told, TVA in due course built or took over twenty-six major dams on the Tennessee River and its tributaries. Here, flung across an enormous region that formerly had only streams and a few small natural lakes, were huge "inland seas" ripe and ready to bring forth billions of black bass. Which they did.

But this was only for starters. The U.S. had almost unwittingly entered its great period of dam building, which still continues today. Many of these dams were needed, many perhaps were not. Many are planned today that may be ill-advised projects. But the fact still remains that from border to border and coast to coast large impoundments have appeared, and these, in today's world, make no mistake about it, are *the* important bass waters. The welter of large impoundments has formed an almost limitless aggregate reservoir and breeding ground for the black bass, and the opportunity for thousands of bass to grow *big*. To be sure, the small lakes such as I fished in boyhood still exist and are fished. The natural waters of the South and elsewhere are still immensely important. But far and wide across the nation the *man-made lakes* are where the *most* bass are, and where most of the *big* bass are, and where at least 75 percent of the *bass fishermen* hold forth. They are the home base of *modern* bass fishing. They sparked it.

THE BIG NEW WATERS

The various trouts were of course the aristocrats of freshwater fishing for many, many years. They still remain so to numerous fishermen today. But the fragile home waters of these fish early began to be despoiled by civilization, thereby in effect progressively limiting their range. Meanwhile, the fashioning of the huge impoundments was ever increasing not only the *amount* of water black bass inhabited, but the amount of *quality habitat,* and these new waters were also extending bass range over enormous expanses of the U.S. where few, or none, had ever previously existed. This placed the black bass rather suddenly at the doorstep of millions of anglers who had never caught one, or at least had caught few, and who had never caught a trout and never would. As tackle became more and more refined, anglers began to understand that the black bass was indeed a fabulous sport species, and just possibly even less predictable and more whimsical and challenging than the highly touted trout.

Thus it has evolved that in this generation by far the majority of fresh-water fishermen are bass fishermen primarily. And, a great number have been brought up hardly realizing that there is bass fishing of any real con-sequence *except* on the large impoundments. As mentioned, the natural lakes are still utilized. But the big man-made lakes are where the heady action is. Most youngsters do their first bass fishing with their fathers on a reservoir such as Dale Hollow, Table Rock, Sam Rayburn. Their fathers may well have grown up fishing other impoundments that were brand new while they were youngsters. The big bass tournaments are usually held on the impoundments. They receive broad publicity. Annual contests and records kept by several magazines show that the impoundments dominate in producing big bass.

These are seldom modest- to small-sized lakes like those that furnished the action early in the century and on into the 1930s. Most have shorelines of hundreds of miles. They require big boats, heavy, fast motors. They demand all the scientific paraphernalia and accoutrements toted by modern bass anglers. They dictate the use of specialized tackle. And the successful fisherman must apply extremely refined knowledge if he expects to be successful. But when he learns *how* to handle himself successfully on these new waters, his success so far outshines that of former years as to leave no comparison possible.

In spreading the range of the black bass and the amount of water avail-able to it, often with optimum conditions for growth and successful bass colonization available, the man-made lakes brought bass fishing in amazing quantity to not a few locations where people had previously had very little fishing opportunity of any kind. Texas, which today is pushing Florida hard for the title of "Bass Capitol of the Nation" and indeed may be well ahead in quantity of large bass annually taken, serves as an excellent example.

At the turn of the century, aside from saltwater fishing and a few catfish and panfish waters, there was little in that huge state to entice any angler. During the first decade of the 1900s picayune progress was made in im-poundment building. By 1930, however, Texas had more than thirty sizable impoundments. Little fisheries management was involved. Not a great deal was needed, or even thought about. But Texans began now to *catch* bass. More and more were drawn to the new lakes. A decade later the number of those lakes was crowding fifty. By 1950 the total had passed sixty. By then Texans were swiftly becoming bass addicts, and by 1960, with over a hundred large reservoirs in what had once been a near-waterless state, the largemouth bass had become practically the "state fish." Today—as this is written—the latest tally gives Texas 157 impoundments, and the number will have grown by the time this is read. Texans are, as they themselves say, "bass crazy."

On the border with Mexico there is Falcon Lake, with almost 100,000 surface arres. And the newer Amistad with, at capacity, 84,000 acres, is already becoming nationally famous. There is renowned Sam Rayburn with 153,000, and terrific Toledo Bend, publicized nowadays nationwide, with an astounding 186,000. Dozens of others each cover 20,000 or more surface acres. What may be loosely termed a "southwestern desert state" has thus moved in a few decades from a near-bassless region to one of the most prominent, possibly the most prominent, bass bonanza in the nation.

The same thing has happened elsewhere—in Oklahoma for instance. Once the "dust bowl" at its worst, Oklahoma is now dotted with impoundments. National tournaments are held at locations such as Eufaula Lake. In Missouri, where once the fame all went—not for large bass but for delightful action—to the doughty and usually diminutive smallmouth of the Ozarks streams, now Table Rock Lake, the fabulous impoundment on the White River, has just been named at the time of this writing as the hottest spot in the nation, this year, for numbers of bass above five pounds.

Indeed, the man-made reservoirs have made bass fishing throughout much of the U.S. the Number One angling sport it is today, and they have changed its technology more thany any other development that has occurred in modern times. Today the basic economy of a whole local area, preposterous as it would have seemed years ago, sometimes depends on the bass fishing created by the impounding of a new lake in a water-short region. As an example, Ute Lake in eastern New Mexico, on a tributary of the Canadian River, brings swarms of fishermen—and dollars—to a locale that at one time might have seen bass boats only as mirages. Up in Northwestern New Mexico, Navajo Reservoir on the Pine and the San Juan has placed largemouths spang in the middle of the desert.

The same phenomenon has spread almost everywhere across the country
—California, the Dakotas, Montana, Mississippi—you name it. And, the
black bass has proved itself the one single freshwater game fish of large
size capable of successfully colonizing the majority of these new waters.
With the astonishing recent upsurge of interest in fishing as a recreation,
the adaptable bass has drawn the lion's share of attention everywhere for
several reasons: they are the most commonly available nowadays to the
greatest number of fishermen; they exist, thanks in great share to the new
lakes, in the greatest abundance over the broadest range; they grow large
enough to offer satisfaction and pride to an angler; they cavort on the hook
below surface and above in a manner calculated to sustain angling thrills.

TRANSPLANTS, A BOOST FROM BIOLOGISTS

By placing bass waters, and abundant bass, near fishermen, man has
helped nature to take her course like boy meets girl. But the rise of the
black bass to king of the freshwater sport fishes has also been immensely
assisted by the spread of its accessibility not necessarily in all cases via
impoundments, but by *transplants* to suitable waters where originally no
bass existed.

As I write that, an example crowds my thoughts and I am transported
in memory back to an exciting few days of bass fishing in a setting that
then seemed completely incongruous, a place where, indeed, a couple of
decades previously no bass had existed. We were spending the entire
summer that year in Montana, and I was doing a lot of stream fishing for
trout. One day Bill Browning, the well-known photographer and writer
from Helena, mentioned bass.

"We'd be just about right to hit them big at Mary Ronan," he said.
"Would you like to try?"

I did know that bass had been transplanted to certain Montana waters,
but somehow I could not help thinking of these fish as definitely not
"western." I simply couldn't imagine anything very sensational occurring
with the largemouth here. But I did know Lake Mary Ronan as an excellent rainbow lake and also loaded with kokanee, the land-locked form of
the sockeye salmon. So I agreed to go.

This beautiful lake lies west of huge Flathead Lake, in far western
Montana. When we arrived, Bill admitted he had fished very little for

bass. His fishing life had been dedicated almost entirely to trout. The time was late June. I was guessing that water temperature should be about the same here in a normal spring as in northern Michigan or Wisconsin, where I had fished for bass a great deal. There the bass usually spawned sometime between early and late June.

By good fortune we visited with another fisherman, who assured us I was correct. "The males are swarming in the shallows right now," he said, "looking for bedding sites."

The shoreline had several areas where dense stands of reeds were in evidence. I suspected these were a tipoff to where the bass would be. Thus, a weedless lure was required. I rigged up a plastic worm on weedless hook. But, I used no weight at all at the head. By rigging moderately whippy rods, we were able to cast the light worms fairly well. They sank with a natural wriggling action and could be worked gently among the reeds. For no special reason, I used "baby" blue, and I kidded Browning that this was my secret killer color. It was highly visible, of course, but as we learned before the session was over, almost any color would have caught those eager bass.

When my first strike came, it was a tentative tug. I fed a bit of line. The fish moved away, and I struck hard. I was expecting a small fish. It still didn't seem to me that western Montana was "bass country." My astonishment was therefore overwhelming when the rod jerked downward, the fish peeled line, and I could not get it stopped. After a good bit of tangle and bumble-thumbed operation among the reeds, I did subdue the bass. It was a beautifully fat, deep male that barely missed the five-pound mark.

From there on we fished along the edges, casting into pockets where we'd have a fair chance of fighting our fish. And we simply mopped up. In two full days of hammering away, we caught and released dozens, many in the three- and four-pound class, and with two going to either side of the six-pound line on our scale. This was as fine largemouth fishing as anyone could desire—and here we were way out in "trout country" to which the range of the bass had been stretched by successful transplant.

This is true everywhere westward. For many years there has been good largemouth fishing in lakes barely inland from the saltwater, in coastal Oregon. Southern California is loaded with bass spots, and indeed nowadays many a bass enthusiast fishes there for the Florida strain of largemouth. These were stocked some time ago and have done quite well. You can catch bass in Nevada desert ponds today, and in fact almost anywhere south from southern Canada, coast to coast, to and beyond the Mexican border and the tip of Florida. The big lakes on the Colorado River, as examples, heavily stocked, have brought bass to high prominence far outside the original bass range, in Utah, Arizona, Nevada, and all down along the Arizona-California line. Presently there's even an eleven-plus pound largemouth record from Lake Mead, and a fourteen-plus from Arizona's Lake Roosevelt.

Especially intriguing are some of the western transplants of smallmouths that have been successful. Odd as it may seem, today some of the hottest smallmouth stream fishing in the U.S. is found in certain patches of the Snake River, where it forms portions of the border between Idaho and Oregon and Washington. There is a backpack trek a smallmouth enthusiast can take, in Arizona, following the course of the Black River, which is the boundary between the San Carlos and Fort Apache Indian Reservations. The current record here is over four pounds, which illustrates how successful the fish have been. There are smallmouths in at least two Arizona lakes also, and in others widely scattered outside the original range.

Farm and ranch ponds, of which there are hundreds of thousands in the U.S. today, have done their share also in spreading black bass, mostly largemouths, to new regions. Great numbers of these exist nowadays, particularly in the arid areas of the U.S. where until recent times bass were unknown. They have proved to be amazingly excellent largemouth waters. They have brought untold numbers of anglers into contact with the sport of bass fishing, initiating them and graduating them to larger waters and bigger experiences.

With bass on hand everywhere, with tackle and techniques vastly improved, the black basses have been making history much more swiftly than writers have been capable of recording it. Modern bass fishing, perhaps more science than art, has indeed become a truly *national* pastime!

CHAPTER THREE

Learning From the New Waters

THE PUZZLE OF "BIG"

Interestingly enough, it has been the swift spread of the large impoundments that has forced fishermen to learn more about bass and bass fishing. This is not to say that the original bass waters—the smaller lakes and streams, the larger natural lakes—are nowadays unimportant. But, phenomena occur on the big man-made lakes that can be witnessed and followed in detail from the time it begins to fill until it becomes "of age" and, in some cases "overage" and into decline.

The "coming of age" and "aging" of impoundments, plus management aimed at rejuvenating those in decline, have allowed fishermen to see and understand as well the basic ecology of thousands of smaller natural waters. Those will never be any different from their status quo, never different from what they were yesterday or years ago, because they have reached— unless carefully managed—what might be termed the "stability of mediocrity." But management of the big impoundments, where recreation is emphasized in today's world, often makes possible a sustained level of fishing quality not found elsewhere. And the attention toward management is often a must, directed by laws set up prior even to the building of the impoundment. All of this has been of immense advantage to the bass fisherman.

30

But it goes far beyond that. On these large waters, anglers would be at a total loss except for scientific approaches and techniques. I will always remember my own introduction to a large bass lake, after I had been used to average smaller waters. It had always been fairly easy to come to know a small piece of water intimately. I knew, for example, numerous small lakes where I could set my course toward a certain dead stub, or a saddle in a ridge, and *right there* near shore was *the* spot. Today, as an added example, I own a small Texas ranch and have my own small lake, dammed up on a stream. It is a virtual bass study laboratory. I know every foot of it, and could almost name the bass—a slight exaggeration of course—and tell where each will be. I have another pond at my home in the country, a smaller one, and this also is like a miniature, to be studied. But when I was suddenly turned loose years ago on a large impoundment, I had not the slightest idea what to do.

Nor did any other bass fisherman. Should he fish blind, hither and yon? Many did, to little avail. Others patiently studied, cove by cove. But the casual fisherman has no time for such prolonged research. And so, little by little, the modern science of black-bass fishing *had* to evolve, right on these large and abundant waters. It spread from there of course until today it is practiced by top-notch fishermen everywhere, on waters small and large, and it rubs off even on the dubs. Once you know "how" on the big lake, as it is said, the small one is easy pickins.

To clinch the point, if you go to the trouble to add up the surface acreage of all U.S. impoundments, you will discover that, leaving the Great Lakes out, there is more water in man-made lakes than in all the natural waters. In a state like Kansas, for instance, once practically a nonfishing state, just during the period from mid-fifties to 1970 nineteen large federal reservoirs were constructed. We are approaching, nationally, a total of 1,500 impoundments, and the time when at least half of all fishermen will be using them for most of their fishing, and the time when these waters will account for at least half of all waters open to public fishing. That last point, incidentally, is important, because the large lakes, built with public money, must keep shorelines, or much of their shorelines, and at the least numerous access points open to the public.

Probably one of the most important areas of knowledge that has emerged from the incessant and concentrated study of the reservoirs by both individual fishermen and official sources, federal and state, relates to how much of any given water is *useful* to a bass and thus to a bass fisherman, that is, how much is *inhabited* for any prolonged period by bass. This obviously is of tremendous importance to the success of any fisherman. Though no specific figure can be set up that is applicable to all waters, it is possible to make a blanket statement that in all probability no more than one-fourth of the lake bottom of any lake (impounded or otherwise) is amenable to the daily living requirements of bass. In other words, a bass may pass across a certain piece of water—or bottom—but it does not pause, nor does it live there. It is only en route to an optimum habitat, or a habitat as close to optimum as the water affords.

The importance of this knowledge is clear on the large newer waters. On a small lake you may fail to catch a bass here, or there, but it is easy to make yourself believe they are rather evenly distributed because the total amount of space is small, and the "catching spots" usually not far separated. However, the small lake has just as much "waste" space comparatively as the large one . . . except that on the large one the unlettered bass fisherman who fishes indiscriminately might go for months without a full stringer, except when he happened to stumble upon the areas where the bass actually live.

BASS ARE "OBJECT-ORIENTED"

Many influences are brought to bear upon bass to influence their whereabouts. Food, safety, comfort (i.e., temperature)—all are important. But without going into detail about these at this point, we can say that large waters have forced fishermen to learn two basics: that bass are not fundamentally wide roamers; and that they are what may be termed totally "object-oriented." That is, they invariably lurk or live near some permanent (or occasionally temporary) inanimate object—obvious examples: a stump, a piling, a weed patch, a dock—any item that offers proximity. It is almost as if they have the same need for security that the proximity of some object affords so well illustrated in Linus, the Peanuts cartoon character, and his blanket.

Now of course anglers have been casting plugs to a stump or tree for years, knowing bass like to lurk in such spots. None of us needed to learn that. But until studies progressed, especially on the large new lakes, few fishermen realized how absolute was this fixation of the black bass. Further, while many fishermen thought they knew the "objects" necessary to bass contentment, few realized until fairly recently that the connotation of the word "object" was far broader than had ever been believed previously.

A great deal of study by biologists, lure makers, and others has been done by actually getting right "down among 'em," in scuba gear. In at least one prominent study a two-man submarine was widely used in an impoundment. We know now without question the type of living area a bass likes best. It is one of the modern discoveries that puts heavy stringers in the hands of the anglers who have done their advanced bassology homework. Of course, there are exceptions, as with every rule. Schooling bass to be discussed in Chapter 4 may be away from home base—but only on temporary forays. Changes in light conditions, availability of food, temperature —all may force bass to move from a fairly permanent bailiwick, but only temporarily. If the adverse condition continues, the fish will seek a new and suitable (and comparable) abode. Spawning season obviously disrupts what we are talking about here, but that is a special time of year for the fish.

What are these "objects" which magnetize bass? There is a word in use nowadays, a modern term I'm not fond of because it is reminiscent of bureaucratic gobbledygook. But it does make the point. It is "structure." Hip bass fishermen say the bottom is "structured" or they have located a "structure." Though the term is jarring, it describes well the wide application of "object." A steep point may be the object that draws the bass of that specific area. An old roadbed flooded when the impoundment filled may serve a similar purpose. A large submerged tree is an obvious one. It may have individual fish in residence among branches on, say, the east side, and others on the west side.

A hump on the bottom may be the "object" that mesmerizes the fish. I know, for example, of an old Indian mound that was inundated when a lake filled. Bass invariably are found along its edges. This is an extreme but provocative example. Another striking example concerns Falcon Lake on the Rio Grande in southeast Texas. When this lake filled, the old village of Guerrero on the Mexican side was partially flooded. Residents had of course been evacuated and relocated long before. As in many small Mexican villages, there was a rather fancy plaza, with stone benches; nearby was the little Catholic church. Many a bass has been caught, by myself and numberless others, from under the seats in the flooded plaza, and boats have been known to drift inside the church through the open front to cast there in the shade!

On Toledo Bend Lake on the Louisiana border, swiftly gaining national fame as this is written, I discovered during one trip the ridge line of an old dwelling barely visible below the water. Looking down, I could see a fence, a small shed, and the crumbling house. Trees still stood, thrusting high above water, in the yard. This was a real bass bonanza. The fish had taken over in the buildings as soon as the waters had come and the humans had been forced to leave.

The type of object-magnets present must of course be related by the fisherman to the specific water. A small lake in the north with a clean gravel shore here, and a muck-bottomed pond-lily patch farther up, with a small bay across on the far side where logs are crisscrossed and stumps thrust from the surface, is easy enough to decipher. These are, as we say, "bassy-looking spots." Now drop down to Florida and consider for example one of those small lakes—similar in size to the northern one above —that has neither a stump nor a lily to draw bass, nor any gravel beach to shy from. To be sure, most southern lakes have more cover than the northern ones, but I am visualizing a small lake where I fished recently in central Florida. One side was open and showed a sandy rim at the water-line. The other bore small indentations, and these were thick with maiden cane. To those who may not know this plant, it is a tough grass growing up out of the water. In the deepest portions of the cane fields, and along the deep drops just off them, is where we caught our bass.

Thus we now take a step further in this bottom study. Bass in any given habitat situation must utilize what is available. They cannot have the place "restructured." In this case, the maiden cane was the only "object." Yet if you move to one of the western lakes situated in a barren, rocky desert setting, everything instantly changes. It might confuse the unlettered bass fisherman. But the modern "bass intellectual" will know immediately that here rock ledges, shady submerged rock caves, even a smoothly weathered rock point jutting into a channel all will form abodes for bass. A hulk of a yucca or Spanish bayonet noted below surface is invariably a bass hang-out. A spiny thicket of flooded scrub mesquite or prickly pear may claim some lures, but it will also produce bass.

Every modern bass fisherman knows also that a certain object near which a good bass is caught will continue to produce more bass as others, moved from their homes by some unexplained urge, discover it. This is like finding a spot, which I have done many times, where a good buck deer hung out. Gather him in with your rifle this season, and almost surely another good one will be there next year. It is a *place,* a very *special* place, that big bucks like as a personal bailiwick. The bass fisherman who pursues the study of objects that draw bass, and who keeps tabs on where he caught what, can find success in the same places year after year, as long as no drastic changes in other influences occur.

DON'T WASTE TIME ON EMPTY HABITAT

One reason expert bass anglers nowadays fish the big impoundments so much is that there are more *big* bass in most of them, for the simple reason that there is more room in which they can grow. The reason the most successful fishermen use high-horsepower motors and swift, comfortable boats is that they know success depends on finding the fish. With, as we've said, in most instances as much as 75 percent of the total bottom (or lake) area practically devoid of bass, they must skip from hot hole to hot hole. Otherwise, they waste too much time fishing in fishless water or at least in less than optimum bass situations.

I can recall, as an example, watching an angler cast his arm lame at a shoreline on a certain large impoundment. He was catching bass, too. Most were about half a pound. The first several should have cued him. While a small bass may be found in a big-bass situation, a big bass, except possibly during spawning time, will seldom be found in a surrounding particularly amenable to little bass.

In this instance, the good bass were all behind him. Much of the time (there are exceptions, as we'll see) a fair sort of a rule is that when you are fishing *to* the shoreline, that is, when it is within casting distance, the really big bass are nearly all behind you! To prove the point, as we watched that shore caster we were fishing an area that appeared from "up top" to be simply a wide-open expanse of water. But what we knew was that the bottom didn't look like the top. Before this lake had filled, there had been a creek coming into it here, and the creek had over the years cut a channel. It had also meandered, making several rather sharp turns. Wherever a stream makes such a turn, the outside of the curve is invariably deeper, because the force of flowing water has gouged that side and the eddy has settled silt onto the inside of the bend.

We knew that the creek had sustained brush along its banks, but that the bottom of it should be reasonably clear. Here was an absolutely perfect setup—a palace of sorts, one might say—to furnish lodging for several large bass. It was a "bottom structure." It served as an "object." We got over the creek, right over one of the bends, and we fished straight down, a technique   discussed in Chapter 11, one that has grown immensely popular over recent years on some of the impoundments. We took three bass over five pounds before we moved along.

I use this illustration because it so well emphasizes how one can "read" the new lakes. Of course all lakes, natural and constructed, certainly can be deciphered by using modern-day equipment—depth sounders and temperature gauges. In fact, that's how it's done these days. But in addition lakes that were once desert or forest or stream channel have long ago been mapped, and in many instances anglers who live near one knew the land before it was under water. They know where the good productive spots are, and can hunt them from up top.

Even without such prior knowledge or any scientific equipment the average angler can do a fair job of reading what is below by checking out what is above. For example, on a strange lake, an arm that has bluffs shooting very steeply from the water is probably a deep one. If the bluffs are rock, with ledges and hanging boulders, it's a fairly sure bet the same condition exists below water, and that excellent hideouts for bass are to be found here.

If a flat bog stretches back from one side of a lake, chances are the water is shallow for some distance out into the lake. But if a steep hill slants up from one spot, it probably slants down underwater, too. A stand of pencil-thin, tall reeds along a northern bass lake tells of sandy soil as a rule down below, and it may indicate water at the outer edges too deep for wading. Cattails will grow in more shallow spots, but may also indicate a soft bottom. Lily pads will almost always tell of a mud bottom, and water may be deep at the outer edge, yet the pads may grow right up to shore in shallows muck.

Thus, once you fix firmly in mind that only a small portion of any lake is truly productive, and that the bass will be where the objects or structures are, you are headed in the proper direction. But, you must change your thinking from lake to lake as to what may serve as the appeal points to the fish. It it patently ridiculous to go looking for tree stumps in an arid-country impoundment where only rocks and short vegetation are found ashore. Conversely, it would be just as silly for a fisherman used to such a spot to go hunting rocks in a soft-bottomed lake in Indiana or southern Michigan.

But of all the errors to be avoided nowadays, what with the wealth of knowledge gained by modern bass fishermen and biologists, fishing without a precise plan is the biggest. Casting aimlessly to cover much water is a thorough waste of time. Trying to fish "all over" a lake is a greater waste. Know what you're looking for, hop swiftly from spot to spot that fits where the bass *should* be, and forget all of that just-maybe water. Weather, to be sure, will change the lie of bass on certain days. So will temperature, brightness of light, and feeding conditions. But there are only so many places where the fish are *most likely* to be. If you try these, you will find them, and you'll find at least some of them feeding at some time during any given day. Experts such as the competitive tournament fishermen on the big impoundments prove this time after time, and at any season. They almost always catch bass, not from luck but from systematic knowledge.

BASS ARE HOME BODIES

Not only have modern bass anglers discovered, chiefly through the nudging of necessity on the man-made lakes, that vast expanses of bottom are bereft of possibilities, but they have also learned in the meantime that the black bass is far more of a home body than many had ever thought previously. And, the larger a bass grows, the more sedentary it becomes.

There are logical reasons for this direct relationship between age (size) and specific place. A small, giddy young bass skitters around here and there in shallow water because it has not yet formed attachments to any particular place. It is reasonably safe anywhere. Additionally, most of the small forage upon which the small fish must exist is to be found in the shallows. As the bass grows, it must take larger food, and it begins to react more to specialized safety and comfort factors. When it has become a trophy-sized bass, it will have selected a lair that is truly home. This will be chosen as a hide, and a place where ample food may be garnered with the least amount of effort. There are untold instances where fishermen have located an outsize largemouth and fished several seasons to catch it, deep beneath the same stump or cypress bowl, or in the same deep trench of a lake bottom.

There are of course reasonable exceptions to his home-body rule. It is mostly a matter of interpretation. I do not mean to imply that a bass selects a spot the size of your kitchen tabletop and stays there forever. The slope of a point, the deep tip of a rocky jut, a stretch of flooded creek bottom, a series of rock ledges, a stand of submerged trees—any such area may be home. And, this "home" or living space may encompass a sizable expanse over which the bass, or groups of bass, cruise, forage, fin lazily along, or in which individuals lie in one pinpoint spot for an hour or so, then in another fifty yards distant during some other period of the day. But studies by fisheries biologists and fishermen have well substantiated that most of the bass, and especially most of the larger bass, have rather closely defined limits to their chosen bailiwicks. Further, big bass up to the super-lunker stage have ever more pronounced and fixed habits.

I have watched my own bass hour after hour. Certain large individuals live at one end of my rather narrow lake and so far as I can determine never cruise to the other end. I can see, from rock bluffs above this clear body of water, movements of these fish in detail. I have noted certain fish, or small groups, day after day in the same general location. The home pond is different because it is much smaller. Here there is not enough room for even the small number of bass in it to stake out inviolate territories. So they all cruise round and round, although a willow tree in the middle of the pond usually has a specific large fish or two under the same low limbs.

Extremely large bass—the super-lunkers—are also not altogether tolerant of competition. Small bass consort helter skelter. "School bass," as they are known in waters where the schooling phenomenon occurs—bass usually of one to two and one-half pounds—hang together because of a common purpose: foraging on schools of small fish. They are, at this growth period, at their most agile. Bass of four to six pounds group ever closer and settle into ever more strict routines and preferences, usually in small areas of bottom. But a bass of ten or twelve pounds is likely to be a loner. It is more awkward than the smaller fish, less inclined to go dashing about, and some of them do very little cruising around except when absolutely necessary in order to catch food. They are by that age chiefly lurkers, letting food come to them. This is why, in most instances, a single extra-large fish is taken from a very specific spot, its lair. Also, this is why the real trophy bass are mostly taken by pinpoint fishing right to them. They aren't much for giving chase. They are simply too cumbersome.

My reason for emphasizing that bass do not roam aimlessly but have clearly defined territories is simply to reiterate that *finding the fish* is the most important part of bass fishing. And we know now, chiefly from the mass of knowledge that has accrued from so much study and expert bass fishing on the impoundments, that the fish are located in very exact, and even predictable, places. And that these places are not always where the more old-fashioned or inattentive bass fisherman might believe.

Bass certainly do move around. But a word that has been used incorrectly and that has thrown a great many anglers off the right track is "migrate." I read recently the theories of a rather well-known bass fisherman who used the term. It is the connotation of the word "migrate" that I object to. The dictionary defines "migrate" as "to move from one country or place of abode to another, with a view to residence; and "migratory," as "roving; nomadic." Bass do move, for specific purposes. But they are by no means nomadic or aimless wanderers.

What that fisherman actually meant in his discourse was that the bass had moved from their hangout on a point to a nearby shoreline during the evening to feed. The spree lasted a half hour or so and then the bass slipped back to their former lie, only fifty-odd yards distant. The bass had moved in because of a specific forage situation and as soon as the forage disappeared, they moved back. But they did not necessarily cease feeding. The fisherman simply kept on fishing where the bass weren't. In fact, when you hear a bass angler say the bass have "moved out" or have "migrated," you can usually bet he isn't catching any, and migrating fish is always an easy rationalization. I've heard bird hunters claim quail or pheasants had migrated when they failed to find birds in a favorite spot. The fact is, such sedentary game birds live on a few acres all their lives. When you don't find them, it is because there aren't any. There has been some sort of natural attrition. In the case of bass, however, it is usually that the angler is just fishing in the wrong place.

Possibly we might say that bass really do "migrate" during the spawning season. Certainly many of them do move from deep waters in mid-lake a substantial distance seeking suitable spawning near shore. And when, in the postspawning period, they move back again, perhaps the same individuals do not find their exact lairs of the prespawning period. There may be an exchange and "shuffle." But spawning is a particular phenomenon, and a comparatively brief one. Most of the year bass are homebodies. The prime "catching" difficulty many anglers have is in allowing themselves to be convinced!

CHANGES IN FOOD AND TACKLE

As the new man-made waters have evolved and thus drastically changed the habits of bass fishermen, they have also changed to some extent the habits of bass. Chief among these changes are certain feeding habits. I said earlier in this chapter that bass in any habitat situation must utilize what is available in cover. The same is true of food, and interestingly enough the impoundments have made some striking changes in food chains. Individual large impoundments have afforded opportunity to certain species that had been denied expansion of their populations until the new habitat appeared. When a certain species suddenly seizes the opportunity to colonize a new domain, and does so because of optimum conditions in a veritable blizzard of reproduction, very often the influence upon other species in the same habitat is enormous.

Let me illustrate by beginning with a converse example. Picture a small lake, let's say of one hundred acres. There are largemouths here, and blue-gills, plus several forage species such as one or another variety of shiner or dace. Some portions of the shoreline have lily pads and cattails and form proper living spaces for frogs. Aquatic insects such as mayflies are fairly abundant. On an opposite shore there is an expanse of coarse gravel and stones and this has long been home to a large colony of crayfish.

The food chain has long been established in this lake. Nymphs, fry, and other diminutive tidbits sustain the minnows, frogs, and crayfish. Young crayfish, aquatic nymphs, and surface insects form most of the bluegill diet. Young bluegills, frogs, crayfish, and minnows feed the bass. The ecology of this lake is static. Certain of the species will see up and down cycles, but the restricted habitat offers no new opportunities for expansion here for anyone.

Now move to the site of a large impoundment. It has been planned but not yet constructed. In the river on which the dam is to be placed there are white bass, gizzard shad, and some black bass and sunfish. Because the white bass (*Roccus chrysops*) has recently moved from obscurity to renown, let's use it as an example of a species seizing new opportunity for massive colonization.

I can easily remember the time when the white bass—sometimes called "sand bass," "stripes," and various other local names nowadays—was virtually unknown. It was a fish chiefly of large, reasonably clear streams of the Mississippi system. In a few places it was abundant, but though it is awesomely prolific it did not have at that time enough living room to expand further. In some of the same waters in the mid-South and South there were gizzard shad. These also are exceedingly prolific, but were held in check because they, too, had no further room for expansion.

Now the new dam is built and the big lake fills behind it. Here suddenly is a huge, new, and rich area for colonization. Because white bass and shad are both school fish, and the one feeds upon the other, a wonderful opportunity for instant explosion presents itself, and a veritable eruption of both occurred. Fisheries biologists were quick to realize that the white bass, a voracious species and predominantly a forager upon small fish, and also a good sport fish, was excellent to stock in other impoundments where it had not appeared natively. Thus it swiftly became widely established in dozens of impoundments, especially across the South, Midwest, and Southwest.

In most instances the shad were already present. In some shad were introduced, perhaps unwisely, because they too often monopolize the living room in a lake, crowding out game species. But the white bass, burgeoning broadly, helped to cut down the shad explosions, and within only a couple of decades became one of the best-known game fish of the impoundments. Habitats perfectly tailored for them had been created, and they were able to seize this opportunity for massive, dense colonization.

What does this have to do with black bass? Plenty! Because the black bass, somewhat less prolific than the white, and with specific habitat preferences whereas the whites are open-water roamers and not as restricted, also was offered this grand opportunity. And it too was successful, although on a reduced scale numerically speaking because of the inherent species differences.

Thus the black bass suddenly found itself not in a domain like the small lake, with only frogs, crayfish, dace, and aquatic nymphs, although there were modest numbers of all those. But there was also a fantastic deluge of shad. These oily, plankton-fattened forage fish were rich food for growing bass. They existed in such massive numbers as to be always available, and they were catchable. Groups of bass could slash into densely packed schools of shad and simply gorge themselves. They could push a school against a shoreline and decimate it. And this is precisely what they did. The shad became *the* prime bass food in scores of impoundments, with young white bass another delicacy.

This is the most striking example of the feeding changes brought about because of the expansion opportunities in impoundments. A whole new system emerged in each one because of the *room* involved and because the relationship among the species was not static but evolving as each new lake filled. In those where shad were not dominant, other forage species, offered similar opportunities, thrived. Further, as bass were transplanted and established in natural waters where they had not been native, they faced certain changed feeding conditions. I think of one unique situation where kokanee—also transplanted—are present, and because the kokanee are stocked as fry or very small youngsters, the black bass feed to a large extent on these salmon—a real switch.

Now the changes in foods did not in all cases change the basic habits of black bass greatly. But they did make specific changes. In many impoundments bass go on schooling sprees for the purpose of ganging up on shad, which does not occur on another, shadless lake because there is nothing to initiate the habit. Thus new foods and at least some new feeding habits had to be dealt with by fishermen. A bass might well eat a frog in a lake stiff with shad. But crafty anglers, realizing that the shad was now a prime bass food, began catering to the new preference.

And this is how literally scores of new bass lures have evolved over the past few seasons. Lures that imitate the look and the swimming action of shad have been sold by millions. Other lures devised to imitate other new forage in certain lakes have come into instant popularity with locals and visitors. With the appearance of the plastic worm, bass fishermen quickly realized that the new lakes, with their rich bottoms strewn with natural debris such as brush and down timber, were perfect habitat for aquatic salamanders, small eels, lampreys, and various aquatic worms. Then new types of lines, sinkers, rods, and reels all were needed as time went on, to fish these new and advanced bass lures.

A great many of these new waters could hardly be fished properly with some of the traditional lures because the lures were not "weedless" enough. In Chapter 11 we'll get to the new tackle approaches in detail, but briefly what "weedless" really meant now was that "brushless-ness" and "tree-limb-ness-less" was mandatory. Otherwise too many lures were lost. Spoons and spinners as previously known and used over ordinary aquatic weed beds were just about useless. Thus the weedless jigs and skirted, feathered, and haired "safety-pin" lures—crosses between jig flies and spinners—evolved. They were fitted to, and a result of, the new waters. All of these things modern bass fishermen have learned, and newcomers to the sport must learn them and understand the *whys* to be successful.

CHAPTER FOUR

Learn To Know Bass Better

THE ALL-IMPORTANT BOTTOM

One of the drastic changes that has occurred in modern bass fishing has evolved in the fisherman. They have slowly come to know bass better. Odd as it seems, the average bass fishermen, even those who caught a good many fish in times past, all too often had incorrect opinions about precisely what sort of fish the bass is. Magazine covers for almost a century have been depicting the colorful lure worked in shoreline shallows around weed beds and a huge bass attacking it. They have overworked illustrations of bass lying in wait beside log or lily pad, hanging immobile in a weedy lair barely below the surface. In the mind's eye of the angler, this view of the bass was all too common.

The reasons were logical. Up here at the surface and near shore was where the *fisherman* was. He caught his bass in the classical situations shown in art illustrations simply because that is where he fished. It was also something he could visualize, whereas those mysterious deeps, unseen by the angler, were difficult even to imagine. Most anglers in years past also were not bass specialists. They fished for anything that would hit. Curiously also, because most of the lakes of modest size that contained the most bass were not very deep, the black bass was thought of as a shallow-water fish.

You can check out old fishing books that will tell you a bass is exactly that, a species of surface and mid-water and shallows, seldom found over fifteen feet deep, or twenty at the most. I so well recall in my early fishing

43

days when we used a big nightcrawler or minnow on a hook with a cane pole, and how we set the bobber so the bait was perhaps three feet under, seldom more. Part of this, of course, was because you couldn't handle enough line to get the bait much deeper. We did catch some bass, but most of the time only because the bass happened to be up in shallows feeding at the time, or because the waters where we fished had no very great depths and so the bass really were "shallow-water fish." They had little choice. I can never recall, as a young angler, fishing out in the middle of a lake for bass, even after I had started using artificial lures. You got as close in to weedy shores as you could get and that's where you fished. Again, I caught some bass. Some of the time it was because they happened to be there feeding, some of the time because they were spawning, and some of the time because they were small bass that lived there.

I remember a large river where I fished occasionally as a youth. It contained smallmouths and an old fellow who lived near the river explained to me how to catch them. "Bait with a crawdad," he instructed. "Use a heavy sinker and no bobber. Hurl it out as far as you can and let it lie on bottom." Now of course this was extremely logical, but I also recall vividly that it did not seem so to me at the time. Nonetheless, I began to catch smallmouths. There'd be a gentle tug and then the fish would run a bit, and now and then when I'd strike I'd have one.

I had begun thus to catch bass *on the bottom*. Yet fishermen learn slowly. usually because of preconceived and false notions. Those shoreline lily pads still looked "bassy" to me. One day I was fishing to them, casting a minnow and small sinker along the edges and reeling it back. A breeze sprang up that kept pushing me offshore. Each time this occurred I'd be all fouled up. I'd drop my rig, seize the oars, and maneuver to get back close to the pads again. I was fishing a narrow arm of a small lake. As the wind pushed me back, I was actually over the deep gut or trough that ran out into the rest of the lake. The first couple of times, as my lead and minnow hit bottom and I pulled on the oars, line would streak off the reel. I'd grab for the rod, figuring I'd hooked up on bottom. But it was not bottom, it was each time a bass that had grabbed the minnow as it hit bottom in perhaps twenty feet of water.

Odd as it may seem, even though I finally caught one of these bass, and a big one at that, I still considered it just some sort of fluke. It took three fish in the boat before I began to believe maybe I should really fish in twenty feet of water. I had begun to learn what kind of fish the bass truly is.

An incident that strikingly illustrates the point occurred one summer on a natural Michigan lake of medium size. The time was August and the days were extremely hot. Much of the lake was no more than twenty feet deep. A friend and I fished some almost every afternoon, but we weren't catching much. Somehow in fiddling around over the lake we began in desperation looking for a deeper area. At one point, simply prospecting without plan, we dropped our anchor but it didn't reach bottom. We were using cheap casting rod-and-reel outfits, with worms for bait. I dropped my bait over the side and let the line down—down—down.

When the amount of black casting line on the reel was beginning to look skimpy indeed, the sinker finally touched bottom. Instantly I had a bite. After a frantic and exciting battle, I finally boated a bass of perhaps two pounds. We really got after it then. The day was still and the boat drifted very little. We lined up markers ashore so not to lose our spot. Next fish up was an outsize bluegill. We sat there and caught bluegills and bass about as fast as we could get a line down. Later on it occurred to us to tie a thread from my shirttail onto the line when it hit bottom, so we could measure when we got ashore. That trough, which obviously must have been well oxygenated and cool, was almost exactly sixty-five feet deep. That is the deepest I have ever found bass.

LEARNING ABOUT LAKE FLOORS

Thus over the years I slowly learned that a mature bass is not a mid-water or near-surface fish which only occasionally seeks bottom. It is a *bottom*-dwelling species that commonly moves up near surface and shore-line, but only for specific reasons of forage or temporary comfort. There are times to be sure when bass may well be hanging at some in-between depth. But again there will be a reason, such as stratified water that offers a proper temperature or plentiful oxygen. There are lake bottoms that over large areas seldom have enough oxygen to sustain fish life, and of course bass could not stay in such spots. But on the whole this is a bottom fish that periodically and temporarily uses other strata and then returns to its "home," on the bottom. This has been one of the most important lessons modern bass fishermen have begun to learn, and it took most of them many years at that.

In fact, when bass fishing began to be chiefly oriented to the new, large

impounded lakes this view of bass was immeasurably important, for these
were nearly all deep lakes. There was plenty of deep water—water from
let's say eight feet on down to a hundred or more—and much of this water
was well supplied with both forage and cover of varied sorts. A small natural bass lake in the North might be typically one with a productive near-
shore rim but an almost barren bottom. A typical Deep South natural
water might be broad and shallow and productive over most of its acreage
because of cover and food. A unique term I recall for such waters in
Georgia is "flat ponds," meaning flat on the bottom!

Certainly it is true that bass and weeds go together not just in the
magazine pictures but in reality. But weeds and weed beds, which are so
often spoken of as just the place for bass, are by no means as important,
and especially in the big new lakes, as are other types of cover. The main
reason is that weed growth in an average lake does not reach deep enough.
In murky lakes it may be restricted to a zone no more than six feet in
depth. In a lake of medium clarity the weed zone will reach down ten feet.
In numerous clear lakes it may go as deep as fifteen feet. But weeds are
not often found in any banks or dense beds below that because not enough
light penetrates to allow photosynthesis.

Weed beds do harbor an awesome amount of food for bass. Bass do
come into and along the weed beds to feed. In shallow lakes where weeds
can grow over much of the bottom, bass may roam almost anywhere. But
the point to be made is that the weeds themselves are not as important to
a bass most of the time as are oxygen and water temperature. An angler
must realize that a bottom without a speck of greenery, but with a jumble
of rocks, or a crisscross of flooded forest debris, or sometimes just of firm
gravel ending against a rocky cliff base will hold bass in the big lakes much
of the time. Thus the "weed-bed syndrome" should be tempered with the
realization that vegetation is only one item among many that hold bass
like magnets.

Right here I believe we should look quickly at water clarity in relation
to weeds and forage. Although an exceptionally clear lake may permit
weeds in deeper water, a general rule is that water clarity is inversely proportional to fertility. That is, in most lakes the clearer the water the less
fertile it is, which in turn means there is less plankton in it. And, where
plankton production is at less than maximum, there is less feed for the
small forage species that sustain the bass.

Most of the large impoundments are at least fertile enough to produce bountiful forage. But because they are large and usually with ragged shore-lines consisting of arms, bays, creek mouths, and brushy shoal indentations, clarity differs from spot to spot. An expanse that is supremely clear may look very good to you. You may deduce that here weeds, and thus forage, will grow at much greater depths. But this is not necessarily true. The water may be too deep for weeds and not fertile enough to produce much plankton. For example, waters near the dams on the large lakes are frequently clearer than elsewhere, but studies have shown that as a rule these are not as productive as elsewhere.

This does not mean you should seek muddy coves. In fact, where a long, high dam curves around, there may be hundreds of yards of shallower water along rocky fills extending on from the dam itself. Pockets of proper depth and temperature along these may produce very well. But in any case, when hunting bass, if you discover two narrow arms, one appearing fertile and one infertile, the choice would go at least for first try to the fertile one. The lake floor here has a better chance of holding bass.

As one learns, he must keep reassuring himself that above all else it is the lake *bottom* he should constantly be assessing. These large new lakes have vast expanses of unproductive deep bottoms, and also vast expanses, added up in patches or pockets here and there, of deep bottoms where the bass live. Certainly top-water fishing is a marvelous sport. I prefer it above any other. But it has been proved endlessly that something like 90 percent of the bass caught in any year in any productive impoundment are taken from the bottom, in water from six to eight feet down to about thirty-five feet deep. If one will fix that firmly in mind, he is pointed toward success. I often fish top water because I like to, and accept the fact that I will catch fewer, and smaller, bass. I also know that there are times—sometimes day after day in certain locations—when bass will move up for short periods to shallow waters to feed. But sizable bass do not *live* there. They are just not that kind of fish. Think of it in comparison to your home. You drive from it to collect food, or for other purposes, and then you return to its comforts. Or if food and comfort are both amply available at home, you stay put.

ARE BASS SCHOOL FISH?

Just as people have traditionally gathered into village groups over the centuries, even with all the pressures and exasperations the habit causes, bass also have long done likewise. But in the modern language of bass fishing the word "school" is often used incorrectly. Much has been learned in recent years about the gregariousness of bass and the gathering of groups in certain favored spots. Nonetheless, the black basses are not truly school fishes.

The average bass fisherman, even up to just a few years ago, fished to spots that he deemed likely to hold a single fish. There were exceptions, of course. The concentration of spawning is one, a time when numerous bass may be found in a restricted area. But this has nothing to do with "schooling." Another is the "school bass" pattern set by large groups that gather to surround and chop up a compact school of forage fish. These are exceptions due to specific purposes. A true *school* fish is a colonial variety whose very existence depends upon the close association of large numbers of its species. The old rule for walleye fishermen, for example, is when you catch one, fish right there. The same is true for the yellow-perch fisherman. White bass are school fish. They travel together, roaming widely in compact groups. They feed in schools not just under specialized conditions of opportunity, but because this is a fundamental habit of the species.

More striking examples of school fish are found among saltwater varieties. The mackerels gather and travel and live in vast hordes. The forage fish, menhaden, consort in untold millions, so compactly it seems unbelievable. Taking an example of colonialism in another category, the now extinct passenger pigeon lived in immense, supercompact flocks. It nested that way, flew out to feed that way, migrated that way. Regardless of the fact that this concentration led to great slaughter of the birds by man, this species could not have survived in the modern world even if it had not been hunted at all. Its awesome colonial requirements could not have been fulfilled in the habitat as we have changed it. Conversely, the mourning dove, which travels and feeds in loose, small groups, and may nest in loosely scattered fashion, a dozen here, six there, over a patch of trees, was not a compactly colonial species but merely gregarious. This small-group way of life allowed it not only to sustain itself in the face of man but indeed to spread vastly and enhance its range.

I use this illustration because it is exactly comparable to the manner of the black bass. Scattered groups gather, sometimes rather closely, because they discover optimum living conditions in certain rather restricted bottom areas. But they do not absolutely require each other's company and so they are not, technically, school fish at all. Yet the fact that for many years they were spoken of as "nonschooling" led most anglers to the conclusion that the best bet was to go round and round the lake shore, picking off one here, one there, in "likely" places, or at least casting to such spots. But the log or stump you see is usually not deep enough to have a bass in residence.

What may be confusing is that many bass *are* loners. Exceptionally large specimens, as mentioned previously, usually are. Some anglers, very excellent fishermen indeed, go from deeply-submerged stump to stump, point to point, catching one big bass at each and then moving on. They like to fish this way. They may end a day with just as many fish as the angler who fishes the gatherings. But it is a fact that modern tools and techniques of bass fishing have now brought to light the fact that groups of bass— sometimes as many as twenty or thirty and all of them husky specimens —are found, under the big-lake conditions where the fishing is mostly done nowadays, loosely grouped in confined and specific locations. Water temperature, bottom configuration, feeding conditions all influence this habit, and how closely or how spread out the consortium may be. This goes back to my earlier statements about acres and acres of bottom being devoid of bass, while certain small tracts of it are inhabited by large numbers.

In addition to the groups of twenty or thirty, there are occasionally loosely scattered gatherings of many more bass spread over as much as a hundred yards. But these concentrations do not exist because the fish have an instinctive compulsion to group; rather they form because of proper bottom conditions. Largemouths are more frequently found in large scatterings than are smallmouths. Part of this relates to the sparser habitat of the smallmouth.

Although some species of fish will be grouped in vertical schools, bass seldom are. That is, they lie all on about the same horizontal plane, instead of "stacking." There can be exceptions. These occur when a vertical stratum of water—about which more in Chapter 8—offers proper conditions from top to bottom. Not often will black bass groups be found vertically through more than ten feet of water. Much more common is the horizontal placement of groups.

Gatherings of bass are noted for groupings according to sizes. This may be a habit of age groups gravitating toward their own. It may also be because bass of like size have nothing to fear from each other, while small bass certainly do need to be wary of large bass because cannibalism is common in the species. There may be some other influences. I have observed bass in my own ranch ponds hanging around together in what I choose to call "pods" of three to six or more. These fish, all large and of like size, appear rather often to be all males. They cruise together, live together day after day. When I cast to them and hook one, it's routine for some of the others to pursue the hooked fish, trying to grab at the lure in its mouth.

This may be why two bass are occasionally caught at once on a lure. I also have discovered that this habit of "buddy bass" following can be used to the angler's advantage. Cast quickly to the spot and you may well catch a second, a third, a fourth after the first has been landed. The stump-to-stump angler misses such chances because he doesn't realize the opportunity is there. But you have to use care in landing the fish. A chasing "buddy" who gets too close to the boat and observes the hooked fish lifted is spooked and appears to have some method of relaying his caution to the others. If several casters are fishing together, it is a good idea when one good bass is fighting the line for the others to cast nearby. Sometimes a small pod that lives together can be hooked up one after the other by this technique.

Because the groupings or gatherings exhibit size likeness, you can pretty well judge by what you catch the first time or first couple of times what may be in store. A spot that sends up one or two two-pound bass from bottom probably has a gathering of this size. Several small bass hooked in a given area may well mean that is what lives here or is feeding here. Basic rules can be set up that are almost infallible. Except under specialized feeding conditions, bass caught on surface will not run consistently as large as those caught deep. Bass caught near shore will consistently average smaller than those caught offshore and deep. Large bass—bass in the three- to five- or six-pound class—will almost always be caught most consistently in deep water, often as deep as eighteen to thirty feet. And sharp impoundment fishermen now know well that a whole stringer of these can on occasion be taken from the same "hole"—a narrow ledge, a hump, a depression.

Most of the time, incidentally, if you locate a gathering along a point, the greatest number of bass, and most of the *larger* specimens, will be on the side of the point that drops away to the deepest water. For instance, two of us were fishing one day and had located a point that sloped rather swiftly from about ten feet to twenty-five feet. At that depth it fell away abruptly to over forty feet. The other side of the point sloped almost exactly like the first, but there was then no falloff to deeper water, for the bottom simply flattened out. We caught a couple of bass here because we happened to try here first. When we went around and checked the other side, however, we were shortly in real hot business. We took six fish in all, each above four pounds.

To go back momentarily to real *trophy* bass—the "mounting" sort that haul the scale down to ten or twelve pounds—these, too, will be found deep more often than shallow, except during specific feeding or spawning periods. But these as I've noted are not usually gregarious. They are like fat, clumsy, crotchety old gentlemen who wish to be left alone. Nonetheless, the *places* where they hole up are in general about like those where average large bass hang out. But the fishing for the monster must be pinpoint as a rule. It is not given much to the chase.

THE PHENOMENON OF "SCHOOLING"

What fishermen have for some years called the "schooling" of bass, or as some say, "fishing the jumps," is a phenomenon related to certain specialized feeding sprees. I well remember my years of living in Florida, after I had fished bass for many seasons in the North and Midwest. The first time I heard of "school" bass and "fishing the jumps for schooling bass" was in Florida. I had never seen this in the northern lakes I knew, nor had I seen it in most of Florida's lakes either.

The fact is, where a major forage species of compact schooling habits is present, bass learn to gather in groups which give them an advantage in preying upon the school. Although this occurred in some natural waters of the South, it came into full flower as the impoundments increased because they furnished a prime habitat for shad. Gizzard shad and the smaller threadfin shad are both school species. They gather and cruise together, sometimes by the thousands, and compactly. The young bass that live inshore are not physically equipped to prey on the schools too authoritatively. The very large, old bass have formed more sedentary routines of letting food come to them. But medium-sized bass—from a pound to two and one-half pounds—are the extremely active "youth group" of the bass world, agile and aggressive and physically capable of fast fin work. These are the bass most commonly found chasing, in groups, the schools of shad.

They cannot simply chase indiscriminately. They have to watch for a chance to pen the forage. This can be done in a cove, against a shoreline, or against the surface, with the surface phenomenon the most common.

The bass, if you were to check out the bottom, in most instances live right here, or at least nearby, along an underwater ridge perhaps, or the side of a point in a cove, or along the hump of an old submerged roadway, or the depression of an old creek. They are of an active size, a restless age, and require a substantial amount of food. They watch for schools of shad that drift up toward the surface. The bass, acting now like a pack of wolves, come up from the depths, shooting upward into the school. The shad break surface and try to get away, but by then the bass are splashing and throwing spray, sometimes in a patch of surface water fifty yards or more in diameter.

Obviously the shad school, most of it, is able to break through the encirclement and dive to deeper water. As they scatter, the bass do not chase far. Moments later, however, the shad may regroup and surface a short distance away. Or a new school may be caught drifting just below surface, and up comes the wolf pack again. The swirls and roils and splashes are called "jumps." A surface lure or a stick-type jumping lure, or a jig or shallow-running plug raked across the area takes bass. They are in a wild momentary frenzy and may hit anything that moves.

For various reasons, some impoundments have more schooling activity than others. For one thing, a large age group of bass of proper size must be present. And the shad—the most common forage species thus utilized—must be present. Further, certain sectors of an impoundment, for reasons not always entirely clear, give evidence of a lot of such school-feeding activity, while others do not.

There are certain requirements that build up to schooling. First of all, this is almost wholly an occurrence on flat water. I suspect this is because rough water surfaces do not lend themselves as invitingly to drifting shad schools, and also because a broken surface makes sighting forage and chasing it swiftly just too difficult for the bass. The shad must be present, and lazing compactly near surface, in order to trigger the phenomenon. They follow this routine most often when the surface is dead calm.

In addition, this is a routine of hot weather. Almost all "jump fishing" for bass occurs in summer. I have seen times when a big lake was almost impossible to fish because of the heat out on open, calm, and therefore breezeless waters. As an example, one of the wildest seasons of school-bass fishing to occur so far on the renowned Toledo Bend Reservoir on the Louisiana-Texas border occurred during weeks when daytime temperatures soared up to 105 degrees. And invariably the most schooling activity occurs, out in the open waters, from around ten in the morning to about four in the afternoon. During earlier and later hours the shad don't offer similar opportunities, and the bass are generally following other routines.

The angler who is used to looking for secluded stands of drowned timber, or weed beds along shoreline, will miss most of the "jump" action. As noted, there may be a bottom configuration that holds the bass, out on bottom in open water. It is here, in the open, that the shad will show up and here that the bass will cut them to pieces most often. However, schooling does sometimes occur "back in the brush." The surface action, when you do locate it in such a place, is likely to last longer at each flurry than out in the open, for the shad have more chance to try for cover just below the surface. And it is not likely to roam over a large area. On an open expanse in a smooth bay, the groups of bass may roam here and there looking for shad. They're up here one minute, then down and over there the next.

When a school stays up long enough, you can take several fish and every cast is a hit. But you have to zoom your boat in to casting distance carefully or you spook both schools and put them down. Then up they come at a distance and you must chase again. The ideal situation is when numerous schools of both forage and predators are working a bay. I recall one session when two friends of mine caught over a hundred bass just as fast as they could get lures out. With a small electric motor they moved along the bay, casting to jumps as they went. Commonly, if you get a hit and the bass leaps and throws the hook, another fish will strike the moment the lure drops on the water again.

This is, indeed, a phenomenon looked forward to today by many bass enthusiasts each year, but one that was known only very locally and in much of bass range not at all a few years ago. It is something of a "happenstance." By modern techniques of locating bass it is possible almost without fail to locate them when they are not schooling. Bass schools are likely to be roaming and cruising on the prod, and the schools of shad may be anywhere at any given moment. Thus you must hunt for opportunity and it cannot be precisely pinned down to an exact spot. Ordinarily, when it is schooling season and time of day, fishermen ease along, watching sharply for the skitter of a shad school, on occasion for feeding birds, or for the splashes and swirls of the bass.

An angler who knows a particular lake intimately, one where schooling occurs, will have learned that certain expanses usually get the most action, time after time. This may be because the school-age bass live there, or find best bottom conditions there. Or perhaps it is because the shad schools like it, too. But it happens swiftly and erratically. One moment the surface is glass smooth, the next the spray is flying.

Hot weather is a time of squalls and thunderstorms. Many a sizzling day furnishes an abrupt but short-lived storm after which the lake surface flattens out again to utter stillness. Such squalls may build up several times during an afternoon. Most school-bass enthusiasts believe action is enhanced by these storms. Each time after the surface calms, there appears to be a renewal of activity.

The bass angler of the old school did not know that schooling occurred, for the very good reason that, until the new waters came into existence, it was a relative rarity. Thus the modern black bass has been changed in its habits in this respect by its environment, and the modern bass fisherman has gained a new sport by learning to know bass better.

CHAPTER FIVE

Science Unlocks Bass Secrets

YEAR-ROUND FISHING

It is interesting indeed to contemplate the fact that within the past ten years more has been learned about bass and bass fishing than the aggregate of all knowledge amassed, more or less hit and miss, during the preceding half century. Men in scuba gear descend into the domain of this foremost of U.S. sport fishes and study it endlessly right in its home. Lake studies concentrate for months on end, pursuing facts about how often a bass feeds, how its metabolism affects its food intake and in turn how the seasons affect its metabolism.

Studies are made on bass movements, on bass population, and their balances and interrelationships with other life in their aquatic habitat. Because the black bass is such an important recreational resource, biologists need to know every fact about it, the better to manage the species. As the knowledge has piled up, it seems sometimes almost too ponderous for a fisherman to sift and evaluate. Yet it can be boiled down and concentrated. Science continually turns up conclusions that have simple and exceedingly valuable bearings upon the chances of success of the eventual "bass consumers," the fishermen.

Probably one of the most important new areas of knowledge concerns *year-round fishing*. Only over the past fifteen years or so have most fishermen realized it is good all year. When I was a lad we "knew" that bass couldn't be caught during hot weather. Oh, an occasional accident occurred (we thought) and we hooked a bass. But in hot weather bass simply did not feed. Don't ask me why, or how they could live without eating. But fishermen told this to each other.

When cool fall months came, there was some bass fishing. But even then reactions among anglers were mixed. Certainly the bass hit better then—in the parts of a lake where they were fished for!—than during summer. Later on, in winter, there was again no bass fishing. I recall that even in the late 1940s when I wrote what I believe was the first book about ice fishing, it was considered all but impossible to catch bass in winter in the North. Down in the South fishing was considered fair to middlin', but time and again it was said, even by official fishing promoters in bass-rich Florida, that "April and November in the South are the hottest bass months."

The truth is, as we know today, bass feed around the year. In extreme cold they may stay in a semidormant state for brief periods, but this is only because, being cold-blooded, their metabolism has drastically slowed down. It has not stopped, and bass do not "hibernate," as was once supposed. They do require a much smaller food intake at low temperatures than at higher ones.

In summer bass are actually *more* active than at any other time simply because water temperatures are higher and their metabolism is revved up. There is a limit, of course. When discomfort from high temperature engulfs the domain of a bass, it will cut down feeding because of anxiety. But seldom are bass forced into such a situation. They are able in most waters and particularly in today's large, deep waters, to find comfort, and this they do. Indeed bass do not slow down their feeding in summer; many fishermen until recently simply fished for them where they weren't. As I said earlier about deep water and bass, this is where they'll be in summer, except for periodic forays into special feeding areas.

Spring was always considered the best and about the only time for bass fishing. This is what every angler said right up to the past decade and a half. There was some truth in the idea. Certainly fishing was excellent, for bass were at the easy disposal of fishermen during spring. Finding them was not complicated because this was the spawning period. That urge brought them swarming inshore; they were concentrated; competition for food was severe; fishermen had them "boxed in." It has been estimated that as many as 90 percent of all bass caught in the U.S. only a few years ago were taken annually in the spring. Some crafty specialists knew how to catch them at other times, but the average so-so fisherman had no idea where to find them, what they did after spawning, or how to fish for them. Today the change is drastic. Many waters give up their best catches at any other time except spring.

Bear in mind now that as the impoundments developed, as fishermen swarmed to them, as bass clubs and tournaments evolved, as studies piled up knowledge, more and more expert bass anglers also were developing, self-taught by the new gadgets and the new facts turning up endlessly. Lately it has become well known that winter fishing for bass below the freeze-up zone is excellent. The fisherman in mid-latitudes may be freezing his fingers up topside, but the bass have only to seek a spot of comfort down deep. To be sure, its food intake may drop, but bass can still be inveigled. Today it is well known that more trophy bass are caught in winter in temperate climes than at any other period of the year. All the accomplished and informed anglers fish deep for them, and have learned to pinpoint the types of places where they're likely to be.

Thus, year-round quality bass fishing has become a fact. Methods may change somewhat with seasons. Bass may switch locations seasonally. Their diet may change to some extent, their activity accelerate or decrease. But modern bass fishermen now know where—and how—to find them at any time, and that they do not cease feeding seasonally. No longer do the fish leave the fisherman whanging away at the shoreline when they move out from it in spring. The new science has left them no hiding place, and because so many states have no closed season on bass, the sport continues in high gear without seasonal slowdown.

CRACKING THE FEEDING CODE

The route of a bass to a hook is quite obviously via its stomach. Therefore, if a fisherman knows what a bass likes to eat, and how often, it simply is a matter of finding the fish and presenting the food, or a facsimile. That of course is simplistic logic, but with a modicum of expansion it can become a matter of rote to a fisherman.

What a bass will eat cannot be said in a few words. The fact is, few if any fish will accept a wider variety of food. However, we don't need to attempt to make a list of foods or lures. In any given water one is certain to know what the major available types of forage are, and which ones are most easily taken. These are what the bass will utilize as mainstays of diet. A good illustration above water in the realm of predatory mammals is the coyote. In the Southwest there are jack rabbits, pack rats, deer, and cattle all on the range of the coyote. Some anticoyote people claim terrible depredations upon deer by coyotes. Some ranchers claim killing of calves. But studies on coyote stomachs show that about 95 percent of their diet during years when there are normal "crops" of forage species is made up of rabbits and pack rats. These are the abundant foods easy to come by.

In the view of a black bass, however, a good many artificial morsels not similar to his most abundant local grubstake will intrigue him, simply because he *is* so profligate in his eating habits. And so we need not be quite so concerned about what, as we are with when. One of the main areas of scant knowledge about bass to this day is why they feed when they do. We can certainly set up a reasonably workable pattern of feeding. But it will have many exceptions simply because so many influences are brought to bear on all life. A long and detailed study on one lake has pretty well authenticated what most expert fishermen already know . . . that the time when heaviest feeding activity may be predicted will be from first dim light of dawn until well on toward midday. Then there will be a slack—or less active at least—period through midday and into the afternoon. By mid to late afternoon activity will begin to pick up and will become progressively more accentuated until dark. There will be some night activity, but consistently it will never match that of daylight, and especially that of early in the day.

This outline is of course rather rough, and there will be all sorts of exceptions. But it has been proved good enough to use as a fundamental pattern. No experienced angler would let it keep him from fishing during the predicted "poorer" hours, but it still is a good general guide, and detailed studies over several years have confirmed it.

No one has more than the vaguest idea what triggers feeding sprees at any given time. But the one wisp of knowledge every bass angler should seize upon is that it is known definitely that on many an occasion feeding begins suddenly, and furiously. That period may be brief. Thus, the angler who attempts to stay with it over the longest period is obviously most likely to be there when the action starts. Many times I have watched for hours on end the bass in my ranch lakes, which I've used as a kind of laboratory of bassology. There will be several large bass lying near bottom wholly unconcerned with their surroundings. Forage fish—varied minnows, small sunfishes—laze about within inches of the big predators. Neither pays any attention to the other. No fear seems to show, no shyness, among the forage, nor any "scheming glance" on the part of the bass.

Suddenly everything changes. The bass become alert. One makes a vicious pass at a small fish. Others begin. A feeding frenzy ensues. When it starts among these fish, it can be observed elsewhere on the lake. Something has triggered the action but studies have so far not indicated what. My observations are well substantiated by many others. In several studies divers with scuba equipment have watched bass and forage fishes at close range and seen the same phenomenon occur. Other feeding periods, however, may be launched more casually, and often these last much longer. In addition, the largemouth bass in particular can quite often be tempted to take a whack at a lure when no actual feeding is going on. It has been suggested that this occurs out of anger, or annoyance, or curiosity. No one knows. It is doubtful that the small brain of a bass has any long list of very well defined emotions.

Where the "feeding code" has truly been cracked is that we do now know quite definitely how often bass feed. Or to put it in a better way. we know how often bass need food. Later on we will discuss at length the immense importance of water temperature. Suffice it here to say that bass are most active, that is most comfortable and with most stable, high metabolism, at somewhere between the mid-sixties and up to 70 degrees. In that temperature range, a full gullet will require close to forty-eight hours for digestion.

Now it is easy to draw false conclusions from those statements. The digestion period has been well authenticated by scientific study. That does not mean a bass will feed bulging full, then not take another mouthful until all food is digested. All of us, I'm sure, have caught bass so full it was impossible to see how they could get anything else down. All have also caught bass with partially digested food. What the digestive rate does offer is a clue to when major feeding periods are most likely to occur—all other influences being satisfactory.

This rate, mind you, is for summer, or at least for what are generally called summertime water temperatures. It is an excellent guide by which to project what may occur at higher, or lower, temperatures. Bass will feed at higher temperatures, but it is not certain that at higher ones their metabolism speeds up much more. It is, at greatest comfort level, at about top form. However, as the temperature level in one place decreases, bass obviously will try to find a spot where it hasn't. Thus, finding the fish is always the single most important chore of the angler. But many times the fish won't be able to find the optimum temperature, so they must make do with something less desirable. Metabolism, and therefore digestion, at 60 degrees and lower slows down comparably. This means that the full stomach is not empty until, let's say, fifty-four hours (rather than forty-eight). The bass does not need as much food, it doesn't take as much, it feeds avidly less often, it does not in fact feed *as* avidly because of slower metabolism. And it may be inclined therefore to take smaller offerings, or one single large one—like an outsize pork eel—but also to take them slower, with a lackadaisical pickup.

I want to mention here that one of the early discoveries of ice fishermen, when that sport was first becoming popular, was that a bait suitable for a bluegill in summer seldom took winter bluegills. They didn't *need* large morsels. They also bit weakly, seemingly with diminished concern. In my ice-fishing days I caught a good many bass, disproving the theory that beneath the ice they didn't hit. But I took most of them on small minnows suitable for yellow perch. And they certainly did not bite often, or with alacrity.

I mentioned that we must be careful how we interpret facts. Just because bass at 70 degrees digest a full gullet in forty-eight hours does not mean all bass keep regular hours for meals. No doubt some bass are feeding at any given time. But all the other influences—such as light and hours of greatest activity, surface conditions, etc.—seem to indicate the general hours of most activity. Also, some curious results have come out of studies of bass feeding times and digestion rate. There is good reason now to believe that on the average perhaps half the bass population of any given water feed most actively at the same time. This means that at some time every day, between midnight and midnight, half the bass will have a major feeding period.

All of this applies, remember, to the ideal temperature range. This would mean that across much of the mid-South and South more than half of the year probably would see bass most likely to be avidly feeding, during the hours noted earlier, at least once each day. In the North this would apply from about June through September. Where this optimum comfort temperature is present *somewhere* in any lake at *all* times of year, the bass will have found those spots and the general guide to feeding times will apply.

I have a little theory of my own gained from study of my own ponds that appears to have some basis in fact. In two different ponds we knew the ages of the bass in each. We also knew that these fish, stocked from hatchery ponds, were from different hatches and therefore each group had started its life at a different time. I began to wonder if each group had automatically established similar feeding habits within its group. Over some weeks it seemed that bass hit well on one pond but during those hours or that day they hit very little on the other, and vice versa. Is it possible that age groups of bass in any lake feed at different times? No one knows for certain, but if it is true this is all to the good for anglers. Some bass are sure to be feeding almost any time. In fact, some usually are.

DAILY MIGRATIONS FOR FOOD

One of the most important areas of new knowledge for the bass fisherman concerns the fact that bass do not spend very much time along the shore. We have touched this lightly in material on the deep-water and bottom-hugging proclivities of bass. But that bass are not shoreline-oriented is one of the most difficult facts for many a fisherman to believe. Most certainly bass feed near shore and spend some time there, but not much, which is exactly the opposite of what bass fishermen believed some years ago.

First we must establish what is meant by "near shore." If a point of land slopes down sharply, as has been described earlier, bass may be found along the slope. But to the fish this is not a "shoreline." It is a haven in deep water. What we mean here by shore or shoreline is what most anglers used to visualize as "bassy waters"—the weedy shallows with gentle slope up to dry land. Many times, commonly once every day and sometimes twice during the most active months (temperatures), bass will *visit* such locations. The term "daily migrations" has been used, but "visits" is probably better, for the other seems to indicate long journeys for long stays.

These visits are for feeding, except during the spawning period. The action here may be of short duration because these are simply "meal calls." There is another factor involved, too, that confuses a fisherman. Because young, small bass *live* in these shallows, size of bass caught during a visit may run the gamut. This may lead an angler to false conclusions, because the little bass may continue to hit after the big ones have stopped— that is, left.

A most useful fact turned up by investigation shows that bass on these inshore moves almost invariably travel along a shortest-distance line, or at least a well-marked lane day after day. They proceed to a feeding spot and operate there. The majority of anglers have for years fished along parallel to a shoreline, believing the fish are cruising parallel also. This is not true. There is only a very modest amount of parallel-to-shoreline movement of bass. They move in toward shore, feed, and return along the same travel lane.

Now it is obvious that bass moving inshore to feed are hungry, and those returning are fed full, or must be assumed to have fed. Thus the *inshore* movement is the one that pays off. It is almost like saltwater fish coming in with a tide in a frenzy of feeding. Lately, knowing this habit, bass experts have learned to seek out both the deep lies of bass and the travel routes or "daily migration" routes to shallow feeding places. By staking out along the route on the inshore movement, the fish can be waylaid and some excellent sport ensues.

One may even get a good many clues as to precisely where the fish will probably travel. Keep in mind that when you travel you go by landmarks and maps. You drive, let us say, from work at noon to the corner, turn left, go a mile, turn right, pass the high school, two gas stations, and you come to the restaurant where you will eat lunch. Researchers now have good reason to believe that a bass follows "landmarks," of an underwater variety, too. Knowing where one is going underwater is more difficult than on land. But a fish certainly is able to tell when it is moving upward into shallower water because of lessening pressure on its body. It does not *think* these things. They are instinctive.

Here is a rocky bank along which the fish moves, with water becoming less and less deep. The surface is closer, the light is better. Ahead is a big log, or a stump, submerged but in line with the shore where the feeding area is located. Beyond is an old tree thrusting from the water, and beyond that the weeds begin and the minnow-rich plot has been reached. When feeding is finished, the fish moves back along the same route, landmark by landmark. Again, it does not mentally check these off as it goes, but by this route and these markers it first discovered the feeding area and by routine it is thereafter guided by them.

Now then, many a modern bass angler has learned to short-circuit the daily inshore visits by bringing food, or simulated food, to the fish in their deep resting grounds. Obviously a hungry fish will whack a lure when it is ready to feed, and it will do so down in its deep lair just as readily as it will inshore. In fact, this is like saving the bass a trip! There are times, however, when it doesn't work quite that neatly. Sometimes the bass will refuse to hit until they are en route to their feeding ground. The "trigger" has not yet been pulled. Or, one may have difficulty finding the lunker hole or it may be in such dense bottom debris that he cannot cope with it. Now he seeks only the route of the daily visit, takes his stand here, and has the fish dead to rights. Or, let's say one is not very adept at deep fishing but dearly loves to catch bass in shallow water or up top. If he knows the migration lanes and the shallow feed patch, he can get it the way he likes it best.

Some of these travel lanes are difficult to work out. My slant is to look first for the easy ones. A deep lie off or along a point or ledge or bottom hump, with a marshy or lily-pad shallows at the head of the narrow cove formed by the point, and with stumps, rocks, or drowned trees plainly marking a route may be just the ticket.

I think offhand of possibly the most perfect daily-visit situation I ever discovered. This was in a northern lake I fished in summer. Out in the lake there was a round weed bed about fifty yards across. Aquatic growth showed above surface. This was "almost" an island. The bottom sloped up neatly like a cone. Fish lying deep at any point around the cone simply moved up in a straight travel line from their given resting point. The weed forest atop the cone in shallow water was a veritable bonanza of forage. In early morning, and again in late afternoon, given proper weather and temperature conditions, bass surrounded and fed in that weed bed. By anchoring out away from it, a hooked fish could be brought into open water and fought down. It was a charming, and charmed, spot.

THE MYSTERY INFLUENCES

There are many apparent mysteries connected with all fishing endeavors. So many influences of various kinds are brought to bear upon all living things that the infinite combinations are bound to prove confusing, and not altogether manageable. Because fishing has always been an imprecise art, it has always been fashionable to "explain" why fish bite or why they don't by myriads of highly contrived theories. Just as many an old-line southern gardener never planted seeds except "when the moon was right," anglers have long hatched ideas bordering on the mysterious.

The old gent who calculated that it was beddin' time for a certain species because the wild honeysuckle buds were showing or the redbud was in bloom or the fresh ramps were laying their pungent aroma upon the spring air might be laughed at. But the fact was that he simply was timing his fishing to a parallel spring phenomenon, and this in turn was timed by air temperature, which in turn affected the temperature of the water which in turn set the fish a-spawning. The sport who chuckled at the old gent was the dumb one. There were those who could never swallow the moon theories, and others. However, the modern angler, and especially the modern bass angler, is beginning to learn to listen and experiment, and never to laugh at any theory, no matter how far-fetched it may sound, because it just may be true.

There is not the slightest question that the moon affects bass fishing. Original theories were identical to those held by deer hunters, for example, who predict poor deer hunting periods of full or nearly full moon, good hunting during the dark of the moon and slivers of moon. The idea is simple: that creatures feed more at night when there is more light. There is probably some truth in this, at least in deer hunting. But a bass is not the same type of creature at all. It is fundamentally diurnal, whereas a deer is fundamentally nocturnal. Each is active to some extent during the opposite portion of the twenty-four-hour period.

Careful tabulations by numerous bass fishermen tend to prove that in general fishing tends to be only so-so during the moon's first quarter. This certainly does not mean one should give up fishing during those days. Again, there are dozens of influences upon the fish. It is almost like a kaleidoscope. When all the particles fall into a certain pattern, so that good influences dominate those tending to retard activity, the lightning may well strike. But by and large a bass fisherman, in the light of today's knowledge, might well give himself every smallest break. In planning a trip, for instance, dodging the moon's first quarter is reasonable thinking.

From a half moon on to a full moon, fishing is usually better. This is not a whimsical guess. Many expert bass fishermen have kept diaries that clinch the point. It is interesting, too, that here the night-feeding theory appears to hold up. Night fishing *is* frequently very good between the half and onto the full moon and as the full moon begins to wane. There are, however, some "ifs." If you fish a murky lake you seldom will find the situation at night improved from the first quarter. A lake or stream that contains extremely clear water, however, will generally serve up substantial action. Some of this is undoubtedly caused by the simple fact of the fish being able to see better. Some also may be that in clear water fish that would feed in the shallows early and late are skittish. The angler himself easily spooks them, and they wait until after dark.

A much more complicated, and just possibly far more important, influence of the moon and the sun is the *tidal* one. Tides, the effect of which are easily visible along saltwater beaches, are not seen inland because the bodies of water are not large enough for a perceptible effect. Nonetheless, the tidal pull, the influence of the specific positions of the sun and moon, is just as great anywhere inland, even though you cannot see it.

Some years ago John Alden Knight, now deceased, devised after years of study his Solunar Tables. They are still printed annually today. The theory, briefly, was that fish responded in feeding activity to tidal effect. There are, he became convinced, four periods of special activity during the twenty-four-hour (plus) lunar day. Two of these periods are rather brief, lasting from thirty to forty-five minutes or so. These he called "minor" feeding periods. Two others, the "major" feeding periods, last for one to two or more hours.

The minor periods may offer hotter fishing than the majors. The term "minor" thus should not be taken to mean the fish feed in any "minor" manner. The tables Knight worked out were keyed to the tides, and then translated to fit inland longitudes and time zones. Each year of course requires new tables. Some years ago I had a long correspondence with Mr. Knight. I became immensely intrigued with his theory. Go back now to my statement earlier that something—nobody knows what—suddenly triggers a lavish orgy of feeding. I began fishing according to the tables.

I recall vividly that when I went to favorite lakes and streams of mine at that time I had to drive invariably across a section of the Pigeon River State Forest, in northern Michigan. I began watching to see what the deer were doing. If I saw deer up and feeding at 2:00 P.M., I'd check my table. If a major period was in progress, to give me time, I'd really race for the lake. Invariably the bass would be active!

Many fishermen I talked to laughed at me. Many have always laughed at Knight's Solunar Theory. But not many serious bass anglers do so nowadays. For example, I remember reading that Bill Dance, who gained national fame as *the* great among bass fishermen, having won an incredible number of tournaments, had quit laughing at the Theory after he had tried it over a period of time. He was convinced it works.

Here again, however, all bass fishermen must be careful about evaluations, and about getting ensnared by a single theory or supposition or opinion. The fact is—and John Knight was the first one to bring it up—other influences may intrude to upset the feeding periods. The periods are set up for what can be termed normal conditions, and that can be translated as optimum conditions. Air temperature lower than that of the water, high winds, high water—such influences can shatter the delicate balance. Nonetheless, the *complete* bass fisherman should be aware of these Tables, study them, and take them into consideration.

One of the all-time mysteries also was named by Knight as an upsetting influence. This is barometric pressure. The idea that barometric pressure drastically affects fishing is by no means new. But more and more bass fishermen today are taking it more and more seriously. Remember the old saw about "Wind from the east, fish bite the least"—etc.? Up to a point it is probably true. An east wind in most places indicates an approaching storm or unsettled weather. That may in turn mean a slowly sliding barometer, or a barometer that has hit a deep low and is staying there.

Some years ago I followed the results of a study carried on for over a decade on a certain trout stream. Among the conclusions drawn was that barometric pressure had no effect whatever upon how much or how little trout fed. I was always skeptical of the result. It was based on catches by all kinds of anglers. Some were better than others, and caught fish under poor conditions. The fact is, almost all of today's master bass anglers know well that barometric pressure is definitely an important influence. But they also know that the old ideas about pressure—and possibly you have long believed them—are not entirely correct.

The traditional idea was that a rising barometer means good fishing, a falling one bad fishing. These are half truths. If the barometer starts down but gently, and keeps sliding slowly, bass fishing almost invariably slows down practically to a standstill. This is not to say that all fish will have ceased feeding, but most will have. Yet suppose now that a front is coming in and it is really rolling. The barometer literally plummets. On this fast fall, other influences being equal, there is almost certain to be a bonanza of action. Thus the modern bass angler's rule: "fast fall, fast fishing."

The reverse is very likely to occur also. That is, if the barometer has been low and steady then starts up in a swift rise, action may well be comparably swift. A slow return up the scale will offer fair to good fishing but ordinarily nothing sensational. If the pressure skyrockets and levels off and stays at an extreme high, or if it plunges and stays at an extreme low, you'll really have to work at it. Fishing can be predicted to be poor. However, most expert bass fishermen are now convinced that a *steady* barometer, at either a modest high or modest low means full stringers. Filling one may take longer than on that abrupt movement of mercury, but a level of fair fishing is almost certainly in store for as long as the pressure remains stable.

Without any doubt some scientists or one of your science-minded bass fishing buddies will come along from time to time with ideas, theories, or assumptions that you will find ridiculous. But don't scoff. Bass fishermen are still learning. Keeping an open mind is frequently a key to success. Science has indeed unlocked many secrets of the black bass. But there are more riddles, and these also will in time be solved.

CHAPTER SIX

Light: A New Consideration

UNDERSTANDING ITS IMPORTANCE

One of the great delights of fishing is that it *is* an inexact science. Or perhaps there is a better way to put it. Though people have been fishing for sport for centuries, have endlessly tried to make their endeavors scientifically precise, and have succeeded fantastically in the modern scientific sport of bass fishing, it never quite comes off in its entirety. The basic reason for this frustration is that fish live in a medium where it is impossible for us to join them over long periods for observation, and into which we cannot look from above with much clarity or continuity. In addition, a myriad of influences are always present in inexact mixtures, so that what appears today to be a sure-fire catching method for all time dissolves tomorrow into a maze of new problems and exasperations.

Nonetheless, it is surprising that the average angler has not recognized more quickly, and studied more thoroughly, those areas of fishing research that *do* permit precise methods and conclusions. One of the most important of these considerations is light. Here is an intriguing field, one that can lead to heightened understanding and success that has been touched by the average angler hardly at all.

One summer out of curiosity I kept asking over and over of bass fishermen what time of day, if they could select but one, they would prefer to be on the water. What period of the twenty-four hours did each feel was the most productive? The dawn enthusiasts were numerous. But they were about matched by the evening addicts. There were also the scattering of avid afterdark fans. And of course there were those fishermen, with whom I cannot quarrel, who would reply in effect:

"I just stick to it as long as I can hold up my casting arm. You can't catch bass with your lure in the boat or your boat at the dock and you waiting for the 'action' to begin. You have to be there when it starts!"

This of course is a shotgun method but it works. However, it has been proved time and again that over a long haul on any bass water in any latitude there are periods when the *most* activity occurs. The two general periods of the day when most bass are caught are from just before dawn until the sun is high at midmorning or before, and the period from mid-afternoon until full dark. Again, no rule is infallible. But detailed studies in numerous locations do show this trend.

Nonetheless, when I followed my question about choice time of day with one asking *why* the angler felt bass fed more avidly at those times, I had such an assortment of answers that they were meaningless. The fact is, though a welter of influences are brought to bear in unpredictable patterns on any given day, or during any given hour, *light* is one dominant factor—the effect of light upon the water, under the water, upon the forage, upon the fish, and upon the lure. It is at least one of the important "whys," and bass fishermen need to understand it far better than most do.

A bass lives in a world that, compared to ours, is always dimly lighted. Even when the sun is bright and high, so that its rays pierce the surface close to or at a right angle, the rays cannot reach with much brightness to any substantial depth. When surface water is in the brightest sun, especially in shallow water and where the bottom is very pale, certainly it is well lighted. We can observe this even from above. But let a cloud cross the sun and the change in lighting in the world of the bass is far more drastic than in ours.

Thus it would seem that a bass, in order to survive, would need to be equipped with vision far superior to ours. To be sure, the vision of a bass is well adapted to its environment, but its vision is not even remotely comparable to that of man. And in addition the medium in which it lives adds to its difficulties in seeing, as does the physical makeup of its eye. In fact, once a fisherman understands some of the basics of vision in fishes, a whole new world of angling lore is automatically opened to him. He begins then to understand far better what the fish sees, how it sees it, and how its visual abilities are related to his approach as a fisherman.

THE EYES OF A BASS

It is surprising, considering the small brain of a bass, that its eye is so well developed. With modifications, it is fairly similar to the eye of other higher vertebrates. There are most of the parts present: cornea, lens, iris, retina. And there are eye muscles. But one item lacking in the eye of a bass—and most other fishes—is a lid. In other words, it cannot blink, or close, its eyes. It will be immediately obvious that even in the poorer lighting of its liquid medium, this is a handicap.

A bass therefore must at times *shy away* from excessively bright light, whereas we are capable of closing our eyes. It can avoid excessive brightness fairly easily, because it is so perfectly adapted to movement in liquid. It simply goes deeper, or into shade. This is why, as we will discuss later, bass lurk in shade. It is also one reason why schooling bass in bright, open waters in midday come zooming up to slash groups of shad but go down very swiftly again. The light is a handicap to their vision, just as it would be to yours if you stepped suddenly into a glare or stayed in it too long.

This is by no means all the difference between bass vision and yours. The iris in the eye of the higher fishes is capable, to a degree, of size regulation, but much less than that of the human eye. For example, when you move from low to high light or vice versa, the membrane in front of the lens of your eye contracts or expands. The size of the pupil thus changes swiftly, admitting or shutting out light, as needed, to the retina. Though the more highly developed fishes can do this to a modest degree, the very medium in which they live, with its smaller amount of light, has apparently not encouraged the evolution of a very agile iris.

In addition, the focusing device in the eye of the bass is totally different from ours, and by no means as efficient. The lens of the human eye is shaped in an ellipse; that of the bass is round. That in itself is no handicap to the bass. In fact, the round lens equips the bass to focus endlessly refracted light rays underwater—a thicker medium than air—far better than we can. However, when we focus on any object, our eye muscles flatten (for distant objects) or round out (for nearby objects) our lenses as the need occurs. The bass doesn't have the muscles to do this. In addition, living as it does in a dense medium, the lens must be firmer than ours to withstand water pressure, and so it could not be flattened easily.

What happens, therefore, when the bass wants to look at a distant object, is that special muscles move the lens closer to the retina; for a close object, the lens is pushed farther away. This is exactly the manner in which a camera is focused. It is important for a bass fisherman to note that what is "distant" to a bass is not what we think of as distant. Thirty yards is an extreme distance for a bass to see with any clarity. Most of the time, in most light situations, in fact, it is less than half that. The handicap of course is the result of the way light and water mix or, more properly, fail to mix very well. But the point for the angler to remember is that a bass does not see his offering at any remarkable distance. The inference should be obvious.

The focus for distance is also neither quick nor accurate. The eyes of a bass are basically adjusted for close vision. It is believed by most ichthyologists, in fact, that most freshwater fishes, the bass among them, are extremely nearsighted. This is logical. The rounded lens indicates it. And there is no great need for a bass to see over long distances, since the opacity of the water restricts clear vision to short distances anyway.

The eye of the bass is also in a fixed position, or very nearly so. That is, the eye can be moved only slightly if at all from side to side. This may not be any serious handicap, but it does mean that to change sighting position the fish must itself change position. It cannot see "out of the tail of its eye" as we can. But it can see on both sides at once because the eyes are set at the sides of the head. However, this means that in most instances, and perhaps in all, the bass sees only with what may be called "monocular" vision. Some few fishes—the sea basses, for example—are capable of focusing both eyes at once. But the black bass probably sees any given object clearly with only one eye at a time. This gives a flat plane rather than a three-dimensional view, and is good for anglers to bear in mind. In other words, the bass sees a lure in a different manner than we do.

This brings up something a bass fisherman may well ponder during sleepless nights, or perhaps pondering it will make his nights sleepless. Not only do bass see lures differently from the way we see them, but they see them *much closer*. I've never heard this matter discussed, and it needs consideration. When you look at a lure, it is lying in your tackle box, or is in your hand. You see shape, size, color. Now bring the same lure up within inches of your eyes and you can't see it plainly at all because you can't focus that closely.

I have watched bass scores of times come zooming up to a cork bug or a surface plug that has been twitched and then left inert. Often the nose of the fish, or one side of its head, is within one or two inches. We cannot deduce exactly what the bass sees, how it sees the lure, what the lure looks like that close. But conceivably it is magnified, or only portions of it show, or perhaps the color looks different at that range. (Keep this in mind when you read the first part of the following chapter.)

To get some idea of what the bass may see, take a strong magnifying glass and look at a bass lure through it. With the glass you can bring the lure nearly as close to your eye as the bass does. Now take the glass away, move the lure away until your unaided eye can see it plainly. This probably will be "reading distance." Now use the glass again. Get the lure in focus at reading distance and slowly move it closer, keeping the glass distance adjusted, too. This will give you some idea, a startling one perhaps, of how a bass approaching a lure views it, minus of course the water medium. If you think about this, it may help explain to you as you read on into the next chapter some of the puzzles of lights and lures, their shape, size, and colors as seen through the eye of a bass.

COLOR VISION AND LIGHT

Without doubt a bass sees better underwater than we do. But the difference in vision for a bass between bright and dim light is undoubtedly like ours, except that extremely bright light disturbs the bass more and, in effect, often blinds it, wiping out any appreciation of color and probably of shape and location too. I have watched bass dart out from a shadow to strike at a surface lure that lay in dazzling sunlight, and observed their confusion. It must be remembered that other senses may take over at such times. A lure making a commotion can be heard. A live bait may be heard and smelled. But an inert artificial, such as a plug, must be seen, after the commotion dies down. I've watched bass rush out, swim wildly about and dart back without striking. I am convinced the bright light in such instances lost me a chance at the bass.

In dim light, however, it is probable that a bass sees dimly, just as we do, so here his other senses partially take over. The less light, the less color the fish sees, too. For it is true that the eye of a bass does have a well-developed ability to distinguish colors. We will examine this later.

In any eye color vision takes place by means of minute nerve ends called cones. These are activated by—or pick up—the varying wave lengths of varying colors, or rather the wavelengths that the eye translates into colors. Some animals, deer for example, have eyes without cones and thus are color-blind. The eye of a bass is supplied with cones. But just as in the human eye, in order for the cone to operate, there must be a fair degree of brightness of light. Think of a brightly lit landscape, with wild flowers, and with the bright greens of foliage. Now let a heavy cloud cover pass across the sun. The human eye records the same scene now with only a low color quotient and chiefly in pale hues with little contrast. This rather dim color range gives us an idea of what is seen by the eye of a bass in its underwater landscape.

The eye of the bass is also equipped with other minute and myriad nerve ends called rods. These indicate mostly brightness. As light dims until the cones translate little color stimuli, the rods take over. Hues become less meaningful, but *intensity,* or brightness—diminishing brightness—is seen, or translated from objects, by the rods. Bass eyes are well equipped with cones and rods but because bass are much more active during light hours, from very dim to almost full dark, and no more than half as active, overall, after full dark, the cones are dominant. This is why lure *color* is not important in night fishing. Color as such has by then become meaningless. Undoubtedly other senses are at that time more important, and sight is only a relatively minor adjunct.

FISHING THE SHADY SIDE

With the foregoing fundamentals we can begin to see why light is so important for the bass fisherman. I have watched scores of anglers casting indiscriminately in all sorts of bassy situations, without any regard to where the lure hit. They were simply "covering the water." But the fact is that bass, for various reasons, select certain places to hide, or lie in wait. Though many influences, again, bear on the fish, light is an extremely important motivation toward taking up a spot in which to rest or feed, or even over which to cruise and forage.

Most of the time the "shady side" is where the bass will be. In fishing drowned timber, for example, or fishing a southern lagoon filled with old cypress stumps, it is all but useless on sunny days to cast to the bright side. It is true that a bass may hear a commotion and dart around to investigate. But in bright light the bass is reluctant, for several reasons, to expose itself. The sudden change of light makes sighting difficult, and there is the inherent wariness of exposure in bright places.

The bass will invariably be lying in the shade, where it can see best, hide best, and be most comfortable. But in addition, keep in mind that forage species, from minnows to crayfish to frogs to aquatic insects, will also select the shade where available. Thus, more food is certain to be here in the shade or else moving about seeking the shade. Forage moving from bright to dim light also has difficulty adjusting to the new situation, just as we do going from bright to dim places. The waiting predator—the bass— is thus not so easily seen until too late, when it has made its pounce.

The "shady side" quite obviously changes during any given day, and it also changes from day to day, depending on the weather. Just because you caught a big bass this morning on the west side of a stump does not mean you should go back there and cast to the same side in the afternoon. Any other bass taking up a position here late in the day will be on the east side.

One must also translate shade vertically. When the sun is high, bass must often move to find other secluded spots. In water where rocks are the cover, bass love to get under the edge of a boulder where it is shady. Or they lie in a crevice. Or they get down among weeds, just as one might rest in a shady thicket during midday. Think how many times you've seen bass lying doggo under a dock. I have watched big ones in Florida, from a position underwater, lying far back in a dark place under a big boat dock. From their view the brightly lighted area at dock edge is like a movie screen upon which forage shows plainly, in silhouette or otherwise. Unseen themselves, they are in perfect position to dart out. But they will dart only so far. They are not long-distance chasers. If you relate these things to your fishing, you will enchance chances of success.

Further, there are many situations in certain bass waters where the shady places are at a premium and may be very small and obscure. I think of a lake of my own on our small ranch in the Texas hill country. Studying bass here has taught me much about their habits. On one side of this lake there is a rock wall that has very few undercut spots. Thus, few bass ever select that space for lay-ups. But there is one spot along it that invariably contains a bass. Most fishermen I take to this lake never even see the place.

It is no more than a foot wide, a small pocket carved out in the rock wall, a tiny cave that reaches back—I saw it before the lake was filled—perhaps two feet. It is an absolutely perfect spot for a bass to lie and for forage to try to hide, too. Many a bass, I'm sure, has made its entire living there since we built the dam.

The moral, of course, is to actively seek the shady places, regardless of how small they are. Except under special conditions, covered elsewhere in this book, if you will fish consciously to the "shady side" you will catch more bass. Besides the objects which offer shade, the secluded arms and bayous where trees give overhead cover from bright light will invariably be good producers. But so will deep lies below open water. Many bass fishermen do fish these places, just on a sort of hunch or "feeling." But light is the factor that they need to understand.

LIGHT AND THE TIME OF DAY

Early in this chapter I remarked that questioning bass anglers about the time of day they liked best, or that gave them the most success, brought forth preferences predominantly for early and late. Further, I noted that studies have shown time and again that the greatest amount of bass activity occurs, over the long term, from dawn until midmorning and from mid- or late afternoon until dark. Now we can more easily begin to understand *why* this is true.

Certainly influences in addition to quality of light are also present. The temperature of shallows at these times is likely to be pleasantly cool and comfortable for bass. Forage, feeling the same influences, is also active. By and large these are the times when the surface is likely to be reasonably calm, too. Not always of course, but the chance is high. Yet all of these items argue forcefully that the *light condition* is a dominant influence allowing and inviting activity.

Note well that the chief times of surface activity for bass are usually early and late. At those times there is no glare. What light there is is spread rather evenly. There is not the *need* or urge to find the "shady side" now, for it is all shady side. Bass are now able to see with more clarity than at any other times.

May I remind you that bass are well equipped with color-translating cones in their eyes, as well as rods that designate brightness in low light.

It is interesting indeed to note that almost all fish of *shallow* water are thus well endowed. Now a bass, even though it spends much of its time in water anywhere down to thirty feet in depth when available, is still considered a shallow-water species. During the periods of the day when light is modest in the surface strata, bass therefore are able to appraise shape and color to best advantage in those strata. This is why so much surface activity occurs at those times.

Before the sun is directly upon the water, and late in the day after it moves off, there is a beautiful overall glow, looking from beneath the surface. *Intensity* of light is even. Deficiencies of sight in a bass are now of lesser importance. Light and shadow have combined to produce an even lighting. *Accuracy* of the strike of a bass is enhanced—and don't be misled by anglers who say a bass never misses. Of course they do. Overly bright light, as I've pointed out, can itself cause a bass to miss its target.

Recall how you have often fished, very early, at dawn, and perhaps again at dusk, in the shallowest water. Many times I've taken bass that were feeding so shallow their backs were out of water. But now, relating this to light, you begin to understand why. In the lowest light, the shallowest water may appeal to many heavy foragers. There will be exceptions. But if you are going to fish close to shore, do so in the very low light of dawn and dusk. We're not speaking here of size, so don't confuse this with trophy fishing. This is quantity fishing. As the light comes up, you will find bass feeding farther out from the shore. They can now see well down somewhat deeper.

DEPTH AND LIGHT

But now the light comes up and up (in early morning fishing) until the sun is on the water. This is precisely when many a bass fisherman gives up. By now he is tired, and perhaps hot and hungry. The heck with it. Yet careful studies have shown that bass do not necessarily cease feeding then. It is at this time of day that we must begin thinking about the "shady side" in a *vertical* plane. As brighter light occurs, it begins to become uncomfortable to the eye of a bass, and the fish may feel unsafe in shallow water. This is especially true when the surface is calm or only barely skirled by whimsical and gentle morning breezes. But now the angle of the light allows it deeper penetration. By retiring little by little vertically, that is, deeper, the bass can match almost exactly the light conditions that were on the surface shortly after dawn.

Of course the same influences are felt by forage. So, as the bass retires and the forage does also, feeding may continue. One broad study carried out over several years shows that on the average, given normal feeding conditions, bass continue foraging until well on toward noon, regardless of depth. Presumably the feeding ceases mostly because they are fed full, but also because they have retired to deeper places to spend the day.

A danger of course is that bass fishermen may take all this to mean that bass are caught *only* in shallow water during the low-light parts of the day. This is not true at all. None may feed shallow on a given day. Big bass, as noted earlier, will usually be caught in deep water. What we are saying is that when bass are feeding chiefly by sight, one of the easiest methods for them, and feeding on or not far below the surface, their activity will be tied irrevocably to light conditions. If you want to catch many bass, and enjoy seeing them hit, the low-light periods of the day are the times to do it, up top. Exactly the reverse of what we have just outlined will occur in afternoon, the fish working up slowly, as light lowers, until that excellent overall glow becomes the prime inducement to lambaste surface or near-surface lures.

OVERCASTS AND BREEZES

Light in its relation to overcasts and broken surfaces is worthy of brief discussion here. When there is a solid overcast, bass waters are so to speak in a state of dawn or dusk, throughout. This removes a severe restriction that the fish may feel at times of bright light. They may roam more. *Everything* is the "shady side." Feeding periods, if occurring, may continue past normal times, and in shallower water than usual. In many ways, though it may seem that fishermen would have it easier now, they don't. There is no longer an opportunity to "trap" bass lying in an exact spot, the shade of a log or beside a cypress bole, or under the edge of a floating weed bed. While they may be in such places out of habit, they can be almost anywhere, and oftentimes are.

A wind may have the same general effect. If there is barely enough breeze to muss the surface, light conditions just beneath and for the first several feet down are almost exactly the same as during calm low-light periods of dawn and dusk. This is why, all of a sudden, a fisherman who has been fishing deep discovers, usually by a fluke instead of purposely, that bass are avidly slamming lures *just under the surface* right out in sunny places. The breeze that roughs the surface but does not make that stratum uncomfortable or ruin the aim of the foraging fish has also scattered and bent the light rays. Just below surface the light is beautiful, for a bass. The effect is almost the same as a modest cloud cover.

But now the stubborn angler who clings to his surface plug or fly-rod popper that was working wonders on a flat surface finds that he has to make many casts to get action. He also finds, if the surface is fairly rough, that he "misses" strikes. Actually the bass miss. They cannot *see* a surface lure from below as plainly because of the crazily bent light rays due to the undulating chop of the surface. The shrewd angler will now drop down to a foot or two below. Here the light is smoothed out and the water action— in a light breeze—also begins to relax. Besides, the fish is now on level with the lure, not trying to look up against the broken surface, and feeding is easier, more successful, and less discouraging for it.

I am sure an entire book might be written about the importance of light in any fishing endeavor, but especially about bass fishing, for bass are so extremely sensitive to it. You can even see evidence of this by penning bass in a cool but shallow place and watching their discomfort and anxiety reactions as the light gets brighter and brighter and they cannot escape from it. Like many fish, black bass have pigmented skin cells that act much like the bits of colored glass in a kaleidoscope. Various stimuli cause reactions within these cells that, in effect, tumble the pigments around so that they form new patterns. Anxiety in bass causes color changes that often culminate in bars and markings unlike those seen in a bass at ease in the water. Too much light from which the fish cannot retire sparks exactly this reaction. If light is that important to a bass, it is quite obvious that it should be at least as important to a bass fisherman!

CHAPTER SEVEN

The Senses of Bass

HOW THEY SEE COLORS

How often has each of us heard some enthusiast declaiming about Old Slabsides, that monster just too smart ever to be caught. Humans have a habit of attaching human characteristics and high intelligence quotients to lower animals. Bass certainly do seem sometimes to be crafty indeed. In reality, however, they have very small brains and little intelligence, if measured the way that of humans is measured. They are creatures wholly manipulated by their complex environment. The very fact of this unwilled manipulation makes them seem sometimes smarter than we are. But this appears to be true simply because we have not learned enough about this complex environment and its effects.

Every bass fisherman should understand the level of development of each sense of his quarry. Though bass are endowed with several senses, sight is undoubtedly the most important as related to feeding. And it is chiefly the feeding urge that attaches a bass to a hook.

We have discussed in the preceding chapter the effects of light in the domain of the bass, and have lightly touched on color vision. I'm sure bass fishermen need to understand color vision in bass thoroughly. Some anglers and even some knowledgeable writers are convinced bass are color-blind. In the light of the masses of scientific knowledge this is no longer debatable. Others believe a spot of red on any lure is what makes the big difference between fish and no fish. Some believe in changing lures every few minutes until just the right color combo is hit upon. Others have two or three favorite colors and stick with them. All these views might be modified somewhat if the anglers were better informed about what is definitely known regarding color vision in black bass.

Color-vision development does vary among fish species. But it is known to be quite well developed in bass. Many careful experiments have been directed at solving the color-vision riddle. Early studies sometimes solved nothing because they confused *color* and *intensity*. For example, if bass were assumed to be able to see yellow as a color just because they were conditioned to feed on and select tidbits of yellow in several varying bright shades, the experimenter erred. The bass might be selecting correctly because of the comparable intensity of light reflection throughout the scale of shades. This has nothing whatever to do with color selection. Later experiments recognized this error and controlled it. An explanation of how these experiments were done is valuable for the bass angler to have.

One of the most conclusive was carried out about twenty-five years ago, but unfortunately few anglers ever heard about it. Others since then have for the most part substantiated those early findings.

Fundamentally the way bass color vision was checked scientifically was by training bass in a laboratory. It was necessary to devise a means that would prove whether the fish were selecting shades of gray, meaning they were color-blind, or actual colors. In white enameled individual aquariums each bass had identical space, identical illumination, and each had electrodes implanted so that light shocks could be administered. Elaborate safeguards were utilized to assure that conclusions could not be mistakenly drawn. The bass were fed larvae from medicine droppers of different colors. Standardized color shades were used, and their intensities measured. The bass were kept at a similar level of hunger, and a way was devised to make certain no bass could hear movement of the larvae—if they were capable of that.

Each bass was assigned a feeding color. It was allowed to feed only from a dropper of that color. When another food dropper of a different color was introduced, and the bass rushed at it, the moment it crossed a certain line it got an electric shock. (If a bass struck the moment a dropper broke the water surface, that strike was discounted because it could have been motivated by the bass habit of striking at motion.) Each bass was given identical response time. It was soon evident that certain individual bass, like people, were smarter than others.

At first just red, yellow, blue, green—were used. Fish trained to see red and yellow were the leaders in correct selection; blue and green trainees had more difficulty. Next each fish was forced to choose only between several shades of the color to which it had been trained. Obviously this would prove if the bass could distinguish shades of the spectrum. But to toughen the test, and check actual color vision, several shades of gray were also mixed in. The blue- and green-oriented fish confused those colors with gray. Yellows had difficulty with light grays. Reds did the best, showing little confusion with grays.

Various combinations were introduced to learn to what extent color intensity was a factor. Fish trained on yellows still did poorly; they seemed to see yellow and light gray similarly. Bass then were tested with several colored droppers, for example, blue and green at once, or a pale pink and a gray. Again, reds won, greens got confused over grays, and blues did very poorly. Further toughening of the test ensued—between varied tints of a single color, between several grays plus a single tint. Emerging results showed that blues and greens, as seen by bass, were colors of low intensity, whereas reds and yellows were of high intensity.

Most interesting were conclusions from still further tests showing that strictly as *colors* bass distinguished reds best, even when forced to make a choice between some red and a gray shade of identical *intensity*. Likewise, strictly as a color, green came next in recognition, followed by yellow. Blue was almost wholly out of the running. There was much more, but the results simply further substantiated earlier findings. In the hardest choice, the fish were tried with color shades clear across the spectrum. Most intriguing was that bass appeared to see purple or violet, and that they just may be able to see both ends of the spectrum—short and long rays—rather like the way a human eye sees them.

By now the scientists had confirmed that *light intensity* fills a vital role in the feeding life of a bass; that strictly as *colors,* regardless of intensity, reds and greens are most easily recognized and seen most plainly; that yellows and blues may be seen much as grays. Further experiments tended to prove that reds were an attractor. But this was not conclusive. It may have been simply more easily recognized as color.

We know that the *size* of an offering is important, depending upon the size of the fish and the rate of its metabolism (which in turn is dependent upon the water temperature). We know that the *shape* of a lure has at least some importance. Some shapes imitate natural foods. Others are designed to create what the inventor assumes to be attractive motion. *Motion* also is important, as an imitation of a natural food, or simply as an attractive "come-on."

Color is far more complicated. Just because a bass can see red does not necessarily mean that he likes red; indeed it's possible that red might frighten him. Color has been used in lures to imitate the shades of natural forage. But there are many more instances of color being used simply as color, in the hope that it will appeal. Does it appeal to the fish, or only to the whim of the fisherman?

We first have to know what a bass can see. A bright, flashing spoon or spinner, remember, is not color. Even a brass or gold spoon cannot technically be called color. The flash of light from metal objects is the attractor. The intensity of the reflection, related to how polished or dull the lure, how clear or murky the water, and how bright or dull the sun, is what appeals to, or frightens, a bass. It may arouse curiosity, which stimulates the fish to follow and strike. In extremely clear water and bright sun it can be frightening.

The above applies to metal lures for underwater use. On the surface, there may be another angle. Dick Kotis, the lure manufacturer and renowned bass fisherman, has long felt that over light bottoms, such as the gravel pits in Ohio where water is extra clear, a lure with color, such as a yellow or frog finish, or even simply a dark lure, say black, will spook bass badly on bright days. Experimenting, he began using a plain chrome finish on his surface plugs, with great success under those conditions. This may be because the fish is looking up at the lure and the chrome has the effect of cutting down the silhouette, whereas the dark or colored lure emphasizes the bulk, which may in bright sun and water make bass skittish. Chrome of course is a noncolor.

DRAWING CONCLUSIONS FROM COLOR VISION

One must be wary of interpreting conclusions about color vision. In my tackle box is a bright yellow top-water plug with a white belly and gaudy red atop the head. Anglers buy thousands of comparable surface lures in various shades. But a bass, viewing the lure directly from below or on an angle from below, sees very little color.

Last year I got into a glass-sided boat so my sighting position was about three feet below the surface. Dick Kotis cast surface lures of several colors and I watched. The white, or pale, undersurfaces of the plugs were about all I could see. As if to emphasize the fact, as we worked several coots swam into my vision. I photographed them, from underwater. Only their feet, and a bit of the belly showed.

When we switched to a diving lure in yellow, of course I could plainly distinguish color. I would have to conclude, however, since the bass confuses yellow with gray, and the *contrast* with the water, which is a matter of intensity, allows the fish to spot it easily. When we ran a shadlike diving lure under the water, it did look to me quite a bit like a small shad. Here was the attraction of shape, size, motion, and color, all simulating natural forage. Up top, I had to conclude that color, except for light or dark— intensity again—might have small importance. Looking up against the light from below, color as such, even on the bottom of a lure, meant little. It may be that the chrome surface lures and black surface lures are all we need!

Another well-known lure maker and an expert bass fisherman, Ed Henckel, made up some top-water popping plugs for gifts at Halloween time, with black heads and orange bodies, the orange below as well as above. Surprisingly, he began getting numerous orders. The plugs, it seems, did well on bass. Motion and sound and the splashing of the water were certainly important. But the orange probably is seen as a shade of red by the bass, and this as "darker" as opposed to "lighter" when one changes lures, using one with a white belly. In a surface-light situation where "darker" was called for, it's possible this is why the plug brought results.

We must not as fishermen confuse what a bass likes or is attracted to with what it is capable of seeing. Take blue, for example. The experiments seemed to prove that bass do not see blue as we do. But I know of an instance of an angler who is absolutely sold on blue plastic worms, the kind sometimes called "jelly worms," because they are clear, like jelly, letting light through. This man exploded when I told him one time about how bass presumably see colors. He had caught dozens of real trophy bass on his blue jelly worms.

"I didn't say they won't work," I explained, "but simply that the bass probably don't see the blue that you do."

What actually occurs is that he fishes these blue worms on the bottom much of the time, six to ten or more feet down. The water of the large Oklahoma impoundment where he fishes could be called clear, as opposed to muddy or murky. But it isn't glass clear. It is of average clarity, the water holding a substantial amount of molecular material in suspension. At the depths where the bass lie, light is not at all as it is at the surface. The fisherman, looking at the blue worm in his boat, sees its glow of light coming through the plastic jelly and it appears bright and appealing. In even eight feet of water several things happen to obscure that color.

One is that light penetrating down this far in water of such clarity is greatly diminished. And in diminishing light those blue worms progressively lose their blue. The bass sees them about as the fisherman would see them at full dusk. In addition, the *color* of light that has passed through water is changed. The color of the water at any given level varies; it is of a different shade than, say, a foot above or a foot lower. Thus, suppose we say that at eight feet the water color (the light) is of a shade similar to light passed through a dark blue-green glass. The plastic worm, held in a simulated shade of this light above water, would not appear the same blue it is in full light.

Without question these factors are what make the blue jelly worms more effective, where this angler uses them, than the ordinary black opaque plastic worms. Even in dim bluish-green light and with low light intensity, the translucent blue will appear more lifelike and simulate a living creature more realistically than the opaque black. Comparably, the "see-through" purple worms so successful and popular today, and the green ones also, give the same effect. We know that bass are capable of seeing the violet end of the spectrum, and that they are capable of distinguishing greens to some extent. Add the "glow" of the jelly plastic in dim light tinged by water color, and no doubt, with added motion, an exceedingly appealing, lifelike imitation is produced.

The somber colors, in fact, may appear more lifelike and believable than the bright ones. However, in excessively turbid water a gold or yellow plastic worm might draw attention—not necessarily because of color appeal or recognition, but because of *visibility*. The contrast leads the fish to investigate, the action nails it. But now what of the angler who swears by red plastic worms, or strawberry shades, which are indeed most effective under some conditions. The answer may be something bass fishermen never thought about. And it may apply to the other colors, too, such as blues, greens, and purples.

Consider as an illustration the red snapper, a deep-water saltwater fish much prized as a commercial table variety. Snappers are bright in color where you see them in the market. But a snapper in twenty feet of clear ocean water begins to lose color to the human eye seeing it from above, or from scuba gear. The red dims and dulls. By the time the red snapper is down at the bottom numerous fathoms deep, the small amount of dark greenish-blue light penetrating there applied to the red sides of the snapper turns it into a *dull gray* creature. This is a common phenomenon known to ichthyologists as "deep-water protective red."

The strawberry-colored translucent worm is laved at ten to twenty feet, or even at six or eight in water of medium clarity, by greenish or bluish light, the effect of sunlight filtered through water of those shades. The strawberry color becomes less and less distinguishable, until at some particular depth it is a translucent gray. This is the same effect illustrated by the grade-school experiment in which a wheel with the four primary colors in equal quarters around the rim is set spinning swiftly. The colors then blend into a neutral gray. In addition, at varying depths the *mixture* of colors will change the lure appearance, exactly as in mixing paint. At some specific depth blue water plus red worm undoubtedly makes the worm appear violet to purple. A yellow lure in blue water may at some point appear green.

The clear worms, as every angler knows, have all but replaced the older opaque colors. Several bass senses may be appealed to by this. These new worms are more limp, have a more wormlike feel. But the see-through factor, which allows light to go through and pick up a shade of color on the way, gives extreme lifelikeness. Those colors, mixed with the color of the water, are translated into natural colors below. This is why, in different waters—of differing clarity and/or depth—some colors work better than others. Few bass fishermen, however, have so far taken these phenomena into consideration.

You may recall my earlier mentioning of fishing with wonderful success in Montana, at spawning time, with baby-blue worms. An angler should interpret such an occurrence correctly, too, or he will miss the correct conclusion. I doubt the color as such had anything to do with the fact that the fish hit faster on these than on black or dull-colored worms. Because of spawning, the bass were concentrated in only small areas of shoreline reeds. Competition for food was severe. The pale blue worm was easily spotted in motion in the crisscross of the reedy habitat. The dark worm was not rejected, but fewer bass saw it quickly and at a distance.

THE SENSE OF HEARING

Bass do not appear to have ears, as we know them in humans, and indeed have no outer ear. But the sense of hearing is well developed, and also important. The attention of a bass is frequently directed toward available food by hearing. A typical example occurs occasionally where I can easily observe it on one of my lakes. There is an underwater shelf of rock that juts out about two feet off the bottom at one point. This forms a dark, cool crevice on bottom and is very attractive to bass. One or more is always resting or lying in wait beneath the shelf.

When I suspect their presence in hiding, I've tried casting a lure onto the surface near the rock bluff. This ensures that the fish cannot possibly see the lure strike. When the lure makes its surface *splatt*, the bass does one of two things: either he will dart out in fright and whisk directly away to a new hide or, if he's hungry, he will come charging out and whirl toward the place where I have left the lure purposely lying inert. Both actions show that not only did the fish hear the sound, but that it knew the direction from which the sound came.

I have also tried casting far past the shelf, so that the lure drops onto the creek bed above the lake. Then I gently pull it free and retrieve so that it eventually crosses above the ledge. Using a lure with fore-and-aft spinners that gurgle, again I can entice a bass that is hungry. It may not strike, but it charges out and orients itself properly for a look. The gurgle, drawing nearer and thus more distinct, has been heard by the fish.

When lures based on "noise," which means vibrations carried through the water, first arrived on the market, many anglers scoffed. Yet some very successful lures nowadays utilize the sound principle. Some shenanigans have been worked on this theme, too, like the lad who called fish with a buzzing bee in a bottle sunk below surface. Those vibrations undoubtedly carry very little through water, and besides there is no reason to believe a bass has ever heard a buzzing bee and therefore would be attracted to it. I will not deny that *any* sound audible to a bass might at times attract it out of curiosity, however.

One current successful lure maker uses a small lead weight in the head of a certain lure to give it proper stance and balance and action. In some of the early models the lead worked loose, and rattled. He discovered that some bass enthusiasts were systematically shaking several dozen in a store to see if any rattled. These they bought, and confessed that the noisy ones got best results.

Numerous "rattle" lures have been marketed. The surface popper and chugger-type lures and the "gurglers" all aim also at hearing as well as the fact that the water movement attracts by sight. But bass hear more than just the loud noises, like lures of this variety, or outboard motors, or clanking on boat bottoms. When close enough to forage, they easily pick up the vibrations created by swimming forage fish, or a crayfish scratching back under a stone. It is now conceded that many diving and deep-water lures with only modest action send out vibrations picked up by bass, and that the line parting water in front of the lure may do likewise.

Sound is important to a bass at any time where safety is concerned, and during periods of extremely turbid water where feeding is concerned, or in deep water where only small amounts of light penetrate. Under such conditions a bass *must* find food at least partially by hearing, and on occasion entirely. Large flashing spinners cut through murky water with a sight picture for a nearby bass, but they also produce sound vibrations audible to a bass. It is not inconceivable that the slow retrieve of a black pork eel over bottom debris in dingy, deep water is first *heard* by a bass, before the lure is seen, or perhaps scented.

How do bass "hear"? They monitor sounds in several ways. Keep in mind that they do not need ears like ours, for sound is conducted via the dense medium of water far better and more emphatically than by air. When passing through water sound is actually amplified, and it also travels much faster. A sound vibration at a pitch within the range of the human ear and emitted in air at a thousand feet would take slightly less than one second to reach the hearer. The same sound—and a bass can hear within a part of our audio range—launched underwater would be heard in much less than one-fourth of a second. Thus, bass are forewarned of danger, or alerted to food, far more quickly than we can even imagine.

The manner in which they interpret sounds may be physiologically different, however. Within the skull there is an inner ear, which is sensitive to sound vibrations that strike the fish's skull. How delicate this arrangement is we can only guess; it may be exceedingly so. This inner ear relays the sound messages to the brain. The air bladder also relays sound because vibrations of varying intensity change the air-bladder pressure, and these changes are relayed by nerves in its covering. There are also sensors along the lateral line. These have multiple purposes, one of which is to pick up sounds.

The bass's range of audible frequencies is quite different from that of humans. They are capable of "hearing" only low frequencies. They may be able to hear vibrations as low as we do, which is around twenty per second, but probably six or seven thousand per second is as high as they can detect. The human ear reaches up to some 25,000 per second.

Of course no one knows if fish "hearing" is the same sense as ours. But it is now thought that the bass uses the sensors it posseses along its lateral line as a kind of sound-ranging device. Recall that earlier we discussed the fact that bass are believed to make daily feeding visits or migrations by following distinct lanes lined by marker objects such as rocks, stumps, logs, or sharp banks or points. This is accomplished, scientists believe, by a kind of sonar such as bats use when flying. Swimming motion sends out vibrations that bounce from objects and are relayed back to the fish. This allows them to know precisely where each object along the swim lane is located.

There is another interesting speculation regarding this lateral-line sonar system. When a lure moves through the water, the vibration is picked up by the fish even though it cannot see the lure. In addition as it closes for the kill, still unable to see the lure, let's say because of total darkness or murky water, the swimming motions of the fish send out vibrations that bounce from the lure itself, a perfect tracking mechanism. This is still in the realm of supposition, but it may account for the bass's unerring accuracy under difficult conditions.

Another intriguing study is presently in progress relative to sounds the fish themselves may make. Sensitive monitoring devices have picked up and recorded on tape numerous underwater sounds that are still not identified. Some of these experiments are being carried on in small lakes, where the exact composition of the aquatic life is known. Thus the sounds picked up must be coming from a relatively small group of species. Lure makers are much interested in these experiments, and in fact at least one is deeply involved in carrying out his own. Is it possible that bass make sounds heard and recognized by other bass? No one knows—yet.

Whether or not one learns to catch bass by appealing to their auditory sense is not as important as realizing that they do have sensitive hearing.

For some reason normal usage of outboard motors does not seem to bother them. The gentle, subdued whirr of the little electric prop apparently does not spook bass either, and indeed may even sometimes attract their curiosity. Vibrations sent out by a plummeting anchor may disturb bass in that area. Particularly in clear, shallow water, boat noises—clanking of gear, paddles, etc.—definitely make bass wary. On the other hand, the knowledge that they can hear lure movement, and can locate lures by sound as well as sight, is valuable. It teaches an angler that he can fish "blind" when necessary and still be successful.

THE SENSE OF SMELL

The sense of smell is not evenly developed in all species of fish. Salmon are thought to be able to smell out their parent streams and thus migrate to where they were born. Sharks detect blood in water from long distances. Catfish partly "smell out" as well as taste bottom food with their barbels. In bass, which are predators, the sense of smell is located chiefly in the paired nostrils that are easily seen on the snout. These do not have inside openings, but come to a dead end. However, water washing into these pores carries scent stimuli that are relayed to the brain.

At this point in research, much is still to be learned about scent and scent fishing, but enough is known now to be utilized by bass fishermen to their distinct advantage. For example, the amino acid present on human palms, and exuded with sweat, has been isolated as serine and proved to be repellent to fish. Some races—whites chiefly—exude more of this than others. Youngsters and women secrete less serine than adult males. Males who perspire copiously secrete more serine than those who do not.

One year a friend of mine who never showed a sign of perspiration even on a brutally hot day, and I, who perspire until my shirt is soaked under similar conditions, did a small experiment. We changed lures every few casts, each of us always using the same type, size, and color. Neither of us washed hands between changes. He outfished me on bass everytime. But when I washed my hands with plain old nonscented laundry soap, and he did not, I drew almost even with him.

You can take this or discard it, but if you are a bass angler who listens to all the "possibles," you will take it. Gasoline and oils are repugnant to all fishes, chiefly because they are harmful. The bass angler is in error who fails to wash his hands after operating a motor and getting gasoline and oil on his hands. A friend of mine, one of the most successful bass fishermen I know, washes his hands with bourbon whiskey after a run by boat before beginning to fish. I consider this a disgraceful waste of good bourbon but cannot argue with results. One researcher who has worked with the sense of smell in fishes has found that alcohol is attractive, and the sugars in a whiskey such as bourbon particularly appealing to fish. Switching lures with the bourbon smell on the hands just may serve as a mild attractor.

A gentleman who did more a few years ago with the science of scent fishing than any other discovered that ordinary soaps, not scented ones, apparently had an attraction for fish. Catfish have often been caught on hunks of laundry soap. Bass, thoroughly predaceous, were not specifically attracted, but were not repelled, whereas both gasoline and insect repellents were obnoxious to them. Washing the hands with soap before changing or touching a lure, or else washing the lure before casting again, he decided, had advantages. The clincher was that a metal lure, which readily retains scent, would give little result after being handled by a person who exuded much serine, but after a half hour, during which it was washed by constant casting and retrieving, it worked much better. This man even washed live minnows with soapy water after hooking them by hand. He felt results were better.

Dick Kotis, the lure maker and well-known bass fisherman, washes his hands after using gas or oil with a motor, and he feels that even carrying reel oil in a tackle box may be a disadvantage. It gets on lures, or at least the smell does, and inhibits fish. These may be ideas to scoff at. But I don't intend to scoff at suppositions from people such as Kotis.

Here are a few items that have been learned about sense of smell in fishes, and in particular bass and other predators. Sweets are attractive. Salt is definitely an attractor. This is thought to be the reason that solutions used to preserve such items as pork rind, which contain much salt, are actually an attractor. I have caught dozens of bass with fly-fishing tackle using a small strip of pork rind taken from a salt solution and impaled on a bare hook. I have watched many of them take the lure. They approach, appear to sniff or evaluate it, then inhale it. Salt, I am convinced, is the reason. Like most fish, bass are extremely sensitive to the relative salinity of the water and have definite limits to their tolerance. They have inbuilt measurement sensors, possibly in the lateral line, that tell them when dangerous salinities have been reached.

Some of this knowledge will suggest to a bass fisherman what to do and what not to do. Some of the most mysterious aspects of the sense of smell in predator fish concern what is now well authenticated as a warning system to others of their kind. According to one Canadian researcher, a fish that sustains injury while hooked, such as broken patches of skin or scraped scales, secretes an infinitesimal amount of a complicated chemical that tells others of its kind to stay clear. Further, a forage fish hooked and used as bait, it has been suggested, may well exude a chemical signal of fright or anguish that tells predaceous species of its travail and inadvertently urges attack.

The soft plastic worm, and other soft plastic lures, have become among the most deadly for bass. One of their early disadvantages was the smell of the plastic and the oils used to keep them from sticking to molds. Then lure makers learned to use what are called "scent masks" (a common one is anise). This has been proved not repellent to fish, especially bass. Some lure makers claimed they had added an attractor scent. What they had actually done was to add a scent that was not known as positively attractive, but neither was it known as repellent. This killed or masked the truly repellent scents of the material and processes. Recently, however, manufacturers have used new plastic coatings impregnated with scents supposedly attractive to bass, and these are released into the water when the lure is wet.

Do you recall the old jars of pickled minnows and other natural baits? I doubt they ever caught anything. The so-called pickling solutions—preservatives—were mostly offensive to fish. Today processors know several methods of overcoming the problems. Freeze-drying is one. Stink baits don't work for bass because they are not scavengers. But it is a fact that when fishing is slow a piece of bait—a section of fresh-dead minnow, a chunk of worm, a crayfish tail—added to a lure such as a jig enhances success. The bass may be attracted by the motion, sound, and color, but not enough to strike. As it approaches, it picks up a scent trail and begins to home in. This is the final promotion that clinches the sale! Again, scent fishing for bass is barely in its infancy. But those who understand that bass do have a well-developed sense of smell, and cater to it protectively or aggressively, will be in the forefront when stringers are weighed.

OTHER SENSES

How well or poorly the sense of taste is developed in fish is difficult to establish. Scientists know that it does exist, and that it is much better developed in some species than in others. There are taste cells on the tongue, the lips, and the throat. Some species have others placed in various locations on the body, from the paired fins to the tail.

Experiments show that some species can distinguish basic flavors—bitter, sour, sweet. Carp will lie under a leaning mulberry tree and eagerly eat falling fruit. Watch carefully when many large tadpoles are floating in a lake and you will never see a fish grab one, even though those of bullfrogs in particular look large, fat, and nutritious, and certainly are easy to catch. This jellylike stage of the frog contains chemicals repulsive to predator fish. Perhaps this repellent has evolved to protect them during their nearly helpless stage.

Taste is probably not of any special importance to most fish, and in the bass not highly developed. It is easy to confuse taste and sense of smell. Scent may tell a bass the food item is edible, and from there on taste isn't really necessary. Even though some lure makers have touted plastic worms with a genuine smell of earthworms, it's doubtful that they taste like an earthworm to the fish. Yet if you observe bass closely, you will note that a hungry fish will seize a big plastic worm, with or without earthworm smell added, close on it, and gulp it down clear into its gullet. We cannot prove that it doesn't like the taste, but the odds are it isn't very important.

Taste as such may serve other purposes. Fish—bass among them—are acutely aware of acidity and alkalinity of water. A western member of the sunfish family, for example, the Sacramento perch, has been established in some of the Sandhills lakes in Nebraska. It can tolerate high alkalinity better than other sunfishes, and some of those lakes offer it. Scientists believe that taste buds may serve as monitors of the acid and alkali quotient in the water.

Saltiness is also thus monitored. Largemouth bass move into brackish water in some places along the coast, along both the Atlantic and the Gulf. Some excellent bass fishing occurs in the lower portions of numerous coastal rivers of the South. Tidal wash adds salt water to fresh and the bass will tolerate the mildly saline mixture. They grow very strong, in fact, inhabiting brackish water for long periods. But they have a limit of salinity. Taste buds presumably are important for determination of salt content. To a bass fisherman, the acuteness of the sense of taste in his quarry has little application.

The sense of touch is of course well developed. It is similar to the same sense in humans. Nerve endings scattered over the body serve to relay messages of touch. Though acute, this sense has no special correlation with fishing methods, either. Nerves of touch, however, also serve to monitor water temperature. Nerve endings or sensors along the lateral line may also be involved. This, of course, is extremely important, because temperature almost entirely dictates where bass will be at any given moment. We will discuss it in detail in the next chapter.

Sensors along the lateral line, and possibly elsewhere, are acutely attuned to water currents and other water movements. There is also a sense of balance, and in the liquid habitat of the bass this is most important. Otherwise it could not tell whether it was rightside up, upside down, or on a tilt. Both the lateral line and the inner ear assist here.

These explanations of how the senses of a bass are developed and utilized show, in a way, what it is like to *be* a bass. The angler who understands them is enabled all the better to "think and feel like one."

CHAPTER EIGHT

The Controlling Influence: Temperature

THE MATTER OF COLD BLOOD

We have said that three important requirements of any life, bass included, are food, safety, and comfort. The last item, to a human, means many things—an easy chair, a comfortable bed, protection from heat and cold, good air to breathe, water fit to drink. The human has myriad means of attaining these ends. So, too, do other warm-blooded creatures. The wild goose migrates back and forth between suitable seasonal climes. The deer grows a special winter coat to protect it from the elements.

In addition, humans and all other creatures of warm blood have a kind of inner fire. The heavy fall coat of the deer helps hold body heat. Humans pile on clothing for the same purpose. Or they migrate like the waterfowl. They can thus sustain themselves well in a broad range of temperatures, from far below zero to as much as 120 degrees F. or more. To be sure, if the body temperature of a warm-blooded creature is raised or lowered only a few degrees, its system fails and it dies. But those exigencies can be reasonably well controlled.

The fish, conversely, has cold blood. Some fishes, such as certain of the oceanic species, avoid the rigors of climate by long seasonal migrations north and south exactly like migratory birds. The black bass, because of its freshwater lake and stream habitat, is far more restricted. Nor can it—or other fishes—grow special coats for seasonal protection. In the search for comfort, the bass may move to some extent horizontally, but most of its search will be vertical. It must try to find a water level where the comfort range exists. That search and its successful accomplishment are possibly the most important factors related to fishing success or lack of it. Few bass anglers of past years paid close enough attention to it, but the modern kind now realize that *water temperature,* because it almost totally controls the whereabouts and activities of bass, is the key to success or failure.

A warm-blooded creature submerged in water of a given temperature has a built-in system of burning food to keep the blood and body temperature up to par. But a bass, cold-blooded, has no such mechanism. Its body and blood temperature approximate at all times the temperature of the water in which it is suspended. When the temperature rises, up to a point limited of course by life tolerance, the metabolism of the bass accelerates. As water temperature decreases, metabolism—all bodily processes—slows down. Continued progressively downward to limit of life tolerance, the bass "motor" slows down until it is barely operating.

But the bass has, like warm-blooded creatures, a precise comfort range. This is the temperature range at which it feels best and is likely to be most alert and active. Its metabolism is revved up and it feeds at its heartiest. Because it is in high fettle within this temperature range, it is always seeking a place in the water where that range exists.

It may not always be able to find such a spot. In some shallow southern waters it may be forced to tolerate higher temperatures because there's no place to go. It may even be forced because of hunger to feed at higher than the "feel good" range. But it may also switch feeding times, to after dark for example under those special circumstances, when its body temperature is better attuned to the cooler surroundings. If the temperature goes too high, it will become so uncomfortable it will feed little. Finally a point is reached where the metabolism shuts down. The blood temperature has passed the limit of life tolerance, and the fish dies.

Increasingly colder water does not affect its comfort in quite the same way, for the following reason. The maximum comfort range for a bass is much closer to its high tolerance than to its low tolerance. Thus, as water temperature drops below the maximum comfort range, the metabolism slows, slows, slows, the fish is less and less active, takes less and less food, until, unable (let's assume) to find any comfortable place, it ceases activity entirely for days at a time. Yet it can still be caught, when bodily processes demand food, although much smaller baits and lures will usually be the only items acceptable, and the strike is now very weak.

COMFORT RANGES

It is interesting to note, and it is logical too, that the temperatures at which bass spawn are within their ranges of maximum comfort. As mentioned earlier, the largemouth spawns normally at from 62 to 65 degrees. It may spawn at higher temperatures, up even to 75 degrees, but seldom much below 60 degrees. The smallmouth bass spawns at from 60 to 65 degrees normally, and it may spawn at temperatures to 70 degrees.

Numerous studies of comfort levels and of high temperature tolerances for bass have been made. Keep in mind that the comfort level is the level of greatest activity and balanced metabolism. Thus, these ranges are the ones the knowledgeable bass fisherman will always attempt to find, and in which he will fish. For the largemouth, outside limits for the range of maximum well-being span from roughly minimum spawning temperature of 60 degrees up to 75 degrees. For the smallmouth, the range begins at about the same temperature, 60 degrees, but the smallmouth dislikes (is uncomfortable in) high water temperatures. A high of around 72 degrees tops its all-out activity span.

A good many expert bass anglers and scientists have attempted to pinpoint the exact temperature considered absolute optimum for comfort and activity. Some have put the smallmouth level at 65 degrees; another places it at 68. Given the 13-degree overall span for the smallmouth, this places the best fishing temperature just about in the middle, and narrows it to a span of *only* 3 degrees. For the largemouth the best absolute level has been placed by one at 73 degrees, by another at 72, and by a third at 70. This puts the optimum within the overall 16-degree largemouth well-being range nearly at the upper edge and covers a range of only 4 degrees.

The exact temperature may differ somewhat according to latitude, and it certainly differs in relation to what is available. Largemouths are able to thrive in water above 80 degrees when cooler water is not accessible to them, as long as the water is not heated abruptly to that level. They have been caught in water temperatures of 85 to 88, and have survived at 90. But water of 90 degrees is nearing the metabolic shattering point. In northern waters, where temperatures seldom get into the eighties, largemouths would die quickly if some debacle caused temperature to rise suddenly above 80. Smallmouths are intolerant in most of their waters of temperatures in the high seventies, and cannot exist if sustained temperatures above 80 occur. A severe, and sudden, temperature change of 10 degrees, up or down, can kill either species, if no swift retreat is available.

What the fisherman must understand, however, is that comfort is a two-edged sword. A hungry bass lying at a level of absolute bodily comfort will forsake that water temperature, if food there is unavailable, for temporary forays into much higher temperatures. After feeding, or pursuing schools of fish—as with schooling largemouths after shad in summer—the fish will immediately return to the more pleasant level. However, the angler would not habitually go looking for those higher temperatures where the bass "may" feed. If he locates the well-being level, and the bass are there, and hungry, they will hit his offering with as much eagerness as elsewhere. And so, finding the comfort level, i.e., the level of greatest probable activity, is the *single most important chore* for any bass fisherman.

A provocative way to look at it is that within this temperature interval the "bass motor," its metabolism, is running the most efficiently. The bass is—and this is extremely important—*growing* at its fastest pace. Because of the metabolic speed and the growth speed, the food intake must be larger, and so the hungry bass feeds more, and is that much more likely to be caught.

Many anglers do not realize it, but (cold-blooded) fish never stop growing. People, and animals, do. Warm-blooded creatures all have an average maximum size. Occasional giants or runts occur, due to glandular and other actions. But there is no such thing as an absolute maximum size for a fish, except as aging and natural attrition cut fish down at fairly predictable sizes. It should be encouraging to know that new records *are* possible, always. A fish that happened to make it past the average allotted span of fish years will keep right on getting bigger until the day it dies.

Remember also that we said length of growing seasons have much to do with size and age of fish. This of course is another influence of temperature. The reason a record bass is more likely to be caught far south than anywhere else is that where bass are able to grow every month of the year, as in south Florida, the older the fish the larger it will be. In addition, you can predict where a new record or any outsize bass is most likely to be caught: in a deep lake of the Deep South. This is because the fish, growing year round, is able in such waters to find temperature ranges most suitable, comfortable, and therefore most helpful to longevity.

Another fact of bass growth anglers should know is that when water temperature drops below 50 degrees, growth comes almost to a standstill and from there on down there is little if any growth at all. In such low temperatures, all the fish needs to do is take in enough food to keep its motor barely turning, but none to grow on. Largemouth bass have been caught in lakes that do not freeze over at temperatures way down in the low forties.

Water is at its densest at 39.2 degrees. But it can drop to 31 degrees before freezing actually starts, even though the water is expanding now and thus becoming lighter and thus rising. The reason I use 31 degrees is that the 32 degrees we've long spoken of as the "freezing" point is actually the point on the upward scale where melting begins. That is, if you raise ice temperature from 31 to 32 it begins to melt. I have caught largemouths through the ice when the bottom temperature was well down in the range between 32 and 39.2. But they were just barely in operation. Smallmouths are regularly caught, by patient fishermen willing to suffer, in water down as low as 34 degrees.

If a bass fisherman will spend more of his time hunting the best temperature range than he does fishing, he will improve his score over the long haul. Further, he must learn that when this range is not available he should seek the one closest to it. Most of the time, he'll be searching for a level that is below optimum, but higher than the general water temperature. That is, in the range let's say from 40 to 60 degrees, he'll always be on the lookout for warmer pockets of water. Every step upward will mean heightened metabolism in the fish, thus more need for food, and therefore more activity. But on the upper end, if water is in the eighties or the high seventies, the angler will try diligently to find some bottom patch or stream riffle or deep pool or spring where the temperature is even one or two degrees lower. Because the span of best action is very narrow and the larger interval of outside comfort limits is narrow enough,, it is easy to deduce that the fish are awesomely sensitive to temperature and that a single degree lower or higher may mean a concentration of fish ready and overly willing.

DEDUCING WHERE THEY'LL BE AND WHEN

In Chapter 1 I mentioned what I termed seasonal "shuffles" of bass. These will occur, in temperate climes, most prominently during some period of the spring and fall. But they may occur in summer during unusually hot spells, or at any time during cold snaps, as in the South. Such movements will not be of long duration, if weather conditions are only temporarily abnormal.

Now it is easy to understand that these shuffles, or changing of locations, are tied almost wholly to temperature. We know that bass are essentially fish of the bottom. They may lie at times suspended in mid depths, and when they do it is invariably because they are seeking the proper temperature. Most of the time, except during surface feeding under specialized conditions, bass will lie suspended only a short distance above bottom. There are instances when a bait or lure fished right on bottom doesn't get much action, yet when it is raised up three or four feet it does much better. Almost without fail a temperature check will show that the bottom water is outside the comfort zone but that a proper temperature exists slightly above. Bass do not rise or dive far after food.

In addition to temperature and the fact that bass are fundamentally bottom fish, we have seen that they are also object-oriented. I have used that terminology earlier because I dislike always talking about "weed beds," which many books have done. Certainly bass do utilize the edges of weed beds to a great extent. But there are hundreds of waters where other "structures" are far more important. In many Florida lakes bass lie far back under floating water hyacinths. It's a great location for forage, and the dense roof of vegetation cuts the sun's heat. Yet a lake in desert surroundings has nothing similar; it does, however, have rocks or submerged cactus and brush, and that's the place to look.

At any rate, we know that bass desire the temperatures already discussed, and that they stay most of the time on or near bottom, and that they insist on some object, or bottom formation or cliff that can be translated as such, in proximity—logs, weeds, rocks, a depression, a hump, a steep bank. So now it becomes obvious that all we have to do is to let those three items guide our search for the fish. But the *temperature* will be the key. When and if it changes, the fish will seek a new spot to their liking of comparable configuration.

In shallow southern lakes there may be many places that offer all three, or at least as close as the fish can come to them. But the farther north one goes, the more will seasonal changes have their effect. Wherever seasonal changes of climate are severe enough to kill aquatic weeds, or at least retard their growth, then wherever the bass are using the weeds these will be less important from fall on through winter and will gradually become more important from the warming trend of spring on into summer.

On a lake where prevailing seasonal winds blow—and on the large impoundments these are always important—a certain shore will be less likely than its opposite to hold bass. For example, if warm winds are usual over a period of several weeks, let's say during May, they will warm the water along the shore against which they blow, and the shallows there may be several degrees higher than on the upwind shore. But a cold wind depresses surface and shallow-water temperature rapidly, and thus the fish might be driven by it from a shoreline even though other desirable factors were present.

Some years ago when I lived in northern Michigan, I went each spring to fish for smallmouth bass along the islands and shorelines west from Mackinaw City. The bass would swarm inshore usually in June. They were going to spawn in due time. But also these shoal waters were warming and comfort temperature brought them in even before it was bedding time. During my first seasons I began fishing the east and northeast shorelines most simply because I happened to be able to get to them more easily. I didn't do very well, except in small pockets of protected water.

I began to realize that these pockets were warmer than the shoreline water, by several degrees, and I suspected that's why few fish were there. Then one day I hiked across and fished the southwest shoreline of Waugoshance Point. I'll never forget my first session there, because I caught twenty-six smallmouths, each about two pounds, in twenty-six casts. I released all. I wanted to continue fishing. But it occurred to me as I fished, wading, most of the time with my back to the shore, that the warm breeze was my right shoulder, from the West. Next day I was back and it was the same. The early summer winds, it now dawned on me, were predominantly from the western quarter, and they warmed these shoals because they were pushing the water against the shoreline. It is a lesson that has stayed with me a long time, and it is applicable to impoundment bass fishing. During cold snaps, or brief periods of extra hot weather when winds blow, there is the same effect—raising or lowering of water temperature—of brief duration.

It is important to note here that many bass fishermen, especially on the big new lakes, head for the shore where the wind is piling waves. The theory, which often is absolutely true, is that small food such as the plankton on which shad and minnows feed is being pushed by the wind and wave action toward shore. The forage fish follow, feeding on this more and more as it is compressed, and the bass follow the forage fish. Once at the shore, the theory goes, the shad and others will turn to face the incoming current of wind-pushed water, scooping up plankton. The bass also lie facing that way, the better to scoop up their meal. Casting at such times from shore and retrieving back in, or else casting parallel to shore, gets best results.

As I've said, this certainly does all work out just that way at times. But the theory is too pat. If the waves are too rough, the baitfish dislike it and don't stay. If the temperature goes down too far outside the comfort zone for the bass, they will invariably seek food elsewhere. The point is, they seldom have trouble finding it.

Seasonally, a bass in fall in any area where the weather is emphatically cooling, will move to deeper water because the shallow water cools first. But where summers are hot the bass will have been in deep water all summer except for feeding trips upward, and they may do just the reverse of their relatives farther north. They may find the temperature they like in shallower water. Later, in spring, the shallows and shoals will warm first in cold to temperate regions, and the fish, still on bottom and near some security object, will move in. But when the summer comes and the temperature of the shallows loses its comfort range, the fish will shuffle back to a similar bottom situation in deeper water, or suspended near a cliff or other structure over deep water.

The clarity of water will make a substantial difference in how fast or slowly it warms or cools. I remember learning this the hard way during a fishing trip a few years ago. Two of us had been fishing an exceptionally clear lake. Bass were coming into shoreline waters in droves and the action was great. We decided to make a run to another lake most of a day's drive distant, and stay over. That one was renowned for its big bass. When we got there, however, and began fishing, next to nothing happened. I was not thinking in those days quite so much in scientific terms and was puzzled. The fact was, this lake was a deeply stained variety. Penetration of sunlight was minimum. In fact, from such waters the rays are to some extent reflected rather than absorbed. Without question the shoreline temperature was still not high enough to draw the bass in.

WATER STRATIFICATION

I have held back material about stratification of lakes—thermal stratification, which means simply layers of water of varying temperatures—until we had established the basic patterns of bass behavior. Now we must add this phenomenon because it is extremely important on large lake waters anywhere in the temperate zone. It is also important for fishermen who fish smaller and protected waters.

There are two general types of lake waters. One is the small, shallow lake or pond with a depth, let's say, of not over twenty-five feet. The other is the large lake with greater depths. A third type may be lumped in with the first. This is the lake, usually of modest size, that is well protected from any heavy wind action. The large lakes such as the impoundments are always open to the wind.

Consider first the small, or protected, types that are not deep. During the summer the water temperature in these will have a uniform progressive temperature drop from surface to bottom. That is, for every foot of depth there will be a gradual lowering of water temperature. Of course clarity, again, will make some difference. But at any rate no erratic lowering is evident at any point from top to bottom. The curve is gradual and even. Finding the proper depth in relation to temperature here is fairly simple. Also very important is the fact that oxygen supply will be fairly uniform throughout.

To keep the explanation of what occurs on these lakes as plain as possible, consider one in the North that freezes over. Late fall cold chills the pond surface. As the air temperature drops, the surface water becomes colder and denser and sinks, pushing upward lower areas of progressively warmer, less dense water. This process is called the "fall turnover."

At exactly 39.2 water reaches its greatest density. When a lake in a latitude where the surface freezes has completely turned over, the water throughout stands at 39.2. But now the surface begins to freeze. From 39.2 downward, water expands, becoming lighter, and eventually it becomes ice. Thus, the surface temperature is now below that of the remainder of the lake, and the water at the surface is expanding, becoming lighter, and floating. Were it not for this expansion and lightness below 39.2, a lake would begin to freeze on the bottom.

During the winter this frozen lake lies dormant. The lightest water is on top, and ice cuts off any wind action. In some shallow northern lakes and ponds fish kills may occur, especially if heavy snow lies over the ice. No sunlight then penetrates. Weed growth, which by the process of photosynthesis releases oxygen and burns up carbon dioxide, ceases. Without wind aeration, oxygen dwindles. As weeds die because of blocked photosynthesis, their decomposition releases more carbon dioxide. The fish, their oxygen supplies depleted, die. I have seen shallow northern lakes in this condition where, by cutting a hole through the ice and looking through it with head covered to blot out light from above, one could see dead bass littering a stretch of bottom. Bullheads would swarm to the hole, attempting to gulp air.

This of course is a specialized situation, but it illustrates why the annual lake turnovers are important. As spring nears and the ice melts, the surface layers rise in temperature until they reach 39.2 maximum density. At other depths the water may be at 36 or 35 or 34, and so the dense water sinks, and the lake gradually turns over again—the spring turnover. Meanwhile wind, with ice gone, stirs and aerates the surface and the turnover redistributes oxygen. Photosynthesis of the remaining sprouting water plants begins, adding more oxygen.

But now we turn to the large, deep lakes. These, which seldom freeze except in extreme northern bass latitudes, still go through the fall and spring turnovers and the winter dormancy periods exactly like the small, shallow lakes. In the deeper ones, the turnovers are extremely important to fish during summer because the depths, even without ice cover above, may have become depleted of oxygen, and of course the turnover redistributes it from upper, better aerated water. We have not discussed oxygen to any great extent but it is obvious a fish cannot stay in water where it is deficient. Bass will attempt to find water of both proper temperature and plentiful oxygen.

In the summer true thermal stratification occurs on the large, deep lakes. As air temperature goes up, wind action causes surface waters to mix with those a few feet down, thus bringing upper water temperature close to that of the air. These upper layers become less and less dense. They of course remain on top. Wind action, which does not reach very deep, keeps mixing them. Presently this top layer is of rather even temperature, but the effect has not reached more than a certain small number of feet down. A surface stratum is formed that is close to an even temperature throughout. It may be anywhere from several feet to fifteen feet or more thick, and from the top down there will be anywhere from no difference in temperature to as little as one or two to five degrees.

Because this horizontal stratum is much lighter than the water below, it does not mix well. Further, let's say for illustration that wind blowing along the surface shoves current eastward, and underneath in the stratum this causes a reverse current westward. In effect this upper stratum lies upon the colder water below and currents glide upon the colder lower stratum. This circulating upper water, of near air temperature, is technically termed the *epilimnion*.

Immediately below it, where air and wind effect have not reached to any extent, the water has been warming gradually but at a much slower rate. The warming has of course been caused by some heat drawn from above. But every foot further down one goes, the warming is drastically less, and so the temperature of this stratum falls off very rapidly. This band of water is called the *thermocline*. The word means "slope of temperature." Water temperature here will drop so swiftly that over a ten-foot span there may be as much as a 25-degree difference. In other lakes it may be more gradual. In some the thermocline may be broader than in others.

The lower edge of the thermocline marks the depth where there is little influence from surface warmth, even over long periods of time. Thus, in the area from here on down to the bottom—called the *hypolimnion*—there is little change in temperature. The temperature drop from the hypolimnion to the bottom may be as little as 5 degrees, or in a very deep lake possibly as much as 20 or so, but the drop is very gradual.

There are many variations, lake to lake, and many influences—wind, currents, temperature, degree of warming—that cause a lake to stratify or not. In a great many lakes that do experience stratification, for a variety of reasons the thermocline may have not only the best temperature ranges for bass but also the most oxygen. Heavy weeds in the shoreside portions of the epilimnion may be short of oxygen in summer. On an overcast day, for example, or at night, photosynthesis slows or ceases, decomposition continues, and oxygen becomes deficient. Or a lowered water level, resulting from evaporation or a purposely lowered impoundment, may decrease oxygen supply.

At any rate, we may say that in lakes that *do* stratify, the thermocline very often will be the home of most of the bass all summer. If a lake is too cold, and the upper limits of thermocline temperature too low, the upper stratum, if thick (deep) enough, will hold the bass. In most lakes that evidence stratification, the deep, cold hypolimnion will be (in summer) the least habitable from the standpoints of both temperature and oxygen supply. In many instances scuba studies have shown that bass in impoundments that stratify spend all summer either high or low in the thermocline.

If not there, they are almost certain to be in the upper stratum, but most of the time in its lower portion.

In many places it has been said that the thermocline is of most interest to fishermen in summer because the most preferable temperatures and the most oxygen are found there. I do not wish to refute the idea but to qualify it. Many bass lakes do *not* stratify. Many that do stratify have improper temperatures *for bass*, although not necessarily for other fish species, in the thermocline. Some have both proper temperature and adequate oxygen content in this unique stratum. When you do find a stratified lake, and optimum situations in the thermocline, it is a virtually perfect situation. The fish are then virtually confined to rather definite places. But the trouble is that some very qualified researchers have assumed that situations they found and studied in specific latitudes were generally the case, which of course is not true.

It is most important that fishermen understand the stratification phenomenon and the advantages to bass—in certain cases—of summer residence in the thermocline. But exceptions are just as important. For instance, a large number of impoundments built on big rivers evidence currents throughout, or else excessive wind action. These waters cannot and do not stratify. On some others, where power plants are operating, the generators at the dam create currents many miles up the lake, inhibiting stratification. Lakes that are not constant-level, where water is let out occasionally for irrigation or other purposes, or where it is accumulated, have currents entering or leaving bays and arms. All such influences inhibit natural stratification. In shallow lakes depletion of oxygen may result, as we've said, from lowering.

Just in passing it should be noted that one of the wonderful attributes of the impoundments is that flooding of natural terrain more often than not fashions lakes with highly irregular shorelines. Most bass food is produced in near-shore waters. Thus, the more irregularities—bays, creek entrances, arms—the better the food (and bass) possibilities. It probably has not escaped the reader that we have avoided mentioning streams. These will be discussed separately, but it suffices here to say that of course stratification cannot occur in them. In addition, the current in rivers where bass live usually keeps the waters well oxygenated, so this is no special concern.

Let us review by means of an illustration. Starting at the top, the upper stratum of a stratified bass lake may be at perfect comfort range for bass, and may be well oxygenated. Let's suppose this layer is ten feet deep and at surface 75 degrees, with a drop at the ten-foot level down only to 71 degrees. Over the next ten feet down, however, in the thermocline, the temperature drops swiftly, to 58 degrees. The upper part of thermocline is thus perfect for bass habitation, too. The lake is eighty feet deep here. From the lower edge of the thermocline, at twenty feet deep, on down to bottom the temperature drops—over this sixty-foot span—only from 58 to 45. Oxygen is low, temperature likewise.

There may be seasonal changes in stratification. During swift temporary changes in surface temperature, strata may be formed that soon dissipate. Twin thermoclines may spasmodically form. But once true summer stratification is evident, the thickness of the upper stratum may begin to increase as the season progresses. The epilimnion (upper stratum) may slowly expand, become much deeper, and the thermocline narrower. This has a profound effect upon the bass.

An upper stratum ten feet deep in early summer may contain all the water in the lake that is at optimum comfort level in temperature. Or maybe this comfort zone is only in the thermocline. But by August or September that upper layer may be forty feet thick (deep), and so even though the surface itself may be too warm, a vast new comfort zone has been opened up, or else the comfortable thermocline is deeper. The bass will be deeper, of course, but they may not also have more bottom acreage within comfort range, which is one reason they are sometimes more difficult to locate at this time. Conversely, a lake of modest size that does not get much surface weather effect or mixing may stratify and stay quite stable throughout the summer. There may be a surface stratum ten feet thick that remains all summer. If the weather is clear, this layer will of course be deeper than if it is murky. Some turbid lakes with stratification may have the upper stratum only four or five feet thick.

Not all lakes, as noted, stratify in summer. Very large, deep, cold lakes open to wind may not. However, a bass angler utilizing either the massive impoundments or the small ponds should be well informed about this phenomenon, and he should ascertain whether or not stratification does occur where he fishes in summer. Such knowledge can be most helpful in finding the fish, and that, after all, is what it's all about.

MISCELLANEOUS TEMPERATURE CONSIDERATIONS

In all situations where a layer of water more than three or four feet deep has very little variation in temperature, anglers must make some careful deductions in order to find bass. I recall an incident related to me by a friend that occurred on an Arkansas lake. On the weekend a swarm of fishermen were in action. There were also other swarms of water skiers and pleasure boaters. The day was gently overcast, which made the light just right for surface fishing, particularly since the water temperature through the first several feet was exactly right for activity.

The man who told me of the incident said he and a partner tried desperately to catch fish in an arm that was known as a fine up-top producer when everything was "right." Fishing, however, was very poor. It finally occurred to him that the enormous disturbance caused by the boats might have something to do with it. Still in all, the temperature up top was proper. But now the angler decided to see about lower level temperatures. He discovered that the water at fifteen feet was only two degrees cooler. This gave him a clue. They moved out over a trough that he knew ran across the arm. They went clear to bottom, sixteen feet down, and began to catch bass. He had to conclude that the fish had gone down to avoid disturbance by the boats. So had the forage fish. But the temperature was still perfect for activity because of such narrow variation.

We have touched on the fact that bass will leave their comfort range when necessary in order to feed. But they will in such instances usually feed swiftly, and then return to the proper temperature level again. The more exaggerated the differences between this feeding zone and comfort, the sooner the fish return to comfort. We have also mentioned that at below optimum temperatures, bass will feed progressively less as the temperature drops because they need less food. It should be emphasized here, even at the cost of repetition, that *small* offerings are most often more productive than large or normal-sized ones in such situations. In addition, they must be moved more slowly than usual.

There is another, more important consideration. A bass is no long-distance chaser even at top form. At a low rate of metabolism it will hardly deign to move at all to seize food. *Pinpoint presentation* is the key to catching bass then. This is not always easy, for it involves guesswork. But the colder the water in general, the warmer it will undoubtedly be in the *deepest holes*. Find those, and drop a lure straight down if you can. The new-fangled jigging on bottom works well. Or drop a lure such as a small plastic worm into the hole and then move it only an inch or two at a time.

Oxygen, as mentioned, is commonly low in deep waters. I know a lake in northern Michigan, without inlet or outlet, that has such low oxygen most of the year on bottom that fish cannot live there. It is a small "straight-sided" lake; that is, the shallow rim is narrow and falls away rapidly. This lake, unsuitable for bass, was turned into a trout lake because the trout lacked the bass's preoccupation with structures and objects, and didn't mind being suspended most of the time at medium depths.

High temperature, as we've said, can deplete oxygen in shallow lakes, by revving up the decomposition process of weeds and by rapid surface evaporation. Without aeration by wind action, such lakes will become difficult for bass. The fish will try to find the best of what is available, and this may be outside their most favored temperature range. Whatever the reason for bass moving outside this comfort zone, they will always be as *close* to optimum as they can find. Thus one should look first for the perfect range, and if something is guessed to be wrong, try the one nearest. It may be slightly above or slightly below.

During periods of the year when seasons are changing, always remember that the surface waters are most severely affected. A quick change in air temperature can heat or cool upper waters rapidly. This will have its effect upon forage species, and upon bass as well. In both spring and fall, there is likely to be a reverse switch in times of day when fishing is best, in any latitude where waters are cold. During the night the upper waters have cooled. Fish will have left them for deeper, warmer spots. When dawn comes and you expect shallow action, it doesn't materialize. You quit in disgust, but you shouldn't. When the sun gets high, it will warm the upper waters of the shallows and shoals and this is the most active time there.

I think of two good illustrations. One March I was in south Texas doing photos of calling coyotes. We had our bassing equipment along and wanted to fish some of the tanks on the ranch were we were operating. We tried one about 8:00 A.M., after a chill night. Not a touch. At 2:00 P.M., when by all the rules the fish should not have been very active, they were just rolling and cavorting all over the same tank. The small pond, protected from wind, had warmed rapidly on top when the sun got high, even though the dawn had been chill. We used surface plugs and simply decimated the bass. But as soon as the sun was off the water, they quit.

The other illustration concerns high-mountain trout lakes. Waters here are always cold, even in midsummer. They are usually not very fertile, and the variety of life in them is sparse. I learned long ago that dawn and dusk fishing on these lakes is almost never very productive. When the sun warms the surface, middle-of-the-day action is the rule, for both fish and forage are then active. On clear waters for bass comparable to the high lakes, the problem then arises of spooking fish that want to feed in upper, warm strata. Invariably fishing is best when a light breeze riffles the surface; in smallmouth lakes this is especially evident.

Shallow lakes, North or South, are never as good bets for fishing by temperature as deep ones. A lake with no water over ten or twelve feet deep may have a lot of fish, and you may catch a lot, but the chance is they'll be small. Further, you can't pinpoint them easily because the temperature will be stable throughout the lake. Conversely, the lake with a highly *varied* temperature pattern—certain to be a fairly deep one—gives you real breaks. You can locate the bass exactly by temperature, for they'll be in very specific locations.

What is so curious about the temperature matter is that none of the fundamentals is the least bit new. Scientists and even thousands of fishermen have known for years that temperature influences fish. But somehow the average fisherman has never quite been able to let it become as important as it should be with him. Part of the reason, of course, is that in past years it has not always been easy to measure water temperature at varying depths. Today, as we will see in the following chapter, it is easy. So always keep it fixed in your mind that a bass is not at all like you are. The bass is cold-blooded. Water temperature actually dictates almost every facet of its life and movements. We too are severely affected by temperature, but we have many ways to dominate it. The only recourse to discomfort a bass has is to move.

CHAPTER NINE

The New Science of Locating Bass

BOATS AND MOTORS

To the bass fisherman of thirty years ago or more a boat was usually an old rowboat with worn and squeaky oarlocks. Its chief purpose was to support the angler so that he could cast from out on the water back toward and near shore. Today a fishing boat is a specialized craft. It is designed for fishing, of course, but today there are more fishing boats conceived and manufactured specifically for bass fishing than for any other purpose. And these have been borne to and on and by the large impoundments. The first thought in design is to make them efficient craft for *finding* bass.

Thus the average bass boat of today must be of a size equal to large and often rough waters and it must be able to get up and go. The distances between stops may be long. The calm waters may be ten miles from dock, or vice versa. To avoid wasting time moving over the 75 percent of bottom that is without bass, the angler wants to make the traveling swift. Then he needs a craft that doesn't require a lot of jockeying by paddle and oar, and one that gives room and comfort for fishing.

Indeed, today's so-called bass boats are designed for just one place and one activity: large impoundments, and bass fishing. It is simply amazing how many firms are manufacturing these single-purpose craft, and how many of them are spoken of as "bass boats."

110

Today's average is a boat of around sixteen feet; a few are eighteen. Some very good narrow-beamed boats have been built over the past few years and have become very popular with bass fishermen on the drowned-timber lakes. However, most makers now believe stability, and a wider margin for safety on the big waters, is needed. Thus, the trend is toward broad beam and shaped hulls such as the trihedral.

My own choice for today's large-lake bass fishing is a sixteen- or eighteen-footer with the trihedral hull. One sixteen I like very much has a sixty-three-inch beam. The choice between fiberglass and aluminum is a personal one. Both serve very well. The largest and oldest manufacturer of small boats in the nation, incidentally, researched all existing models by all manufacturers just prior to this writing, and from the lot, and from questioning scores of tournament bass fishermen, came up with what in general a "bass boat" should be. They came up with a sixteen-footer in fiberglass, with a beam above five feet and a trihedral hull.

The reason I emphasize size and stability in a bass boat for modern fishermen is that newcomers to the big lakes have little idea how rough and dangerous they can become. On a body of water, for example, fifty miles long and as much as twenty to thirty miles wide in some places, a wind can kick up water altogether as tough as on one of the Great Lakes and often worse than the open Gulf of Mexico under a similar breeze. Thus for safety a craft about as noted is a good place to start making a choice.

Bass boats as such only got started in the 1960s. But the spark really started a flame and today the choice is broad. Interior appointments on most of the craft are rather similar. In a boat of this size one needs a center depth of about two feet. An average on several of the better-known models is 24½ inches for a sixteen-footer. The entire interior trend is toward comfort but with lots of space and nothing in the way. Steering wheels, always inhibiting to movement of man, rod, or net, are swiftly giving way in these specialized boats to stick steering, located as a rule at the forward left side where it offers no interference.

There is a foredeck broad enough to stand on when necessary. If you're prospecting, ready to buy, beware of a foredeck that bends under your weight. The latest in bass boats does away with chrome rails around this foredeck. Just another nuisance, and besides that the boat will have a small electric motor mounted up front and a rail would not allow that. Most of the bass boats use high-back-rest swivel seats with no arms; a few have stationary seats with arms. The former usually get the nod. But the modern bass boat is not designed to carry a large group. Two fishermen is the design of most, although many carry three. Of course other designs are available, for families, but we're describing here the modern craft for serious bass fishermen.

The swivel seats are sturdily attached, and one should be certain they are. Everything is kept out of the way inside. Rod racks and storage trays line the sides. These should be roomy, but the boat is not a camper. Most models have a molded-in splash well for the motor. Bait wells are of course optional. But the fact is that few of today's impoundment bass anglers use live bait. Some like a fish well in which to place their bass. Most, however, hang them on a stringer over the side where they stay alive better.

One of the musts of the bass boat is shallow draft. It must be able to get into the drowned timber and the shallow spots as well as take the open water. To get an angler up high, some models sport a deck with a "throne" to which one of the seats can be moved. The forward stick steering, incidentally, eliminates the steering console in the center but also in some models eliminates the "throne" seat. Some fishermen prefer a rear or center console.

Most bass boats in the sixteen-foot class are powered with motors up to seventy-five horsepower. Some use one hundred. Less will do. However, the reason for the large power plant is twofold: it gets one from hot hole to hot hole in a hurry, and it is a large safety factor in a bad blow. An electric motor tilt is preferable, to avoid movement and noise inside the craft at each stop. The electric motor up front in today's bass world is a must. The ideal mount is one that is jointed. This allows the skipper up front to lay the little motor on the forward deck so that it does not thrust out over the front. It is swung up and out and down on the jointed mount by a rope. Controls for the electric, which is used once the destination is reached so the boat can be quietly jockeyed among drowned timber or into narrow pockets, are of the foot-pedal type. This leaves both hands free, and the fisherman who practices a bit can keep full control every minute, even while casting or playing a bass.

The bass boat is carpeted with the outdoor type of material or has vinyl flooring. This is to make it nonskid and quiet. There is ample room for the battery for the electric motor, and the angler owns a charger. Most leave them at marinas, to avoid carrying them in the boat. Anchors

—two—are an integral part of the bass boat. And they're rubber coated to avoid noise. Pinpoint fishing to bass located in a good lie requires a boat that remains in place. Once the spot has been ferreted out, no experienced bass man wants to have to do it all over again because of drift.

These, then, are the basic attributes and equipment for the bass boat on today's big lakes. I've gone over them, albeit briefly, because this rig is one of the mandatory instruments utilized in the new science of locating bass.

MAPS AND COMPASS

Average bass fishermen of a few years ago would have thought today's dedicated member of the clan had lost his mind, if they could see him show up at a new lake, and the night before his first try stay up half the night studying maps of the lake bottom. But it is a fact hard to hammer home to anglers that at least 90 percent of the catching is in the *locating,* and that at least 75 percent, sometimes 90 percent, of a lake contains no bass. These statements or facsimiles thereof may become awfully monotonous before you finish this book. We've already repeated it several times. However, it is absolutely the case that most fishermen who fail to catch bass have been fishing where there weren't any. They imagine the fish weren't hitting, but they weren't getting lures to them. A good map, if one will study it, and knows what he is looking for and how to interpret it, can really help put one over the fish.

Remember how all successful fishermen tell others that they must "get to know the waters"? What most have meant even though they perhaps did not know it was "getting to know the land on bottom." One who fishes day after day on a small lake does get to know the bottom well, even if just from dropping anchor. But a large lake is quite another problem, and the map is where to start.

There are several varieties of map available. On some of the big lakes, marinas have them. As a rule these are simplified maps that show details of shoreline only. You can orient yourself properly with a good one, but they cannot permit you to do a meticulous enough job of pinpointing where the bass will be. However, many such maps, and those available from Corps of Engineers and Bureau of Reclamation on lakes they have constructed and administer, will have at least some depth contours. Also, they will show where old roads run into the flooded lake, and where creeks once were, and sometimes where old submerged buildings stand.

There are topographic maps available at low cost from the U.S. Geological Survey. Some of these show what the land beneath a lake looked like before it was flooded. But as a rule the scale on these maps is not as fine as you need, for the land contours may be shown only at hundred-foot intervals. The most valuable maps are hydrographic maps, which give the depth contours of the bottom. The contours on most are at ten-foot intervals. These are excellent. But if it is possible to acquire one that shows five-foot intervals, it is even better.

Hydrographic maps are available from two sources. Some states either have all or most of their lakes mapped, or are in process and have some. Where these are available, the cost is generally low—from fifty cents to a dollar per map. Fish and game departments will know what are available. Federal hydrographic maps may be obtained from the U.S. Geological Survey, GSA Bldg., Washington, D.C. 20242. For specific maps of lakes east of the Mississippi, contact U.S. Geological Survey, 1200 S. Eads St., Arlington, Va. 22202; for lakes west of the Mississippi write the Survey at Federal Center, Denver, Colo. 80225. On some large lakes, sectional maps are available. You can also get from the Survey an index of available lake maps.

The first chore is to learn how to read the map correctly. Contour lines close together will mean a steeply rising ridge, those far apart mean a gentle bottom slope with little rise or fall. With a bit of study you can "see" what is on the lake bottom quite accurately. A submerged island, a long ridge or reef, a steep-sided deep hole, a drop-off, a shoal—all are important. A point of land above water that appears on the map contours to show underwater stairstep ledges and then a sudden fallaway to deep water may be exactly what you want.

The best approach is not to try to make an overall appraisal of the map, which is likely to be difficult and confusing. Instead, mark off a small section and study this closely. Let's say that you have talked to a few successful fishermen as they came in to dock, or to guides or the marina managers, and you learn that most bass have been taken the past two days in fifteen feet of water. On the portion of your map you have marked off for intense study, you carefully go over the contours. What you are looking for are places of fifteen-foot depth or very close to it that appear to be the types of locations bass will like. A stretch of fifteen-foot bottom with broad stretches between contours won't look like much. But a narrow one where an old creek used to come in will bear scrutiny. Perhaps the contours indicate a curve in the creek bed, with a fifteen-foot depth in the bottom. Circle that spot. You want to hunt it down.

Out on the water, you'll discover, that may not be as easy as it sounds. But after you have had long practice it will come much easier. So, the best plan in the beginning is to mark off the section of map that is adjacent to the place where you launch—the marina or a dock or ramp somewhere. This gives you a point of orientation. Now you can run the boat slowly up the shoreline and see the bays, islands, and other physical markers that show on the shoreline of the map. Every bass boat should certainly have a compass mounted on it. Check the compass with the map as you go. Then you will be properly oriented at all times. And here and there you can jot landmarks on the shoreline of the map. "Big white rock." "Tall dead tree." "Old road comes in." "White house on shore."

In a single hour you have that section of lake well fixed in mind, by shore contours and the depth contours on the map. Further, at the start, don't try for the tricky places. Try to find the fifteen-foot spots easiest to locate. Again, where creeks come in, or prominent points where rocks are submerged, or the old road. By selecting the easy ones—at least those plainest to work out on the map—you will learn the technique faster.

A pitfall is the water level of the lake. If it is a constant-level lake, and is full, that's fine. But on some impoundments levels are manipulated for irrigation and other purposes. Thus, on such lakes you will need to know whether the lake is full, and if not, how low it is. If it is ten feet low, that first ten-foot contour doesn't count.

Few bass fishermen go the one further step of carrying a pocket compass. It's a valid idea. If you want to get things down really fine, outfit with a compass of the orientation type. These compact compasses have a base plate with markings, use of which is described in the brochure with the compass, that allow you to keep travel direction by use of landmarks, and by degrees on a course. Used as the instructions explain, in conjunction with your map, you can not only find an exact spot on the surface below which is what you hope will be the school of big bass, but the same course settings can be used to find it again.

Whether or not you elect to get it down this fine, always triangulate a good spot when you locate it, even though you have marked it on your map. Line up shoreline landmarks that will allow you to return as close on the button as possible to where imaginary lines from landmarks intersect. A map will help you, incidentally, to estimate about how far from shore the spot is, if it is near a shoreline and not out in a broad expanse of open water. If the lake is full and stable, the depth contours will show with fair accuracy, when translated into map-scale measurements, the distance from the shoreline. Obviously you have to have a small ruler to do the measuring.

THE MAGIC BOX

The appearance on the market only a few years ago of the modern, compact depth sounder or depth finder at a reasonable price just about revolutionized all fishing from boats, but had its greatest impact upon bass fishermen. Today no bass fishing enthusiast would be without one. Many are now on the market, tens of thousands are in use. New ones are appearing regularly, several of them more and more compact and at ever lower prices.

The idea of the depth finder for sport fishermen is a result of adaptation of the sonar used in World War II for locating submarines. In simple terms, "sound navigation range" (from which the "sonar" abbreviation originated) is a means of sending out a sound wave via electrical conversion. The sound wave, audible neither to fish nor man, is sent through the water, bounced off any object and back to the sending point, where it is picked up. Timing of the interval between sending and return tells precisely how far away the object is.

A few years ago there was a rather sudden flurry of interest by numerous manufacturers in producing variations of sonar for use by anglers. At that time a national magazine assigned me the chore of tracking down as many of these experimental gadgets as possible, trying them, and reporting on them. One was a design held in the hands, the far end of it underwater. There was an earplug that allowed the user to check not only on depth by listening to varied noises, but also to hear fish as they swam. I discovered that I actually could hear a swarm of small bait fish, like a sudden breeze, as they swirled across the field of pickup. We tried still fishing and at certain depths I could actually hear a game fish seize the bait. It was an eerie experience, but I had to conclude finally that the invention was not very practical.

Another, made in Japan, was a fishing rod and reel and line, with a sensor at the end of the line, a ground that had to be stuck into the earth beside the bank-side angler, and an ear plug. Supposedly he could "hear a bite." It was worthless, but nonetheless it was evidence of a push toward "electronic fishing." By now commercial fishermen along the Atlantic coast had begun using large sounder (sonar) units. They were trying these not only for checking depth and type of bottom, which could be read in differing light flashes on a dial or on a graph by means of inked lines, but also for actually locating large schools of fish, or small pods of large fish.

From this kind of gear, which operates with high success today, it was but a step to build small, compact sounders for sport fishermen inland. I have always felt it was unfortunate that these were hawked originally as "fish finders." It is true that fish can be located with them, and frequently are. But the advertising had too many prospects visualizing the ease with which they would pinpoint the smallest minnow a hundred feet below, or the largest trophy game fish hidden in a deep crevice.

Fortunately, the growing popularity of bass fishing and the growing number of impoundments coincided with the soaring popularity of the small sonar units. Moss bass fishermen began to realize that the really practical application was in checking depth and bottom type. And even though the units are used by all varieties of anglers today, bass fishermen are by far the most important group, the group that has developed sonar potential to the fullest.

The little "magic box" is now virtually a must item of bassing gear on the big lakes. The transducer which sends and receives is in most cases permanently mounted in the boat, although it does not require permanent installation in every case. The compact "box" contains the dial on which the light signals are flashed, plus batteries and the necessary electrical equipment. Or some may be hooked up to storage batteries. Most fishermen have the finder mounted in a rack on a seat or on the side of the boat, for easy viewing.

It works roughly as follows. When turned on, the transducer, mounted just below the surface, sends out the impulses aimed toward bottom. The area of water through which the sound waves pass expands the deeper the waves must travel. From boat bottom to lake bottom, the pattern is like an inverted cone. The size of the cone differs in some units, but roughly it would be about two feet across at five-foot depth, double that at ten-foot depth, and progressively larger until at thirty feet it would cover a circle on the bottom ten or twelve feet across.

Signals are sent back, and translated into flashes of light on the dial, indicating the depth and also the type of bottom. A hard bottom of sand or gravel gives a specific width of flash and type of signal. A mud bottom causes the signal to fade badly. Rocks on an uneven bottom will show as several signals, because they translate as varied depths here. Each high rock bounces back its own signal. In general the width of the light signal is directly proportional to the depth of the water. The tilt of the bottom also is indicated. That is, a steeply slanted underwater bank within the sound wave cone will cause a broad signal because cone diameter is on a slant. Debris such as submerged trees and brush will be indicated in numerous scattered signals, but the one solid signal will still show where the bottom is.

Every manufacturer of finders naturally furnishes full instructions for mounting and use with the units. Thus it is our intention here only to sketch the rudiments. But it must be emphasized that you cannot simply zoom out across a lake, read every figure on the sounder dial and thus every bottom configuration as you go. Pinpoint checkups must be done slowly. Study of how to use the finder is mandatory, and also a study of what signals are caused by which objects and types of bottom. The more you study your finder in action, the more you'll come to know what it is trying to tell you.

For instance, you can learn how to read weeds on bottom, or weed beds. You can tell when you pass over cliffs or ledges underwater. You can spot a single submerged standing tree or snag, or read crisscross logs and jampiles of brush. Knowing what you are looking for and how to recognize its signals is obviously the most important.

CHARTING THE TEMPERATURE

What the "magic box" can't tell you is what the water temperature is at any given depth. You could inquire around the docks as to what depth most bass are being caught, then go out and look with your finder for those depths. While dockside information is never amiss, you don't have to have it to find bass, because there is another little gadget that will assist you. This is the so-called "electronic temperature gauge," which in some ways is more important than the finder. But the two together, plus your maps, open up amazing vistas in the new science of locating bass.

There are a number of different temperature gauges for anglers now being marketed. In general the principle of all is the same, although certain

Landing a bass in one of the Highland Lakes in Texas. Once nearly waterless, Texas today is a bass bonanza.

Largemouths from Lake Panas-offkee, Florida.

Catch of Florida large-mouths on plug.

Small lakes often furnish good bass fishing but seldom do they produce any great number of bass of trophy size.

Excellent smallmouth specimen coming in.

*Leaping smallmouth on spoon on north-
ern Lake Michigan shore.*

Catching smallmouth on flies in northern Michigan.

I started my boys early. Here's my son Mike with his first catch of smallmouths on Lake Michigan.

Spotted bass in mid-south latitudes tolerate murky water better than largemouths. Look for debris in shallows when they are up top.

Fishing the Rio Grande River above Espanola, New Mexico, for smallmouths. Few fishermen know they are here.

"Doodlesocking" among the cottonwoods, Ute impoundment, New Mexico.

Largemouths are found nowadays in every conceivable terrain. This is Ute Lake in arid eastern New Mexico.

Strip mining pits in southeast Kansas leave great land scars, but, when refurbished and stocked, they make wonderful bass fishing.

Largemouth leaps from mesquite bush in southwest. If you want to catch bass, you have to get hung up some, and "fish dangerously."

Leaping largemouth, caught on plug. Water is murky—the best type to look for when fishing shallow.

I land a bass on the lower Bushwhack Creek Ranch lake.

Typical of the many new bass boats. Note high perch up front. Many have high adjustable seats, both front and rear.

Wading northern Lake Michigan shore for smallmouths—using a casting rod.

Fishing the big timber of Toledo Bend Lake. Note building roof, inundated when lake filled. This narrow, slope-sided craft is another extremely popular model, born to the drowned-timber lakes.

Approaching line of timber, angler lets electric motor down over bow so we can move quietly.

I use one of the early model plastic floats.

Both largemouth and smallmouth have "gone west" far outside their original ranges. This scene is in Montana.

Fishing from rocky shore, Dale Hollow Lake, Tennessee. Spinning, with good smallmouth on.

In Lake Mary Ronan in western Montana largemouths like this one live in company with rainbow trout and kokanee.

Bringing in a smallmouth while wading Lake Michigan shore west of Mackinaw City.

Fly fishing with popping bugs for largemouths in Florida.

Sometimes regulation trout flies in fairly large sizes intrigue shy bass.

Shot from near water surface, big Florida bass seems to be flying. Fisherman is Dick Kotis of Arbogast.

Wading for smallmouth bass along shore of northern Lake Michigan in spring. Inshore concentrations offer action.

Spotted bass from a Texas stream. Most are of modest size, but a few southern impoundments furnish real trophy fish.

ones are handier than others to use, and some give more meticulous readings than others. You would not find, for example, that a temperature gauge showing only ten-degree intervals is very effective. I have one I use that shows five-degree intervals. This is all right because I know that it is accurate, and I can guess very close by the needle position the degrees in between. However, a gauge marked by single degrees but with numbers, say, five or ten degrees apart, is really best and easier to use. It gives exact readings most efficiently.

The average gauge works about as follows. Small and compact, it contains a battery for operation and a reel with anywhere from twenty-five to one hundred feet of "line," actually a covered wire. At the front end of this line there is a tiny sensor unit with a small eyelet to which a sinker is attached. Be sure the line on the one you purchase is marked in feet, not with five-foot markings, for you want precise readings and no guesswork.

The line with sensor is let down *slowly,* after the switch has been turned on. On some types a needle swings across a dial and shows the temperature at any given depth when you press a button. One some a needle shows in a centered slot when a dial is turned until its indicator points at the temperature being read below. Careful operators will give the sensor element at least thirty seconds to "acclimate" and send back a correct reading. Much of the time the reading will be almost instantaneous. But it is important to know it is correct, and then to believe your unit.

In a boat, where most bass anglers will be, you must of course come to a dead stop in order to read correctly. Otherwise the line will slant and you won't have a correct depth reading. When you do have a straight-down reading, then as you reel up the line (the better units have a reel and handle) you count the feet.

There will be times, obviously, when the temperature will be a kind of riddle. For example, it is always a good idea to test the surface temperature first. Suppose it is exactly right for comfort range for bass. Then just possibly you are in for good surface action. But now progressively test down to, say, ten feet. Maybe you'll find that temperature outside the optimum range. Or maybe you'll find there is only a one-degree difference. This would mean the bass could be at any level in that ten-foot span. In a stratified lake you would, however, quickly discover the depth of the upper stratum, and where the thermocline begins and ends. You'd have a fair idea at what general levels bass can be comfortable, and from there dope out the answers.

In addition to the electronic devices for measuring water temperature, there are simple mercury types that can be lowered to read temperature and that hold the recorded temperature at a given depth while being hauled back up. Although these are far cheaper than the others, the big electronic models are handiest and best. It may seem like you're investing quite a bit of money in all this "machinery." But the modern bass hunter knows well that it's worth the expense. One catches more fish this way. Besides, there is a new kind of satisfaction in finding the fish, even if you release every one.

GETTING IT ALL TOGETHER

Once equipped, it is now a matter of using all the items simultaneously to help you home straight in on the bass. Let us suppose that you have blocked off a single sector on your map of a certain lake, and by studying the map you have concluded that three or four places should offer the best types of habitat. You already know the outside limits of temperature comfort span for your quarry. And you know the narrow band of optimum-comfort range within the outside limits. Thus, you would like to locate that temperature, the best of the best.

You know the types of situations the bass like best. A rocky bottom will appeal to smallmouths, if that's what you are after. It will also appeal to largemouths. A firm bottom of any kind will be better than a soft one. Mud is not the best type, except under specialized feeding conditions, such as a hatch of aquatic nymphs. But ordinarily you would pass up mud in favor of firm bottom. And you know that submerged trees, a bend in what was once a creek, a rock ledge, a sloping point falling away swiftly are bass hangouts. All such configurations are what you are seeking.

Now you move to spot number one you've marked on your map. Drifting slowly or scouting with the small electric motor, you use your depth finder, not especially for depth yet, but to check out the bottom. Let's say it turns out to give a weak or fading signal: mud or decomposing weeds; also shallower than you had thought. Nonetheless, you stop and let down the sensor. Too warm at this shallow depth. You cross that one off and go on to the next. Here you are on the side of a point. The finder appears to be showing you by a complicated signal that there is a rocky cliff here. From the multiple signals you suspect stairstep ledges. There is also a solid jut down at twenty-five feet, the signals show, and as you move out a bit this falls straight off to forty-five feet.

This place has possibilities. You stop dead still now and let the sensor down. You feel the sinker actually touch the shelf of rock down twenty-five feet deep. Temperature here is four degrees lower than you had hoped. Slowly you take in line. You are now right along the stairsteps of narrow ledges. At exactly eighteen feet your dial reads 70 degrees. Perfect. You raise up, very slowly. At fourteen feet you get a reading of 72.

So now your map has led you in a rudimentary way to the general area. Your finder has told you the underwater configuration and the depths. Your temperature gauge has relayed its information that conditions are excellent. What you have located here is an absolutely perfect *type* of spot. This can be a real bonanza, not only today, but on many other days as long as the temperature remains constant. In fact, this type of bottom configuration can undergo numerous temperature changes because it has good potential from five feet on down to twenty-five at least.

It is certainly possible that this may turn out to be a total dud. But because, as we've seen, most of the lake bottom has no bass in residence, the chances are excellent that a spot such as this that has everything the bass need—we assume food is here or nearby—will at some time of the day have bass over it.

I have a friend who fishes this new way, and last summer he located a spot almost exactly as I have described. He found it about 11:00 A.M. We fished it tentatively and caught not a bass.

He was a most experienced scientific angler. He said to me, "I am positive that some time today there will be bass here."

We checked it three more times. The last round was at approximately 4:30 P.M. He took a four-pound bass on his first try. He caught it at exactly the spot where we had read off proper temperature on ledges from fourteen to eighteen feet. We guessed it had hit about in the middle, at around sixteen feet. Within an hour we caught and released thirteen bass here, all of them about the same size. I have to assume that we had found not only all the necessities, but had intruded upon a major or minor feeding period as well.

There is more to the story. This fine bass fisherman, like many others, uses what he calls the "pattern method" of hunting fish. Any given lake will offer a bottom that is predominantly of one type or another. In it there will be certain types of configurations or structures that seem, during a given period, to attract the bass. If bass are lying along ledges, such as I've described, on one point, he assumes they will be utilizing similar conditions along other points.

I fished with him two days last summer, during which he checked just such points as I've described. We discovered that several that lay roughly north-south had both sides very much the same in structure. The water was quite clear; thus light penetrated well. Almost without fail, each north-south point had bass on the west in the morning, on the east—the shady side—in late afternoon. On the east-west points this was not as pronounced, but the fact was that when we had found the "pattern" for the day—the points with rocky slopes and drops—he forgot all else and went searching more of the same. Many experienced bass fishermen pursue this tactic. This is not to say that bass may not be elsewhere on such days—in an old creek bed on a bend, along an old roadway, etc.—but when one good pattern is found, following it pays off.

I said in describing the bass boat that anchors—two of them—are a part of the gear. They are particularly important when one fishes by these scientific methods. On large lakes there is invariably a breeze sometime during any day. When a hot hole is located by diligent effort, it may be of small extent and one may be forced to fish pinpoint. Therefore the boat much be anchored in order not to lose the spot. In addition, even when hunting bass by these methods, a breeze can shove one off a good spot before it can be properly plotted and marked by lining up shoreside markers. Bass may indeed be run off by dropping an anchor while taking readings. But they will be back.

The friend I spoke of who fishes by patterns utilizes a marking method suggested by the firm from which he purchased his depth finder. He carries several small blocks, of about brick size, of white styrofoam. To each he ties a sixty-foot length of fishing line, which is wrapped around the block. To the end a sinker weighing several ounces is attached. When tossed out to mark a spot, the weight unwinds the line and the marker is set. He feels that for bass he does not need more than sixty feet of line, and sometimes uses less.

Last summer he carried several blocks marked "60" and some marked "30." Most of the time where he fishes the bass will seldom be below twenty-five to twenty-eight feet. The thirty-foot markers thus serve and stay right above good spots. In a narrow place, like running checks on an old creek bed, one has to do some very exact marking. It is not easy to work out the details of the course by boat. And it is important to fish very exactly to, let's say, that outside bend. In such instances, markers are indeed useful, and can be left in place if need be.

FISH FINDING

Several years ago I was producing a TV film about bass fishing on Toledo Bend Lake. At the large marina where we stayed and docked, scores of people were always on the long docks fishing for crappie, for this was the spring season, when one could catch them by hundreds. One evening two of us came slowly along the dock, going in after the day's filming. A lady with a cane pole had to move it to let us past. I asked how she was doing. She shook her head. Not very well.

Hap Noble, from whose boat we were operating, stopped and turned on his sounder. We could easily read the bottom. We knew there was no bottom debris here. Still, about five feet above bottom there as a flurry of signals. While I hung onto the dock, he continued reading. The signal kept flashing erratically. This indicated movement. We were over a huge school of crappies.

I said to the lady, "Pull your bobber way up and see if you can get a bait down ten feet." We estimated line length for her and she did as I had advised. Immediately she had a bite. While we watched a few minutes just for fun, she caught sixteen. How many more after that we did not wait to see.

Now then, this is a typical instance of finding fish with a so-called "fish finder." It certainly is possible, and it is fun too. Compactly schooling fish are easiest. For the person who is able to fish every day, it may at times be a handy method on bass. But I am of the opinion that though users of sounders should know the fish-spotting rudiments, this is by no means the important use for their unit.

You know, let's say, that bass like a firm bottom more than a muddy one as a general rule. You can pick up signals made by large fish, and if you were over mud you'd probably discount these because they are not likely to be made by bass. Large schools of forage fish, particularly of shad, which are common in so many impoundments, give out solid signals. They would ordinarily be in only a few feet of water and massed. Thus you can read the bottom and also the mass of bait fish. Some fishermen go all out to locate large schools of bait fish first. It is a valid rule that somewhere near the forage there will be bass. Commonly the bass will be on bottom in deeper water, like a family in a living room but within a quick move of the kitchen when mealtime arrives.

When you find a bottom configuration that looks good, by stopping the boat you can actually see bass on the dial by the signals they make. Those that appear and then disappear mean very simply that fish are moving down below. There is certainly nothing wrong in knowing how to "read fish" on your dial. But I believe too many anglers get caught up in trying to locate fish with their sounders instead of spending the time looking for the several conditions that indicate a hot hole. The consensus among many bass experts is that locating proper temperature, proper depth, and proper submerged structures will eliminate any need for trying to see the fish on the dial. The bass will already have been found.

I mentioned asking questions around a dock as to depth at which bass are being caught. Nowadays many large lakes have several marinas along the shores where rooms, meals, boat storage, bait and tackle shops, and every conceivable service is offered. These large operations like to see fishermen successful. Invariably several guides work out of each marina. The more fishermen, the more money for the dock owner. The more who catch bass, the more who flock to the place. *Depth* has become such a fixation with most such places that reports are in day after day concerning the level at which most fish were caught.

By checking for this information, much time and effort can be saved. A year ago a friend and I were told when we arrived that the expert anglers and the guides were taking most of their bass in seventeen feet of water. We assumed of course that seventeen feet was where the proper temperature was located. Obviously there might be many places in such a huge lake where the proper temperature was at other levels. But why experiment when the word was out?

We went looking for places that should have appealing configurations. As we passed a cove we could see several cars with boat trailers on them parked in the woods. This meant a road of some sort. Did it simply end at the shore? We moved in to have a look. No, it did not. What we saw was an old paved road full of chock holes that continued on underwater. Checking the map, it was easy to find where this road had once crossed what was now the lake. It seemed to bend in toward a side of the cove from which a high ridge thrust.

We followed the road by using the sounder. There had been a ditch on either side and so the hump we were able to follow was certain to be the old roadbed. In a short time we hit the seventeen-foot signal. Moving on a bit we could tell we were going "downhill," for soon the hump dropped several feet. We backed up to seventeen feet, then on back until we were at about twelve. Here we gently anchored. We had not read the temperature because we felt it was as logical to give the spot a try first. On the second cast I had a hit. We caught a number of fair fish here. Meanwhile the boats that had launched here had passed right over this gathering of bass without knowing they were here.

When we decided to quit, just for our own information we moved out over the seventeen-foot level and took a temperature reading. This was during a severe cold spell and the surface temperature had been dropped considerably. Over the first six feet below surface it was in the high fifties. Below that the weather effect waned, and we found 67-degree water at seventeen feet. To check this further, we moved out over twenty-five feet. Here it was colder again, even though by only two degrees. Apparently the seventeen-foot level was the best the bass could find. Two days later the weather was hot again and by midday bass were hitting on top in a frenzy.

Such are the methods used by modern bass fishermen who pursue the new science. Occasionally I, like others, wonder if some of the spontaneous fun isn't removed by eliminating the old guesswork. On the other hand, most of the guessing has been eliminated from the "funwork," too. Nothing beats catching! As I said way back in the beginning of this book, the science hasn't really killed the modern sport, it *is* the modern sport.

CHAPTER TEN

Selecting the Best Waters

NEW LAKES COMING OF AGE

Bass fishermen have an awesome number of lakes from which to choose. Most, however, will fish within a limited range of their home, except for special trips once or twice a year. An area of bassology that has not been studied to any extent by average anglers is the difference in lakes. Which one is best? On which will your chances be best?

Much of course depends on what satisfies the individual bass fisherman. Some are happy catching a lot of bass regardless of size. Some would prefer a chance at fewer fish but of larger size. Some would rather fish a week to catch one real trophy than to catch fifty bass of a pound each. Acquiring at least a basic understanding of freshwater ecology as it applies to bass lakes can help immensely in making a choice of fishing waters. It can also help one understand what occurs or may be in process of occurring on the single favorite lake he fishes.

Bass lakes are, broadly speaking, of two different general types. One is the fertile lake of modest clarity. Most impoundments and southern lakes fall into this category. These are the lakes where the food chain, from plankton on up through the small forage creatures to the predatory fishes,

126

is one of abundance all the way, at least up to the predator level. These are called *eutrophic* lakes. We hear a lot nowadays about "eutrophication" of lakes—Lake Erie is an example of advanced eutrophication, a "dying" lake. So keep the term in mind. For as we shall see, the very lushness of fertile waters, when carried to extreme, is their downfall.

The other basic lake type is the one with a sparse ecology. Usually such lakes are deep, cold, clear, have a minimum of vegetation, infertile soils, and only modestly fertile waters. They are not necessarily poor fishing lakes. Many of the best northern smallmouth lakes are in this category. The variety of life in them is limited. These are *oligotrophic* lakes. In a very general way it may be said that these lakes are "newer" in that they were produced by the last push of the glaciers, whereas the others are farther south and are "older" lakes.

What fishermen seldom realize is that nothing is static, not even a lake. It may sound a bit ridiculous to speak of the "aging" of lakes. But we can see it happening, in our modern world, because we see new man-made lakes coming into being year after year. Thus, we are present at the creation of these massive waters. However, the small, deep, clear northern natural lake of glacial origin, or the broad, cypress-studded shallow southern lake also had its day of creation. A classic example easily seen is Reelfoot Lake in western Tennessee, formed literally overnight by a tremendous earthquake in 1811 that changed the course of the Mississippi River.

What needs to be understood is that every lake, from the time of its forming, whether overnight or over a period of years, began at that time first to come of age, then to age, and then to decline. In some the process, just like the life process of any human, is much longer than in others. There are lakes of the past, both north and south, that have become bogs or marshes, or that have disappeared entirely through total aging until sediments and vegetation took over. If we could all live long enough, we would undoubtedly see the clear, deep smallmouth lake we've fished for years pass from existence. It might take ten thousand years or more, but as organic matter decomposes and falls to its bottom and silt is washed in, sometime in the far future it will probably disappear.

This is a long-term illustration. But the point is that the impoundments, our most important bass waters today, are, curiously, among the fastest-aging of all waters. They change rather rapidly. In much less than the lifetime of most bass fishermen, a new, wondrously productive lake comes of age and achieves distinction, then swiftly begins the dying process, becoming so ordinary that it disappears from the news. Every bass angler needs to understand at least the fundamentals of these phenomena.

A few lakes, especially natural waters, happen to have everything fall into place precisely right, so that as they have come of age a unique balance is formed. There is little siltation from incoming current. The food chain stabilizes, the latitude may be such that cold seasons abort any too-swift weed growth and decomposition. For many years such a lake will have excellent fishing. I know a small northern lake that I fished for twenty years and it always had a perfect bass-bluegill balance. Curiously, there were also yellow perch in the lake. Often they multiply too swiftly and ruin a lake. But for some reason—perhaps poor spawning possibilities—in this lake they did not. The lake still produces very well.

When a new lake is formed by a dam, large acreages of rich soil are inundated. Vegetation of terrestrial varieties dies, enriching the bottom, and is quickly replaced by aquatic forms. Here a whole new ecosystem suddenly erupts. There are of course differences in the quality of original soils from lake to lake. Some are richer than others, and pass their vivacious youth quickly. In some impoundments stocking of fish is accomplished solely from the river that was dammed. Usually, however, stocking is done to launch the first bass population. Forage fish may also be stocked.

Everything now is young. This is an *upbeat* time in life for this body of water. Young bass, wholly uncrowded, have vast areas to roam and settle down in. They are alert to feeding possibilities. Young forage of varied kinds is furiously blooming everywhere. It is small enough for the young bass to eat. There are no population pressures. Oxygen is plentiful. In other words, this is a most vigorous time for this water. Fish, to be sure, can multiply swiftly under these optimum conditions. But that is fine, for living space is no problem.

Many bass fishermen already know that the new impoundment, during its first several years, furnishes tremendous fishing. Bass are not yet large. There are a few Old Settlers, perhaps, that had lived in the tributary streams. But the new crop is growing swiftly and bass of one to two pounds become awesomely abundant. They are also eager strikers. This lake is "coming of age." In northern lakes, bass growth will of course be slower than in their southern counterparts. Many a new southern impoundment has been swarming with one- to two-pound bass in its third year.

Not only are the bass multiplying at top speed, but so are all the other species. A lake like Toledo Bend in Texas had fabulous fishing for big bluegills and a veritable blizzard of crappies before it got to its real peak for bass. Shad, too, multiply astronomically, in all impoundments where they are present, and that includes a great many indeed. Such species as buffalo, carp, and suckers all have ideal conditions for growth. Thus—and note well—as the lake comes of age, which means a peak of quality bass fishing, the living space is actually diminishing, imperceptibly perhaps, and in a very predictable, orderly, and progressive manner. There is still lots of room, but the stage is being set for an eventual decline.

Most impoundments will have between four and eight peak years for bass. This spread is of course arbitrary, for individual lakes will differ. But by the fifth year, let's say, given good spawning success and the original stocking, there will be a very large *number* of bass present, and there will be age classes old enough to furnish a substantial number of *large* bass. From now on, every year will see still better results in big bass. In some lakes—as this is written Eufala in Oklahoma is a good example—six-pound bass are no longer uncommon. Strings of them are caught. By the seventh or eighth seasons real trophy fish turn up regularly. Meanwhile, plenty of one- and two-pound bass are present to furnish fast action when large ones aren't located. But the occasional nine- and ten-pound fish turn up in the news.

Again, length of the coming-of-age span is arbitrary, and differs widely among lakes. There are, for example, several Tennessee impoundments, clear, rocky, with only modest weed growth, lakes somewhat less fertile than those in richer bottomlands, where smallmouth fishing, with large specimens present, has been good for two decades now. Aging is much slowed because of sparser fertility and less actual food production. Conceivably such a lake might peak out and remain fairly stable in production throughout an angler's lifetime.

It is not difficult to spot such lakes. They are always well known to anglers because they have produced so steadily for such a long time. Further, the smallmouth enthusiast will know that a lake he proposes to fish, if it has ideal smallmouth habitat, is certain to come of age more slowly and remain at peak longer than the very fertile largemouth water. But as new impoundments are built, nowadays the best-informed fishermen watch them closely, and plan to make their "attack" when any lake, as they say, "peaks out." This will invariably occur somewhere between, at the broadest span, four and ten years, and will probably be at greatest big-bass volume between years five and eight.

AGING AND DECLINE

Many anglers who fish a lake as it is on the upswing in production and while it is at peak for bass become so attached to it that as it declines they just cannot understand and don't want to believe what is happening. They wonder where the bass are. They berate the fisheries people for not stocking more bass. They make every imaginable excuse. The plain fact is, the bass are now not there, and cannot be.

A classic example occurred on what once was called Granite Shoals Lake near Marble Falls, Texas, and is now known as Lake LBJ. This impoundment was for some years a hot one. Then it fell on hard times. Biologists who studied it and took net samples knew exactly what was wrong. Several rough-fish species had simply taken over. The big lake, fortunately, had to be let down to about one-fifth its surface acreage in order to build added power-production facilities. The fisheries department seized this opportunity to rotenone the lake. They were aiming for a total kill, biggest ever tried in Texas, so a new start could be made.

On the day of the much-heralded kill, some fifty thousand people swarmed to the lake to pick up dying fish. Rotenone does not harm fish for eating. Over 2,000 boats were on the water. Occupants had flocked to grab up a limit of those lunker bass they were positive would be killed. But of the several hundred tons of fish killed, less than 1 percent were bass!

Let's follow now what happens on such a lake to produce such a condition. As the years pass, tons and tons of vegetation have grown, and decayed to form new soil layers on bottom. Plankton by the ton, too, dies and filters in billions of infinitesimal specks to the bottom. The lake bottom is building up more and more muck. This may not in all instances be especially detrimental, up to a point. In some cases it will eliminate ideal spawning grounds for bass while having little effect on the fish that do not build nests but simply drop eggs indiscriminately.

In the many lakes where gizzard shad are present and form one of the most important forage items for bass, millions of them soon become too large for the bass to eat, and in particular too large for the young bass to eat. Spawning of shad near shore occurs simultaneously with bass spawning. But as the young bass are hatched the shad leave for open lake waters and after that are not present inshore very often. Bass large enough to eat half-grown shad have difficulty finding and successfully pursuing them. But this is only part of the problem. The shad multiply fantastically, much faster than the bass. Living room is important. Especially living room in the shallows, where life cycles chiefly begin. Other species such as crappies eat bass fry and fingerlings. Bass nests may be ruined. Bass eat some of their own young. But all told the less prolific bass cannot remotely begin to control the tremendous colonization of the less important species.

In other words, though the black bass is the top game fish in the lake, it is actually poorly equipped to dominate the ecosystem of which it is a part. Other game fishes are to a lesser degree in the same category. The so-called rough fishes do best, because, less specialized, they can tolerate the poorer conditions and the crowding of the declining habitat. Perhaps we might say that it is *not* declining for them, not swiftly at any rate. They are able to cope with it.

Thus the lake by recreational standards is aging. In some cases it becomes more and more fertile. When it passes a critical point in fertility, then it becomes too fertile for the best interests of fish such as bass. In lakes where raw sewage and other effluents pour into the water, though we think of this as "dirty," basically it is all fertilizer. In this superrich water some forms of life can grow profusely, such as algae and "scums" not in the best interests of bass production.

While all of these forces are working against the bass, man, the craftiest predator of all, is whittling away at the adults of the tribe. It was common a decade or so ago to say that bass could "never be fished out of a lake." Biologists are having second thoughts about that. It all depends on how ideal are the conditions for bass *production*—and how many fishermen are concentrating on the lake as well as how successful they are. Today they are far more successful than they once were. They have all the tools to work with. They fish year-round. There are millions more of them. Tournament promoters are presently beginning to be concerned with the "monster" they have fashioned. Tens of thousands of pounds of adult bass are removed from some of the hottest lakes by the swarming tournament anglers. Without question the rules will have to be revamped to make sure that fewer fish are kept.

Experiments done on small lakes where controlled conditions are possible have shown that bass *can* be fished down. The classic study that has been noted by a number of writers is an experiment in Missouri during which a lake of 200-plus acres, stocked with known numbers of bass, sunfish, and catfish, was opened to fishing and a check of catches made. Almost half the bass present and within allowed length limit had been removed from the lake in the first few days. During the first season almost three-fourths were gone.

On large impoundments obviously a decline in bass numbers caused by hard fishing is less noticeable. But it is having a decided effect nonetheless. One reason is that, as we have seen, successful spawning becomes more and more difficult as a lake ages. Plenty of fry never live past that stage because there are more predators after them. In many instances probably no more than a few bass—one or two, a half dozen—come to adulthood from any given hatch, whereas the rough species apparently have better luck because several of them do not have fry concentrated in a few restricted locations.

As bass begin to decline during the period following peak—the "leveling off," as some call it—there are fewer and fewer of them compared to other species. Further, no bass lives, even with the very best luck, much more than ten years; at least the chance of catching a bass over ten years old is very slim. Adults that make it past six to eight years are indeed old fish. Natural attrition from varied causes takes thousands before they reach ten or twelve inches in length. Even if the rate of attrition remains stable—which is not likely as the imbalance turns more and more against the bass—the bass will become scarcer as time goes on.

Thus we begin to understand what aging can do to a lake and its bass population. Once again, this has to be a generalized discussion, for each lake has a different timing and situation. While the discussion of shad serves as a good illustration, of course many lakes contain no shad. Nonetheless, they have other problems. I've used the shad for this discourse because so many impoundments of renown do contain them, and because they have long been a classic illustration of an important forage species bringing a debacle to the very predator it serves. By and large, therefore, we can say that a bass angler who will plan his fishing to take advantage of peak bass populations and then move on to a newer lake after the leveling off has occurred, will always be putting himself in the best position for action and success.

Some lakes in certain latitudes are difficult for bass not so much from the decline and aging process as from other adverse conditions. In some lakes where winters are long and spring spawning conditions precarious, the combined effect is one of constant ups and downs for the fish. Colorado, for example, has many eager bass fishermen but many disappointed ones year after year. Young bass of four to six inches have difficulty finding proper forage during the fall. Exactly like deer that must store up fat for the winter, the young are in a precarious situation. They cannot find enough food of the proper size as fall progresses to allow them to fatten up for winter. They literally starve. Larger bass do not have as much difficulty. But because so few young can become large, the total population remains small, and only in mild years can it move upward. Other examples might be noted, but these should serve to show the difficulties bass have, and how the angler's success is influenced by them.

REJUVENATION

Much more is known about lake management today than in previous decades. And frequently lakes once famed for bass but aged past greatness can be and are being rejuvenated. However, lake-management techniques are still in their infancy. Biologists know what is wrong, but righting it is another matter. The most common applied method nowadays is fish kills with rotenone.

On a small lake, other methods are tried. Netting of rough fish can be helpful. Killing of weeds also is done to improve habitat for game fish. Fertilization is possible on small waters, to block out sunlight and thus cut down weed growth. But most such methods are practical only on ponds and small lakes. On a large impoundment the expanse (and expense) is too vast to cope with. Fundamentally, costs are too high to make known management methods feasible.

In fact, the chief problem with management *is* the size of the water that needs treatment. Much depends on the use of the lake. I know of one lake built strictly for recreational purposes. It had come to the end of the line, with an almost exclusively rough-fish population. Authorities decided to close it to use and drain it, thus killing everything in it. When it had dried down, shorelines were cleaned. Then the lake was filled, and stocked for proper balance. Within a year there was fair fishing, and in the third year it was excellent. Probably it will remain so for some years, and then the process can be repeated. From the angler's standpoint, if he keeps check on lakes so managed, he can tell which years are certain to be good again.

A method now being used on smaller drainable expanses is to drain and then dry out the bottom thoroughly. Then it is totally cleaned, with bulldozers. Afterward it is seeded with a crop such a rye grass. When the crop sprouts well, the lake is refilled. The dying grass on the bottom ensures fertility and plankton rapidly fills the water. Forage and game fish then stocked form a perfect balance for at least a few years, after which the sequence is repeated.

Obviously, on large impoundments used primarily for power production or for irrigation, total drainage is not possible. The drastic drawdown of LBJ Lake, mentioned earlier, was a lucky circumstance, but such an opportunity for fisheries biologists will not often present itself. Because of the much smaller expanse of water there after drawdown the cost of a total fish kill was feasible. And it was accomplished. During such a kill, sample fish of the several species in the lake are let down at varying depths in wire baskets, to make certain the rotenone is accomplishing the desired results. In that case fish at all levels died, and a completely new start was thus made possible.

On lakes at full level, costs for 50,000 to 100,000 acres would be prohibitive, and whether or not a total kill would be possible is problematical. A halfway measure called "selective kill" is sometimes taken. Here enough rotenone is applied to open water to kill off, hopefully, a substantial percentage of shad in order to give the game fish a breather. Occasionally it works out fairly well. But it is at best a stopgap.

Presently some new approaches appear to have better potential. For example, in new impoundments where gizzard shad are not present in the watershed, or have been destroyed, the smaller threadfin shad is being introduced. It has been under investigation as a forage species for some years. In fact, some of the first use of it was made in reservoirs of the Southwest where the problem was not that too-abundant forage eventually took over living room, but that forage was too scarce.

The threadfin shad has several attributes that appear to make it a perfect forage species over a vast range of impoundments. It grows at maximum to roughly six inches, and it also is a slow grower. A six-inch specimen ordinarily would be about four years old—and life expectancy is only half that in most waters. This means that a preponderance of the shad are always in the two-inch class or less. Even at maximum they never grow too large for adult bass to eat, and there are always plenty of young ones for small bass to eat. The gizzard shad on the other hand is a fast-growing species, and at maximum is as much as two feet long. Immense numbers of gizzard shad are in the eight-inch class by the end of their first year. Thus they have outgrown their status as forage for most bass and meanwhile only compete for living room.

Greatest success with threadfins has been in the South and Southwest because they cannot tolerate water temperature lower than 46 degrees. Thus, in northern waters where it falls lower than that, a total annual kill would occur. However, in middle latitudes, in some impoundments, they are becoming a unique asset. They gather in the warmer locations, such as near steam generating plants and in outflows from industrial installations, and are thus able to winter over. Only a small percentage of the total lake population is able to pack into such restricted locations and survive, but enough survive to replenish the supply. Thus, in the future species such as this, assuming there may be others with similar useful attributes, may be a means to rejuvenation of lakes—or rather, they may assist in making rejuvenation unnecessary because a balance may be maintained.

A field of experimentation that may hold great promise also is cross-breeding of smaller fishes. In some lakes where a bluegill-bass balance is attempted, the bluegills (and other sunfishes) far outbreed the bass. They are supposed to act as the forage species, but there are cases where lakes, especially small ones, have wound up with a few large bass, thousands of stunted sunfish, and nothing else. The sunfish are simply too prolific. Most deposit from twice to five or six times as many eggs per female as black bass.

Hybrid sunfish, however, have been "tailored" to perfect forage specifications in hatcheries. The most important of these to date is a cross between a male green sunfish and a female red-ear or shellcracker. The red-ear at maximum grows normally to large size, from one to two pounds, and thus is in numerous lakes an important small sportfish. Green sunfish are much smaller. But it is well known that hybrids of any species often tend to grow larger and also to be hardier than either parent. The most important attributes of this particular cross, however, are that the fish for some reason produce few females. The ratio runs about one female to four males. In addition, females drop an extremely small number of eggs, an average of only about 300.

Because of swift growth and large size—this hybrid has been known to reach two pounds in two years—the cross becomes an attractive species to fishermen. The young furnish bass food during the first year, but because of lack of females and low egg production they cannot possibly usurp the bass's living room. To date this hybrid has been useful only in small waters. But it has set biologists thinking that there may be something here highly important for future study and application to large bass waters.

One other possible management tool is the introduction of large, predaceous species that do not compete directly with black bass. The saltwater striped bass, an anadromous species that runs up freshwater streams to spawn, has now been acclimated to year-round freshwater living and is doing well in several impoundments across the U.S. In some cases spawning has not been evident but swift growth of stocked fish is. Conceivably this could become an exciting means (for management and fishermen) for keeping forage in balance, avoiding interference with black bass, and giving an extra and dramatic bonus in sport.

Another such predator of salt water is the redfish, or channel bass. This one is strictly a saltwater spawner. It has been tried in inland lakes of fairly high salinity and been found to be able to survive and grow swiftly. I believe I was the first writer to report in a national publication about the original experiment, and at that time I saw one red, stocked at four inches, that in less than four years weighed over seventeen pounds. Spawning has not occurred in any of these experiments. But it has become evident that reds just possibly might sustain themselves in large freshwater lakes, even of rather mild salinity. If so, put-and-take stocking might make, in effect, "policemen" of the redfish, predators roaming the lakes gobbling up surplus forage, growing only in size not in numbers. These ideas may lead to many future management innovations of great importance to bass fishermen. A lake, for example, where such methods were used might well be a clue to an angler that here was the best one to select for his sport. The future will decide.

THE REPRESSIVE FACTOR

New and coming-of-age lakes, as we've seen, are predictably important waters to watch. There may seem during the first several years to be overpopulation of bass and their relatives, the sunfish. If one knows the age of such a lake, and that it *is* new, then the "catching" is almost certain to be excellent. But an older lake, let's presume without a shad or rough-fish problem but simply solid with game species, is probably due for trouble. Particularly if a lake is notable for the massive numbers of small sunfish, it is a fair bet that bass fishing will not be very good in it. Many of the bluegills or other sunfish may be several years old and only three or four inches long. They are stunted from overproduction and overcrowding.

At such times influences are brought to bear that are still not fully understood or even authenticated by ichthyologists and freshwater ecologists. One of the most important of these, which apparently is common in the bass-sunfish relationship, is known as *repression*.

Original experiments concerning this phenomenon were done with species of *Cyprinidae,* the minnow family to which carp and suckers belong. Placed in ponds and left there for months, the fish failed to spawn when the time arrived. But spawning *was* accomplished when the same fish were placed in another pond where none had been living. Yet when water from the first pond was run off into a second pond where other ripe fish were held, they gave up attempts to spawn.

What was suspected was that the fish themselves pass into the water a substance, possibly a hormone, that inhibits spawning. And it was also supposed that crowding may be the trigger for the production of this substance. Thus, a limitation would be placed upon the population. Obviously this is not a "thought process" but it could be set off by some basic and instinctive anguish caused by overcrowding.

Presumably numerous fish species utilize this type of population repression and control. Among sunfish it is thought not to occur to such an extent that they cease reproduction. In fact, they keep right on becoming more and more stunted and abundant. But the suspicion has grown among experimentors that the bluegill, for example, may utilize this repression secretion in some manner that prevents or inhibits the spawning of bass present in its environment.

No one is certain how it works. But one of the chief studies done a few years ago tended to show that healthy, growing, uncrowded bass were inhibited from spawning when in the presence of an overabundance of bluegills. Such bass, tested in fresh new waters without other fishes present, proceeded to spawn. It is believed that bass themselves may even exercise this type of population control among themselves.

Ordinarily the large impounded lake has enough new water coming in to overcome such influences. Current is present; in addition, in the spring spawning period it is usual for more water to pour into a lake. If it has lowered somewhat during winter, new water in spring brings up the level. The same situation is true of course in streams. Thus the repressive influence—if indeed it does exist—would itself be inhibited by a diluting and renewing of water that might contain the secretion.

Without doubt future research will turn up more exact knowledge in this field, and certainly new directions will be pursued. There is still much to be learned about fishes and their relations to their complicated environments. But for the present, a bass fisherman wondering how to apply this type of presumption might well shy away from a lake known to be swarming with small fish of species such as bluegills. It probably will be supporting only a small bass population—whether for the reason discussed here or because of a combination of others.

BASS HATCHES AND CYCLES

It is frequently difficult for an angler to understand that the life history of fish is exactly comparable to that of birds and mammals. When there is a normal spring season with a proper mix of wet and dry weather, quail and pheasants and wild turkeys have what we term a "good hatch" and are abundant that year. Other conditions may so drastically reduce hatching success that few birds show in the fall season. It is the same with fish. Those like the black bass, that make nests so that the eggs are deposited in concentration in a small space and in highly specialized areas, are particularly susceptible to what may be termed "weak year classes" and "strong year classes." Under some debacle conditions of spawning, there may be no year class at all. In other years it may be only modest-sized, but at least reasonably successful.

I recall a season a few years ago when bass on a northern lake of medium size where I fished a lot were furnished by nature with a near-perfect set of conditions for spring spawning. Water temperature came to proper level quite swiftly and because of stable weather it stayed there. The shallows were alive with males making beds, and then with depositing females. It was as concentrated a spawn as I had ever observed.

About a week after the eggs had been dropped, a real whistling late-spring blizzard blew in, an unusual piece of weather that dropped shoreside water temperature by actual measurement fifteen degrees. The males that had been guarding the eggs were driven from the nests and into deeper water. Beyond a doubt there was a total kill of eggs. A few fish were observed later on prowling back into the shallows, but no evidence of life in the nests was observed and there was no further spawning.

Here was a striking example of a big gap left in the bass population. There would be no production, or very little anyway, that year. What would have been that age group or year class of bass were missing. In a small lake with little fishing the effect might not be noticeable later. But a debacle such as that on a heavily fished impoundment, one coming to peak condition, would mean that the gap might very well be felt from three to four years later. If two poor hatches occurred consecutively it would be still more noticeable. Some very large bass might be caught. But assuming that the lake already had optimum conditions and was moving up toward peak or was at its peak years, fishing could be poor indeed. It would never be made up, because those age groups would constitute a gaping hole in the bass population. An angler aware of such a situation could well skip this lake but might have great fishing on it two or three years later, when a new and abundant year class came along.

On the small lake that is able to sustain a good balance over many years, periodic losses of year classes make fishing definitely cyclic. In fact, in some middle-latitude and northern waters certain lakes never do very well because the weather time after time plays havoc with spawning. Strong year classes seldom occur. Colorado, for example, has this problem. Earlier I mentioned a lake in Montana, Mary Ronan, where I had found excellent bass fishing. These bass, however, appeared to be from no more than two year classes. Probably they had had a fair yield those previous seasons. But in that lake very little bass fishing is done anyway because trout and kokanee are the mainstays. If fishermen really swarmed after the bass during spawning, the generally weak year classes probably could not keep up.

It will be obvious that in general the incidence of strong year classes will be higher in the South than even at middle latitudes. At least in the natural lakes there will not be drastic influences of weather to hold back or destroy a yield of fry. Other influences—too many rough fish or spawn eaters; poor spawning soils; improper chemical mix in water, such as high or low salinity or too much or too little nitrogen—may appear intermittently to cut down production and leave a weak year class. On the whole, however, stable production has at least a better chance in warm climates.

One serious matter on impoundments, however, is that the purposes, and therefore the operation, of any given lake may in itself raise the odds against bass production some years. A lake built primarily for irrigation or power production has built-in complications so far as bass production is concerned. Undoubtedly anglers know the terms "constant-level lakes" and "drawdown lakes." It can be said unequivocally that the constant-level impoundment will always be the best bass producer. When water level is tampered with, it disturbs the lives of fishes, and it can and often does wipe out entire year classes of bass and other spring-spawning species.

As I write this, for example, there has been a prolonged drought in the Southwest. Falcon Lake on the Rio Grande is spang in the center of one of the nation's largest vegetable-producing areas. Millions of dollars ride on quickly-grown crops that require irrigation. Thus, when Falcon begins to get down to a point where more water must be forthcoming, it can be requested from the next lake upstream, Amistad. If Amistad experiences a drawdown that coincides with the spawning season, the entire year class of bass can be wiped out.

Environmentalists are beginning to understand that sport fish are important, financially as well as recreationally. Whenever possible, spring spawning *is* considered when drawdowns are contemplated for any reason. A two- or three-week respite can mean good production, and though fry may be dislocated and some lost as water lowers, at least the eggs are not destroyed. However, on some lakes it is not always possible to wait on fish.

Drawdowns have other numerous negative effects upon the entire ecosystem of any lake. For example, life in the "littoral zone" of a lake—that rim or near-shore region where light reaches the bottom and where it is possible for vegetation to take root—can be totally wiped out during a heavy drawdown. This will occur of course at any time, but is more influential during spring spawning of bass and other spring-spawning species. Not only are spawning areas destroyed, but the plants and hordes of small aquatic denizens are wiped out with them. This is the most productive portion of the lake. Its entire destruction produces drastic changes in the entire living picture for all life.

Bass are forced to find new locations where temperature is proper and cover is present. They may be dispersed because of these needs and because of lack of food or thinness of food. Relationships between these predators and their prey are totally upset. For instance, one lake I know well was let down last year thirty feet in a few days. Imagine the shattering impact of this change in what had been a stable habitat for several years. Then, when the fish had settled into new ways, the lake began to rise again and gained back twenty-three feet within six weeks.

Even changes in the volume of water, especially when it is lessened, can be most disturbing. Overcrowding can occur and alter every relationship among creatures of all varieties in the lake. Not all impoundments are so affected. Some are designed originally as constant-level lakes and seldom fluctuate except in emergency—as I described in discussing the grandiose LBJ fish kill. The bass fisherman who selects a constant-level impoundment for his major efforts comes to know it perfectly. Because of this and the possibility for settled routines among the fish, success is certain to be better. So is bass production. On inconsistent lakes, the angler has almost as difficult a time as the fish. After each fluctuation he must start all over trying to locate productive places.

TROPHY LAKES AND OTHERS

In the beginning of this chapter I said that selection of a lake depends to some extent upon what a fisherman is willing to be satisfied with. Some shallow lakes are wonderful and consistent producers of many bass, but seldom do they produce large numbers of trophy bass. Lake Okeechobee in Florida, large and shallow, has long held quite stable in bass production. There one can catch a great number of bass in the two- to four-pound category. But the lake has never been renowned as a spot for mounting fish.

This is not to say large bass never come from such lakes. I well remember a bass I caught one time in northern Michigan while fishing for bluegills before bass season opened. I had to release it, but I measured it before doing so, length and girth. It almost certainly weighed nine or ten pounds, and came from a small, weedy shallow lake. But such catches are exceptions.

Many small lakes anywhere in the U.S., and especially in the North and middle latitudes, will produce numerous bass, good fighters and husky enough, but seldom over three to four pounds at maximum. In some of the most stable, well-balanced small lakes this is true. Check such lakes and you will find they are seldom over twenty to twenty-five feet deep at any point. In a few exceptional lakes, a number of large bass are taken from shallow lakes, but as a rule there is some fundamental reason for this. One famous southern lake seldom gives up small bass. But it furnishes numerous trophies. Yet, when one carefully dopes this lake, it is apparent that for some reason few bass from any hatch survive to adulthood. Growth is swift, and the few survivors therefore have optimum conditions.

By and large, most of the trophy bass come from deep lakes. These may be at varying fertility levels. Some extremely husky smallmouths have been hauled from low-fertility lakes. In fact, they are seldom found in excessively fertile habitats. Large impoundments—this can mean anywhere from 5,000 to 100,000 acres—furnish most of the trophy bass today, with the exception of a few natural lakes of Florida. One reason is that they are deep. Commonly large bass lurk deep, and in secluded spots. Another reason is that there are *more* bass to choose from, even where a lake is under severe pressure.

Thus, the large, deep impoundment that has come to peak and is producing its years of large numbers of adult bass is the one in which trophy fishermen are most likely to find success. In the South, where the growing season continues around the year, as we stated earlier a deep, clear, and only modestly fertile lake is the spot to pick if you want a true trophy bass. Such lakes may contain fewer fish, but with a better chance of a high percentage growing to old age. With year-round growth even at a slower rate than in more fertile, teeming lakes, life expectancy is longer, and the bass continues to grow until caught.

CHAPTER ELEVEN

The New Tackle and How To Use It

RODS

One of the first fishing outfits I ever owned consisted of a casting rod five and one-half feet long, made of solid tapered steel and stiff as a poker, a reel that then was called a "bait-casting" reel, but of course with no level-wind device because there was none at that time. The line was not selected with any special care. It, too, was just what was available. It was black and stout, probably stout enough to use to rope a calf. This was used for all sorts of fishing, but chiefly of course—as the bait-casting appellation indicated—for catching bass and other common species with a worm, frog, or crayfish on a hook.

It is curious that today, though this outfit would look like the relic it is to most modern bass fishermen, the "new" attributes of rods, reels, and lines for bass mark a return to those of earlier days. The only difference is that early in this century tackle such as I had was used simply because that's all there was. Today bass anglers have learned that some of the primitive qualities inherent in this type of tackle are precisely what is needed in the new waters. Certainly tremendous improvements have been

143

made, but the stiffness of the rod, which went almost completely out of style for several decades, has returned, and the "old-fashioned" bait-casting reel, immeasurably improved, has come from partial obscurity during the early heyday of the spinning reel to become the firm choice among practically all of the scores of tournament bass anglers and among the vast majority of experienced nontournament bass fishermen. Further, the "stout" line has become standard.

I do not mean to short-sell spinning, or spin casting. As a matter of fact, I use spinning tackle for bass a great deal. But the consensus among modern bass fishermen is that the very nature of spin tackle, with either open-faced or closed-face reels and the attendant whippy rods and lighter lines, is a strike against it on the majority of famed bass waters, where drowned timber, submerged brush, and hang-ups of all kinds form cover for the quarry.

A few years ago I went through a stage of fiddling with what is commonly called "ultralight." I confess I did not find it very appealing. Because I had long been a dedicated fly fisherman, it struck me that ultralight spin tackle was a poor excuse for something better. By the time this fad had run its course, sides had been pretty well chosen between the spin casters who used fairly substantial gear, and those stubbornly clung to the rejuvenated standard casting reel and rod.

The great sales pitch on the side of spinning was that anybody could do it. Learning to cast took only a few minutes. This led, in many cases over the past few seasons, to arguments over what is and is not sporting in bass fishing. Leaving fly fishing out of it for the moment (we'll touch that later), the dedicated bass fisherman felt that finding the fish and getting them to hit *was* the sport and challenge, whereas many an enthusiast of lighter spin tackle felt that *playing* the fish was the big thrill. Casting-rig people claimed that in today's impoundment fishing—most of it at least— you had to have power to ram a hook home in the bony mouth of a bass, and then super power to haul the brute from its lair. Getting it into the boat, or releasing it without breaking off so that it did not swim away with a lure embedded, was immensely important.

Nowadays, of course, spin tackle has been improved in ruggedness until many bass anglers use it most successfully. Some of the tough new open-face reels do an admirable job. A few husky closed-face push-button types do as well. And the new rods in all categories copy what has fast become practically standard equipment for all of the modern bass fishermen who use "bait-casting" outfits: the so-called "worm rod." These new rods, first brought into the casting-rod field and now developed in spinning, too, but with not quite the solid action possible in the former, originated because of the specific needs of the plastic-worm fisherman.

We already know that by far the majority of bass are caught deep, most of them near or on the bottom, and invariably in situations where cover is involved. None of the rods, casting or spinning, available even as late as the mid-sixties, were wholly ideal for this fishing. What was required was formidable body and power, so that once a bass had picked up the worm, often in twenty to thirty or more feet of water and usually in brush, the fishermen could stab him solidly. Bass specialists had slowly come to realize that this takes some doing. Many a fisherman simply could not understand why he missed strike after strike. The fact was, the hard mouth of the fish was difficult enough to pierce anyway, before you added inter-ference of the line by debris and the length of line hauling back through water medium. Most rods "gave" too much on the strike, regardless of its force. The bass was not hooked, but simply felt the yank and dropped the lure.

However, a simple stiff pool-cue stick was not the whole answer, either. In fishing the awesomely popular and effective plastic worm, one had to be able to detect the gentlest touch of the bass. In deep water and among submerged shinnery, a "deaf" rod tip would not relay the whispered mes-sage. The tip had to be sensitive, yet also powerful. The glass rods of today can be made to practically any specifications. The material is without any question the best used to date for fishing rods, and the most adaptable to design. And so it was that the so-called worming rod was born, a powerful casting rod with a responsive forward sector able to telegraph the good news yet stubborn enough to carry out its part of getting the hook home. That is, sensitive but stiff. One rod firm has even named their worm rods "Lunker Stiks." The latest innovations as this is written are the various powerful rods in one-piece design; many bass men prefer them.

As I have said, the principle of the worm rod was quickly translated for the spinning-tackle enthusiast. Nor did it stop there. What anglers began to realize was that for many years the basic problem—the hard mouth of the fish—had gone more or less unrecognized. Once it was understood that 90 percent of "missed" strikes were really rod failures, it soon dawned on people that the so-called worm rods could utilize the fundamental power principle but be varied to suit all sorts of bass-fishing needs.

For example, many a bass addict had long believed that a noisy surface plug could best be manipulated with a long, limber rod. That was because, he imagined, the agitation of the whippy rod imparted action to the lure. After the appearance of firmer rods it became obvious that precisely the opposite was true. To properly manipulate a surface lure of the noisy variety, the *angler*, not the rod, needed to be in full control. Also surface strikes must be dealt with instantly and with authority. Today the expert bassers select variations of the worm rod, with tips slightly faster than those used for deep water and plastic worms, for use with quiet surface lures, such as the thin, light "stick" types, and many use the standard stiff tip for the rougher action of the noisier surface lures.

Thus the solid, powerful rod has become in the past several seasons practically the standard bass rod, with some variations in tip action and length. While still called, as this is written, a "worm" or "worming" rod, it serves all purposes and is the new look in bass fishing rods. Those new to the concept should not think of these rods as special, additional rods, but as *the* most *advanced* type for all bass fishing in today's quite changed waters. Not only worms and surface plugs, but diving and deep-running plugs and jigged spoons can be more precisely handled by this type of rod than by any other.

Interestingly enough, length has not changed much since that long-ago old steel rod of mine. Although one can buy virtually any length, practically all of the expert bass anglers use models averaging five and one-half feet. A few add extra rods of six feet for special purposes, but the five and one-half-footer is the modern bass fisherman's stock in trade for medium to heavy action. Note well that throughout I'm speaking of casting rods.

Again, this discouse is not to put down spinning. It is simply a report on what the vast majority of the most successful bass fishermen use nowadays on those large waters, the impoundments, where most of the bass are caught. There are certainly places where spinning tackle, even fairly light rods, can be used with much pleasure and success. One example would be the streams of modest size—about which more in Chapter 13—where smallmouths of average size abound. Another might be farm and ranch ponds that have very little solid submerged cover but rather fertile waters that in themselves serve as a kind of cover. Or in open waters of rocky lakes, spin tackle of "sporty" weight can be used successfully, although there still remains the fact that no long, limber rod can possibly set a hook as well as a stiffer one, and as we all have learned none can "work" a lure with as much precision as the full-bodied rod that puts the angler in total control.

REELS AND LINES

Reels have been partially discussed in speaking of casting versus spinning rods. To me it is interesting that the truly old-fashioned bait-casting reel has turned out to be the best tool in this category (not counting fly reels, which are a totally different matter), notwithstanding the inroads made over past years by spinning. Whether or not one is in favor of bass-fishing tournaments—and this writer has mixed emotions about them, what with poundage of fish seemingly so all-important—the plain fact is that the myriad of tournaments, national, regional, and local, attract in the aggregate the best bass fishermen in the nation. It is a fact that 90 percent or more of the reels used nowadays by these people are casting reels. And, down the ladder a bit, one can check out any important bass water anywhere in the U.S. today and discover that the majority of the fishermen who are catching the lion's share of the fish use casting reels.

There must be a valid reason, and there are—several. First of all, the new reels are a far cry from what were known as the best even a few years ago. There is no question that, though American casting reels were originally among the best, they drooped in the furor over spinning when it became popular, and it was left to imports—one in particular and extraordinarily well known—to bring the bass fishermen back to the casting reel. However, today's modern bass reels are certainly quite different from even the finest of a few years ago. They have borrowed first of all from saltwater reels. A check of several score of the most famous bass anglers of this period shows that every one uses a free-spool, star-drag-type casting reel.

Over many years this has been the type of reel used in salt water that most easily handles tough fish. Its unusually sturdy construction has been brought to the freshwater models. In fact, many of the bass reels of today actually double as saltwater reels for light and medium work. Or rather, the light-to-medium marine item has been adapted to freshwater use. The star drag has long been known as the best of the lot, quickest and most efficient to operate. It is interesting that its use in fresh water stems from the character of bass waters in many impoundments, with submerged brush and crisscrossed bottom debris. But oddly the average bass fisherman keeps his drag set so it won't slip. The reason for this is that fish must be hauled out of all sorts of brush piles and jam-ups. Stout lines, about which more shortly, make it possible to keep the drag nonslip. But it can swiftly be adjusted if the need arises in order to control a bull bass—that is, let him run—in open water.

It has been said often that learning to use the casting reel expertly takes diligent practice, whereas other reel types are far easier to manipulate well after only a few minutes of use. I'm sure this is true. By the time the serious bass angler has mastered his free-spooler he has come to realize its full potential of line and lure control, and he has become a "pinpointer."

He also knows that with the star drag snubbed up he can strike with fantastic power. I needle several friends of mine about fishing "just for the heads"—they hit reared back and often rising from their seat, especially when fishing deep and in brush, with enough steam to yank a bass in two. The line, which we'll get to in a moment, makes this possible. Nonetheless, the star drag is always there to be relaxed when lighter line may be called for in a special situation. And, the free-spool mechanism is extremely valuable in plastic-worm fishing, so that a fish may pick up the lure with no line drag whatever, yet with the angler in full control. It is also useful in straight-down jig fishing, to get the lure quickly to bottom in deep water and through brush.

Probably I should not call these reels "new." They've been around quite a few years. But they are new in the sense that they are part of the look of bass fishing in this era. Day by day more fishermen become converts. The brands of reels used by the majority are exceedingly sturdy. They also are fairly expensive—anywhere from twenty to fifty dollars or more—but they last for years, with reasonable care.

It is a fact, as noted, that the free-spool casting reel requires more expertise than does the spin reel. It demands more practice and finesse. But that is its great advantage. Once you have mastered it, accuracy and careful manipulation of lures is enhanced to a degree not possible with other reels. Further, among the current innovations are wooden rod handles shaped to the grip, designed to fit almost any make of bass rod, and oversize "power" reel handles designed to fit practically any make of casting reel, both of which give more comfort, more efficiency, and more accuracy to the fishermen. Further, the new reels now in use by most of the knowledgeable bass experts allow absolute control of the *catch*—when coupled with the new matching rods—to a degree unknown with other tackle.

Of course the effectiveness of all this power would be dampened without the innovations in fishing lines. Although some braided lines still remain, monofil is so far in front among bass anglers today that there is no competition. But it is not the monofil that old hands once knew when spinning first brought it to prominence. And, for the modern bass angler, it is not wispy stuff.

I am always amused to remember a guide friend of mine who, seeing a customer step into his boat with what appeared to be light line, said, "That looks like about six-pound test to me."

"It is," replied the customer.

"Then change it," said the guide, and he wasn't smiling. He went on to explain. "Where we're going to fish you'll be in submerged thornbrush all the time. You'll break off time after time and by midday you'll be mad at me because you have to blame somebody. Nobody fishes in my boat with less than ten-pound, and I'd prefer to see you use twenty!"

Amusingly, this idea goes back to the old, old heavy black lines of my youth. But nowadays, as with rods and reels, bass fishermen use them for a reason, whereas earlier there was little else available. Two most important improvements in monofil over recent years have made these lines precisely what bass fishing requires. One is that most of the stretch has been removed. To be sure, some stretch remains, and there appears to be more of it in the lighter lines than in heavier tests. But the reduced stretch has made it possible to get a hook set much better than once was possible. Obviously, when fishing deep, or with a long cast, a line with substantial stretch takes much of the steam out of the strike, no matter how powerful. The second improvement, immensely important, is that strength has been upped considerably while diameter has been either reduced or at least not enlarged.

Most experienced bass fishermen do not feel that this species is as shy of lines as, for example, a trout is of a dry-fly leader. They also know that a twenty-pound test line makes up in "haul-out" qualities for whatever damage it may do in causing some bass to be skittish. However, modern monofil of good quality nowadays may be of twenty-pound test and still be very little if any more obvious as a string attached to the angler's proposition than was ten-pound a few years ago.

The major share of the important bass waters today simply demand stout lines. Certainly small, debris-less ponds, or certain streams and small lakes with modest weed beds can be fished with light lines. But it is not in these that the majority of modern bass anglers do their fishing. And so a survey of the next hundred experts or bass-club members you meet will show conclusively that heavy lines are the rule for all impoundments where brush or drowned timber is found and medium-heavy for more open waters.

In certain situations ten-pound will get more strikes by far than will twenty-pound. In surface fishing often it will suffice, depending on what cover is being utilized. Lines of twelve- and fourteen-pound test are more commonly used, however. Certainly it is possible to get better lure control with these than with twenty-pound. A friend of mine whom I consider one of the best bass fisherman I know uses lines of fourteen- to seventeen-pound test for average fishing, but always has one rig set up with twenty-pound for big fish in cover. One nationally renowned individual uses fifteen-pound much of the time, especially with lures that are not raucous in action, but steps up to twenty-pound with all others and with bottom-bumping lures. Another famous tournament bass man utilizes seventeen- to twenty-pound test in any cover that can be described as heavy. Still another has told me he uses twenty-pound most of the time in all situations. My own approach is to use ten or twelve when fishing quiet surface lures in quiet water and in situations where cover is light, but to step up to fifteen or twenty for everything else.

HARD LURES

A vast amount of research has gone into the development of new fishing lures over the past few years, especially in the field of bass lures. In fact, at least 75 percent of all artificial lures manufactured today in the U.S. are slanted at the bass fisherman. It is true that a good many new lures that pop onto the market seem suspiciously to be just attempts to catch fishermen, but the fact remains that a tremendous amount of serious new knowledge about lures, their designs, and their bass-catching attributes has been gathered during the past decade.

Basically the *types* of bass lures have not changed much. There are surface lures, surface and diving lures, medium-depth runners, deep runners, and bottom lures. There are plugs, spoons, spinners, and of course the fantastically successful soft plastic lures that are strictly a product of this generation. But the design and intent of many of the old basics have changed drastically as more has been learned about what attracts—and holds—bass best.

For example, wise lure makers who are themselves bass fishermen have experimented lately with hook size and bend and have discovered that in modern impoundment fishing larger hooks, very sharp but sturdy and with a wide, round bend by far excel in efficiency those used for years on plugs and spoons. They use great care not to overbalance the lure or change its action by adding these, but they find that hooking qualities are much better with the large hooks. And, in submerged snags and brush—right into the middle of which today's bass anglers put their lures, not always along the edges as was once the case—the large, round-bend hooks shake free very easily.

To illustrate how meticulous and scientific lure makers have become, one who makes surface plugs for bass went all out a year or so ago to fashion a floater that would dive to a specified depth when correctly manipulated by the fisherman. The reason had do with oxygen content of the water. He had discovered that very often in quiet water the amount of dissolved oxygen will differ radically two or three feet down from what it is at the surface. Experiments tended to prove to him that bass hesitated to move up actively into the top layer because of lower oxygen, yet might strike readily a couple of feet down. At least *he* believed this—and it may be true.

In fact warm water contains less oxygen than cold, and we know it doesn't take much to affect a fish. Earlier we noted that in some instances bass (and other fish) grow faster in water temperatures slightly lower than those that characterize their favorite strata. Oxygen may be an influence. At around 40 degrees water can hold at saturation roughly 12 parts per million of dissolved oxygen. But at 85 degrees the saturation point is reached at roughly 7.5 parts per million. Thus in quiet water the comfort range for bass certainly is influenced not only by temperature but by its influence in turn upon oxygen content. Whether the lure maker was on the right track or not, his lure that could be fished on top or a few feet down became immensely successful.

Lures for quiet water have also made specific strides of late because of new knowledge. It was once believed, even in my early plug-fishing days, that a surface plug such as the chugger or popper should be fished noisily in all types of water. When this didn't work, we said the fish weren't hitting. Now we know without question that this was wrong, and the knowledge has sparked the introduction of a family of surface and near-surface lures that are amazingly deadly. Usually when a surface lure drops to the water, bass nearby will flee, but will turn and come back when the lure begins to "work." However, when the surface is calm, and particularly when the water is clear, too much noise and splashing make the fish wary. The numerous newer plugs that some fishermen currently term "stick" lures work wonders in quiet, clear waters.

These may be tapered toward each end, and are without spinners. Some of them sit slanted, that is, tail down. The slightest rod movement makes them jiggle and quiver and dart, but gently and quietly. In timber and above brush, when bass can be inveigled into hitting up top, these lures are murder. It takes very little room to work one and it is never raucous. Some bass men will remember an old bass lure years ago that had a very similar action and is I believe still being manufactured. But though it was often immensely successful, many anglers fished it too violently, and in other than quiet waters, which cut down its effectiveness. New knowledge has proved this.

In the surface-diving category the long, slender lures, many with only moderate action when worked in long or short jerks or with steady retrieve, are a whole new category, extremely effective and productive, that were launched I believe by the introduction of the original from Scandinavia. Hordes of near-copies now flood the market throughout bass territory. This design has of course been enlarged to include deep-running models and medium-depth models. But the shallow-diving types, some with a lip, some without, some with a spinner and some wholly unadorned, have lent themselves admirably to quiet-water and clear-water situations.

On the other hand, we have learned that noisy surface lures—the noisier the better—are mandatory in *rough* water and at times when bass are clinging to cover and must be alerted. Thus, many of the old standby plugs still serve as well as ever at such times. Of course, all of the oldies still catch fish. But the point is, lure design has made great strides due to new knowledge. For example, we know now that the surface type with noisy spinners fore and aft is mandatory when water is murky, and in fact we know that fishing in less-clear areas in the impoundments offers the most productive surface fishing—other influences being equal—simply because the bass are less wary and less likely to be disturbed by the fisherman.

The shad-imitating lures (plugs) are a whole family of killers born of the new era in bass fishing characterized by the huge impoundments with their hordes of shad. These are for the most part blunt-nosed, short-bodied lures that run at medium depths, and that are retrieved by most anglers at a steady rate. For that reason they are among the simplest of lures to fish properly. And they are immensely effective. The one problem with them in some situations is that they hang easily because of the depth and steady retrieve. However, since schools of shad usually cling to open water although commonly near bass cover, these lures are excellent for use in close "bypassing" of bass hangouts. They are also deadly for school bass, for use along rock ledges, and in similar places where they are unlikely to hang up.

It should be noted for those who fish in impoundments or other bass waters where shad may not be present that the shad imitators do just as well in these. Conceivably they may resemble small sunfish and other comparable forage. For example, I often use one of these lures in a dark-back, silvery-belly model in my study pond on my ranch, and it is one of the bass-catchingest of the lot. Yet there are no shad present.

In Chapter 7, on the senses of bass, we mentioned noisemaker lures of the underwater type. There is now a whole family of these. The "rattle" type lures, also mentioned in Chapter 7, apparently are important because of the noise. As I stated, many makers of underwater lures use a lead shot molded into the head for balance. When it gets loose, it rattles, and bass fishermen who used many of these became convinced the rattle was important. Undoubtedly it is, and particularly in murky water.

As this is written, one of the latest additions to the family is a shad-shaped lure that not only has the lead shot purposely loose inside the head but has in addition a sounding chamber behind it. It makes an exceptionally loud rattle, and it is doing very well on bass. Like the shad lures, medium runners, this one should be fished close to obstructions at either a steady pace or with a sweeping and intermittently relaxed manipulation of the rod. Interestingly enough, when this design was first tried it lacked a tail fin. Now it has a small fluttering tail of silver-colored metal, and numerous users claim that the flash draws bass in once they are alerted by the rattle.

The so-called "sonic" type lures were the first ventures into the sound vibration field a few years ago. The vibrations were made by the rapid "shimmy" movements of the lure as it was retrieved, and some of these were meant for swift retrieve, the better to create the vibrations. Now the new crop features shad-shaped lures that have the head designed with a fairly broad but flattened, down-curved snout. The tie-on eye is set above at the back of the head. Thus the snout plows a furrow in the water. This produces pressure waves and these in turn send out vibrations easily picked up by bass. It is like an exaggeration of the sound of a swimming forage fish. Most lures of this new group float at rest, run a couple of feet under on retrieve, and are fished either with steady retrieve or short floats and fast dives.

Ever since the early invention of spinners and spoons, these have been great bass producers. Past decades have seen many very graceful and even beautifully shaped and polished lures. It is odd that in this day of modern bass fishing the new-look spinner family that has become a group of the most productive of present-day bass lures is—at least in my estimation— the ugliest lure type ever conceived. It is what bass anglers call the "safety-pin" design.

Basically this is a piece of stiff metal wire shaped quite like a safety pin. A spinner is attached to one end of the open "pin," a lead-head jig rigidly affixed to the other end. The line is tied to the "eye" at the bottom of the open "pin." Some of these lures utilize two spinners. Some have a short plastic worm attached to the jig. Others use a rubber skirt, or various hair hackles. In some the spinner or spinners are large, in some small. The lure rides with the spinners flapping above the upturned hook of the jig below. Some have long spinner arms so that the blade is considerably behind the jig hook.

There are an infinite variety of designs and combinations in this new lure family. One I've seen has a snap, or snaps, at the end of the spinner arm or arms. Thus spinner blade *size* can be changed at will. Some anglers use the spinner-jig lure with no material around the hook, so they can add their own—pork rind, a long plastic worm, a reversed rubber or plastic skirt so the water pressure holds the lure up better on a slow retrieve. One design, lately conceived and made by a Lubbock, Texas, bass expert, util- izes a flat-headed jig, with spinners of rather small size above it and affixed to short shanks. On Amistad Lake where drowned thornbrush is every- where, this has proved to be virtually unstickable.

The idea of the safty-pin-type lure is to use a slow and steady retrieve— at least most of it so—and to plunk it right into the thickest stuff imagin- able. These lures have proved almost unhangable, and when they do hang up they can usually be shaken loose. They get to the lairs of the bass and are pure murder. Many enthusiasts cast them right into a submerged tree- top or thicket, let them sink to the bottom, and then begin the retrieve. Of course they can also be used with excellent results along edges, near shore, and over weeds. Some cast to stumps or trunks or rock walls and let the lure fall free. Bass take it as it goes down. Some believe twin blades of good size are especially effective in murky water because of the sound vibrations they emit. These should be fished as slowly as possible, however, to give bass opportunity to home to the sound and then see the flash. A few enthusiasts fish the safety pins just about as they would a plastic worm—cast, let it sink to the bottom, and raise the tip to make the lure active for a few inches, after which it is allowed to sink again.

The jig-and-eel is another modern combination. I presume most readers are aware that what we know today as a "jig"—the lead-head lure with single, upturned hook surrounded by nylon, hackle, feathers, etc., and with the hook eye on the upper side of the lead head—originated in salt water. It became popular in Florida immediately following World War II and was considered the first artificial lure ever to take pompano, previously thought to be all but uncatchable by hook and line. It was first brought to fresh water in some of the Tennessee impoundments, mostly in small sizes and as a successful crappie lure. Later numerous manufacturers developed it. Virgil Ward, the Missouri jig maker, was one of those who showed fishermen that jigs—just plain jigs, no "eel" trailer—could catch everything from walleyes to lake trout to bass.

Later, with the fabulous success of soft plastic lures, the leadhead jig, often with some hair shrouding the hook, was wedded to the plastic worm, or to a soft plastic strip made in segments that was called an "eel." Various weedless devices were added, the upturned jig hook assisted debris-dodging also, and the lead head served to get the eel to the bottom swiftly. It could be crawled along, or jigged so that the lead head bounced and the eel wriggled. A deadly combination had been formed. These lures are fished as a rule slowly, and right down into the brush. They are obviously bottom lures, but again there are endless variations—some with the eel tail floating buoyantly out behind the jig, some with extralong eels nine inches or more in length, and so on. A great many expert bass anglers now swear by them, and to some this is the "only" lure.

The so-called "jigging spoon" was slower in getting into the act. This is really not a new lure at all, nor even a new method. It simply utilizes a common wobbling spoon somewhat revamped in design and weight and has come into high popularity recently because of its astonishing effectiveness. It is a way of fishing a spoon *vertically*, that is, straight down from the rod tip, right into the brush and among the bushes and jampiles on bottom. Here and there throughout the South a few anglers have been doing this for years. A common name in some areas for it is "dodlesocking"; another apt colloquialism is "yo-yo-ing."

Today many bass anglers call these lures "shoehorn spoons." It may be interesting and worthwhile to relate where I first learned the basic principle of this method of fishing. Some years ago a number of Russian immigrants settled along the shores of Lake Huron's Saginaw Bay, in Michigan, and in winter made their modest living fishing through the ice, with handlines on a short stick, for yellow perch, at that time an important commercial species in the Great Lakes. The lures they used were fashioned from the cut-down bowl of a kitchen spoon, or from the curved portion of an old gold watch case, or some such piece of polished metal. It was a unique spoon, the top possibly three-quarters of an inch wide, and tapering down to a narrow bottom end. A single hook was brazed to the concave inner surface so that the bend and barb were just below the narrow end of the spoon.

The hook was barbless. The fisherman dropped the spoon to the bottom through a hole in the ice and immediately began jigging it, fluttering it upward and dropping it back a few inches. When a perch struck it was kept coming in one long sweep as the angler hauled out the line. As the fish was flopped onto the ice, it immediately became unhooked from the smooth hook, and the spoon was dropped back again. Some of these adept old Russians caught hundreds of perch a day by this fast and unusual method.

Years ago I used spoons exactly similar to catch perch in nonice seasons, and then used them experimentally to catch trout and bass and several other species. During my first years in Texas, before the new "shoehorn" spoons had been heard of, my boys and I caught numerous bass on the Highland Lakes by drifting slowly and jigging ordinary wobbling spoons along bottom. Thus the idea is not really new. But what *is* new is the gimmick of dropping the newfangled spoons right down into the brush piles and treetops and jigging them.

The point is, when you let the heavy spoon straight down usually you can drop it through some sort of hole, right to the bottom. Then you lift it only a few inches to a foot, which gives a good chance for no hang-ups—and in this little opening you jig it. Lift, twitch the rod tip, let the spoon flutter back down. Most of the time the bass—just like those yellow perch—will take the lure as it falls fluttering downward. At the slightest tap you have to really slam into your fish and keep right on hauling to manhandle it out of the brush. Most of the better jigging spoons now are equipped with large, wide-bend hooks, which is a help. Also, when you do hang up, it is advisable not to use brute force but first to jiggle the spoon hard. Its weight usually loosens it and you can keep right on fishing.

It is true that a few avid surface fishermen use all year the stick baits, the chuggers and poppers, the spinners-fore-and-aft surface raker plugs, and the slender floaters that dive a bit simply because they love to see one surface smash rather than catch a lot of bass. But by and large, the gentlemen who want to catch fish use surface lures, even to spinner types that, with tip held high, burble along the surface, mostly during spring spawning season, unless they are fishing exceedingly shallow lakes, where surface action may be had at almost any time.

Before spawning, and again afterward, the safety-pin lures and the jig-and-eel are favorites of a great many bassers. The medium runners such as shad types and rattlers are utilized as in-between types, for days and times of day when needed. The same types are saved for winter, with a fall flurry at times of surface action but with all these others doing duty. The jigging spoon is utilized at varying depths but gets chiefly a hot-weather and a cold-weather plan. One lure, however, that we've saved for last is an all-year favorite nowadays, was developed as this era of modern bass fishing began, and is without any question the most phenomenal bass lure ever invented. This is the plastic worm.

GREATEST BASS CATCHER OF ALL TIME

It does not take a long memory to recall the first of the plastic worms. A good many fishermen scoffed. Bass would never touch them, they said. A friend of mine, however, told me in amazement that he had caught a bass on one—and that the bass had actually swallowed the worm. Early in the soft-plastics game, I was handed a magazine assignment to try a welter of these lures—worms, small fish, tadpoles, and a host of others in salt water. I remember that a blue crab literally ate a big worm down to a nub.

No one at that time knew anything at all about how to fish plastic worms, except just as they'd been used to fishing live nightcrawlers. I took some to my small lake on my Bushwhack Creek Ranch. The water is very clear and from the dam I can stand in shadow of an oak and watch bass below me. I dropped one in with no hook or line—a "worm" colored specimen—and watched a bass seize it on the way down and swallow it. A bit later my boys and I tried experiments with real nightcrawlers, and real crayfish, pitting them against soft plastic facsimiles of each in our lake. The catch ran almost even as between the real and the imitation—and we let the fish carry them off and swallow them.

As everyone now knows, the plastic worm was here to stay. It literally skyrocketed to fame. Numerous improvements were made, chiefly making them tougher, exceedingly pliant, and translucent. Trying to sell worms, makers flooded the market with every conceivable color and combination of colors. Styles in worms changed and so did materials. Today there are "bead-chain" types supposed to reflect light better, corrugated types supposed to send out better vigrations, flip-tails, floaters, semifloaters, sinkers, worms on a harness, lead-head jigworms, and just plain bulk worms without hooks or rigs.

The latter are today far and away the most popular, for anglers meanwhile had been learning how best to fish plastic worms and which colors seemed to be most productive and in which waters. They learned hookups to make the worms practically weedless, and they learned how to keep them placed properly on a hook. In fact, both sinkers and hooks especially for plastic-worm fishing have been perfected. The amazing fact is that today, in the dozens of tournaments, some of them with a hundred to as many as five or six hundred entries, annually held here and there on the U.S. impoundments around the year, actual surveys show that in almost all cases at least 95 percent of the thousands of bass caught are taken on soft plastic worms!

It is easy enough to say this is because these experts fish them. By the same token, of course, the reason they fish them is that they are so surefire. This lure is without any question the best black-bass lure, particularly for largemouths, that has ever been fished anywhere on earth.

One friend of mine with a devastating reputation as a tournament winner told me, "Of course all sorts of lures will catch bass. Maybe I could catch as many at certain times on something else. But the fact is, these worms will take bass in any water, and at any time of year. Why experiment? I would prefer to spend my time seeking the fish, which is the most important part, rather than experimenting with lures, because I know that when I do find them, the worms will take them."

As I have said earlier, some people don't fish worms, or other bottom lures, simply because they enjoy some other type of fishing more. To be very truthful, I am one of these. I love top-water fishing, for any variety that will strike on top. I have fished days on end with dry flies for trout when wets would have better filled my creel. But I fished the way I liked, and enjoyed lesser but what I felt was sportier action. To this day, when we go down to our ranch and I fish my own lake for a quick session, even —as this is written—midday during deer or turkey hunting, I try a surface lure for a few casts. Then if there is no response I usually switch to a shad-type underwater plug for a few casts near the dam in open water. If no results—I resign myself to worms. Almost without fail, I can catch at least a couple, and on this small lake my record to date was twenty-one in two hours during a heavy feeding season. Thus, if your chief aim is to catch bass, there isn't much question about the type of lure that will give you the best odds—at all times, and under all sorts of varying conditions. The soft plastic worm has indeed proved phenomenal.

There are numerous ways to rig plastic worms. The so-called "Texas" rig, which has become more or less standard among thousands of experienced bass fishermen, is done as follows. If the worm is to be fished deep and on bottom, as 90 percent are, a small, cone-shaped sinker is slipped onto the line first. This weighs from one-quarter to one-half ounce, the choice of weight depending upon water depth. For extreme depths, the heavier weight is used. The cone shape evolved specifically because of its need for use with the worm. It is a slip-sinker type. Some of the late models have the bottom (large) end of the cone slightly concave, so that the head of the worm fits into it.

Hook size may be debated among anglers, but most use a 4/0 Sproat design. The point of the hook is shoved straight down into the *top* of the head of the worm, then the hook is turned and the point brought out the side about half an inch or a bit less below. The hook is now shoved on out around the bend and the shank pulled down through the head until the hookeye is buried in the worm head, but not deeply. Some new hooks are now marketed with a crook in them at the top and a little hooklike protrusion at the eye for the specific purpose of holding the worm head stable, so it won't slip down the shank when cast. The makeshift nonslip method used by numerous anglers is to shove a toothpick horizontally across through the worm head and through the hook eye, then break it off closely on either side. But before that is done, the hook, with most of the shank and all of the bend protruding alongside the worm below the head, is turned around so the point now faces the body of the worm. The point is thrust into the worm until the barb is covered, but is not allowed to come through on the far side. This makes the worm weedless. For proper action the worm should not be crooked at this point, but should hang straight with the line.

As noted, there are many ways to rig bare worms, and there are many rigged worms on the market, some with two or three hooks on a harness that runs down through the body of the worm. Certainly any of these devices will catch bass. But the consensus among expert anglers is that the rig described is far and away the best. When the worm is picked up by a bass, the sinker slips and thus does not disturb the fish.

There are as many theories on how the worm should be fished as there are colors. However, again the general method used by the most successful bass fishermen is to make the cast, let the worm go to the bottom. Then with the rod held at an angle of roughly forty-five degrees, the worm is *pulled*, not twitched and jiggled, until the rod is about upright. The rod is instantly relaxed so that the worm drops back to bottom again. The tip is held low while the slack is swiftly retrieved, then the process is repeated. How fast the worm is worked depends upon the fish—and the fisherman. Some fish very slowly, waiting in between. Some use a fairly stable rhythm. If the bass are active and eager, they'll give the clue. If they are not, one must experiment.

Individual worm fishermen have differing ideas about what to do when the bass hits. Some bass strikes, on certain days, are slammers, unmistakable. Others may be a gentle tap. These one must feel with the sensitive rod tip. In brush especially, the most successful anglers strike immediately. This is because a bass allowed to run may hang the line on brush, and there may be others following it as it runs with the "food." It is best to leave them where they are. If you have rigged properly, the bass will have the hook in its mouth on the first grab, for it will invariably take the head of the worm. I have watched bass do otherwise, nipping at a worm tail when it is reeled fairly fast through the water. But you can depend on it that those bass are not serious, and when they do that they are exceedingly difficult to inveigle. They are simply playful or curious.

Nonetheless, some fishermen allow the bass to run, and stop, before they strike back. A great many fish, and lures, are lost this way. In addition, the bass will now have swallowed the lure and if it is a small or medium fish you would have released, you can hardly keep from killing it in the process. Regardless of which method you choose, your strike must be severe. Brush, water resistance, line stretch, the hard mouth of the fish, the fact that the hook point must be shoved on through the worm by the strike—all these are against you. The pros often strike in a manner that would startle the beginner, holding the tip close to water and swiftly taking slack, then heaving back violently until the rod is, literally, above their head. It may seem awkward and unnecessary but it works.

When bass shun worms used by the pull method explained above, it is obvious that one should try other movements. A friend of mine gives a twitch of the tip that hops the worm along, as much as two or three feet per hop, bouncing it off the bottom. I often move the worm in quick little bounces only a few inches. At times you may wish to try taking the sinker off, using somewhat lighter tackle in open water when bass lie suspended or are in shallow places. Cast just worm and hook, let the worm sink slowly and naturally, with only a gentle twitch occasionally, then retrieve with spurts of action to make the lure wriggle. At times this is very effective. When bass are in shallow water it is utterly deadly. For deep fishing many fishermen prefer a floating-type plastic worm, used with the cone sinker. It tends to float up off bottom and is thus more visible, while the head end near the sinker stays down.

Although it is impossible to state which colors are best in worms, it can be stated that a great many of the "wild" colors and color combinations probably make their biggest sell to the fisherman. As we have seen in Chapter 6 dealing with color vision, the clarity of the water and the depth greatly influence which color will be seen most easily and which may be termed more "natural." Time of day also makes a difference, for the light will be of a different quality at any depth as the angle of the sun changes. Probably the darker colors are best seen in slanted light, which can be translated as early and late. The lighter worm colors, and the transparent or translucent models, probably show up better in higher light.

I have checked numerous experts and even professional bass fishermen to see what their worm color preferences are. And it is especially interesting that they invariably favor the same list of colors, give or take one or two for each individual. The purple or grape-colored worm is a great favorite. Black is universally considered excellent, but for specific times, depths, water and light conditions. Blue and red (strawberry) are invariably high on the list. Dark green also has its enthusiasts. But when asked which pair of colors they'd select if they could have only two, most experts choose black for one, and blue or purple for the other.

This is not to say you should avoid experimenting with colors. Lime green has its takers. I've caught a good many bass on translucent gold worms, and on speckled ones. Any worm will catch a bass. But it is good to know that you don't have to outfit with every hue. The standard colors mentioned are undoubtedly best. Odd as it seems, almost nobody fishes a "worm-colored" worm. In modern bass fishing, even the color of the real thing is passé!

Worm sizes differ. You just have to try small, medium, and oversize and see what works best for you. By and large the standard length will serve best, for the largest variety of situations. Incidentally, refer back to the portion of this chapter about jigging spoons for another excellent way to fish the plastic worm. On occasion letting the worm down to the bottom through the brush, right beside the boat, and jigging it, will produce fantastic results. Some anglers even team spoon and worm for various methods of use; such combinations are even marketed.

The discussion of lures in this chapter is not at all an attempt to discredit the scads of old standby plugs, lures, spoons, spoons-plus-pork rind, spinner and fly combinations, etc., that have been catching bass for many years. It is simply to fill readers in on the lure categories and methods which seem to have been bred from the new waters and the knowledge gained in the past decade or so. The deep-running, lipped plugs that are reeled furiously to make them bump bottom, or trolled fast to achieve a similar result, are still tremendously successful; a few bass fishermen use nothing else. However, it might be pointed out that in most cases the energy expended could be cut down considerably by using a worm, and the result would be just as good.

Going back a moment to topwater, I still fish some old plugs that are in design literally almost my own age. I do so perhaps partly from nostalgia and partly because I am used to them and have confidence in them. They are great producers. That's why they've been around so long. I intend to continue fishing such lures. Just try to tell an old Georgia flat-pond boy that there is a better lure than the old "Lucky Thirteen" in a specified color and he'd think you were nuts! Nonetheless, the new fashions and methods in lures have added tremendous success to bass fishing, and only the angler looking back over his shoulder instead of ahead would fail to utilize these tools.

CHAPTER TWELVE

Fly-Rodding for Largemouths

TRADING TROPHIES FOR THRILLS

When the renowned Dr. Henshall wrote *The Book of the Black Bass* and did his bass fishing close to a century ago, at a time when fishing tackle was to say the least rather crude, it is worth noting that he loved fly-rod fishing, and even developed a deerhair bass bug. There are indications that various Indian tribes used primitive floating bugs, of deerhair or light wood, two hundred and perhaps more years ago. While there certainly are numerous bass fishermen today who love to fish with fly-fishing tackle, this fishing is by no means as popular as spinning and casting and undoubtedly never will be.

Most fly fishermen are trout fishermen. Trout waters lend themselves far better to general fly fishing than do bass waters. The largemouth, a fish of weed beds and varied cover, is plainly difficult to reach with underwater flies. Smallmouths in streams are a different matter and we will look at that fishing in the next chapter. Not only are largemouths hard to reach with sunken flies most of the time, but it has to be admitted that surface flies and bugs limit the angler to rather seasonal activity, when bass are in shallow water or at least in water not more than about six feet deep.

Nonetheless, fly-rodding for largemouths is without any question the *sportiest* way this fish can be taken. There is immense enjoyment, to the experienced flycaster, just in the technique of his fishing. And there is always a great battle because of the character of the tackle. Thus what we are talking about here is first of all crystal-pure pleasure and drama, not total poundage of fish taken. Make no mistake, when the bass is situated so that a fly-rodder can properly present his lures, this is a thoroughly deadly manner of fishing. But it must be admitted also that the size of the bass caught is, over the long haul, not comparable to the trophies possible with other tackle. This is not what could be called trophy fishing.

Occasionally of course some very husky bass are caught on bass bugs. I personally have taken one fish of over nine pounds, which I considered purely a fluke, and I have caught a number in the five- and six-pound categories. But because I have been addicted to fly fishing for many years, and have caught hundreds of bass on surface bugs and underwater flies, I feel I can judge pretty well what the average will be.

For example, I well recall a few winters in Florida when I fished for largemouths almost exclusively with fly rod and bugs. I could take a limit practically any day with the fish running from one to three pounds; now and then a larger bass would decide to have a go at my bug. One of the chief reasons for these averages is that both surface bugs and underwater flies for bass are adapted to shallow waters. The very best bugging lakes are shallow lakes, because in these bass can be caught year-round up top. They are cycled for surface feeding. And most shallow waters, as we have seen, do not produce any great number of large bass, but rather a blizzard of medium fish.

There are fly-rod enthusiasts who bristle at the suggestion that they are limited where bass are concerned. But just check the trophy bass brought in anywhere and you will find the fly-rodders have few indeed. Nonetheless this is no drawback. I've often had far more sport and thrills with a limit of largemouths in the two-pound class caught on bugs than with a string of larger fish taken, say, on plastic worms. And so, make up your mind that if you intend to join the long-rod society on largemouth waters, you are in effect trading trophies for thrills. It is a good bargain. While you may not wish to become a fly-rod-only bass fisherman, switching to it particularly during the spawning season and when fishing shallow lakes or farm and ranch ponds brings many delights.

THE TACKLE

My ideas about fly tackle for largemouths may not be quite like those of numerous other writers. First of all, the fly rod and fly line were designed to most efficiently, and pleasantly, cast light lures. As readers surely know, in spinning or with casting tackle, the weight of the lure carries the line to the destination; in fly fishing, the weight of the line carries the lure and deposits it gently. Whenever one moves up from such lures as bass bugs of hair, feather, cork, or plastics, and large dry flies and underwater lures such as streamers and bucktails, and attempts to cast the so-called "fly-rod size" plugs, or the tiny spoons, or a hunk of bait with a split shot on the leader—this moves entirely out of the realm of fly-fishing. It is an abominable exercise in awkwardness. The casting gives no feeling of grace or pleasure, and any such lure can better be handled by a light spin rod.

I know many persons who use a fly rod and sideswipe bait, even with a cork bobber above it, out to bass pockets. Sure, it will catch bass. But one can far more adeptly handle the same bait on a light spin outfit. I know others who flail away with heavy spinner-and-fly combinations, small metal spoons, and tiny plugs. Why? The lures have to be hurled, not cast. They are not well fitted to fly-rod use, and again spin outfits do the job far better. If you concoct a fly rod heavy enough and a line like a rope that will fire such lures to the bass, then you really aren't fly-rodding anyway, and I can tell you (if you don't already know it) that you won't have much fun.

I have one little trick I use that I like to call "trout fishing for bass." This calls for using exactly the same tackle I would use for trout fishing, and even using various trout flies, mostly of fairly large size. When largemouths are feeding on hatching mayflies, for example, you can use a replica and have great action. A favorite rod of mine, which many lovers of the heavy fly-rod for bass will perhaps scoff at, weighs three ounces and is a bit less than seven feet long. I have taken trout to six pounds on dry flies with it, and scads of bass in the three-pound class, plus a few double that. This has been done with regular trout fly patterns, as I've said. An excellent bet for small lakes in summer is a grasshopper pattern exactly the same as used for trout. The reason I spoke of this method as a "trick" is that certainly it is specialized. Much of the time a largemouth wants a fair-sized bug and strikes more avidly at more action of the lure, whereas the trout-type dries are simply "crept" across the surface.

In the open water of small lakes and ponds where one can cast to the edges of weed beds or along them, or into shallows where bass are feeding, there is another trick I have long used that is not common. This is what I might call using a "pork-rind fly." I often use the same light fly rod. The leader is level, possibly seven feet long—about rod length—and of ten-pound monofil. To this I tie a hook of light wire, round bend, which keeps the casting weight down. Then I place on the hook a strip of white pork rind. If I cannot find strips about one and one-half inches long, I cut down larger ones. Full size (large strips) are too difficult to cast.

This hook and rind serves as one of the most successful sunken "flies" imaginable. It should be allowed to settle naturally, then be fished slowly along weeds, beside stumps and other debris, over weeds in shallows, and so on. Always try to keep your fly-rod lures in a position so that when you have a hit and hook a fish you don't allow it to get into the weeds or into cover from which your tackle cannot easily extract it.

Most of the time for standard bug fishing I personally use a rod shorter than what most manufacturers—and a good many writers—recommend. I feel that one after the other has simply copied the old idea that for bass and bass bugs you must use a rod of around nine feet long. This is utter nonsense. I have several of those, have had others, and I never use them. They are unwieldly, tiresome, and unnecessary. It is true that a good rod of eight and one-half feet is fine for bugs. If it has power it handles a heavy line well. My choice much of the time lately is a seven-and-one-half-foot rod with glass-to-glass ferrules—that is, ferrule-less—that weighs about four ounces. It has all the power one needs. If you are insistent upon using heavy bugs and lines such as the old GAF and wish to heave a bug across the pond, then perhaps you'll need a six- or seven-ounce, nine-foot rod. But I can assure you you are cutting down on the pleasure by such a choice.

Much will depend of course on the types of bugs you use. There is not much problem with underwater flies, because they have less wind resistance. But large bass bugs with long feathered tails do fight the wind. I try to select bugs that have as little resistance as possible, yet appeal to the bass. Deerhair bugs are not as popular nowadays as they once were. They have some disadvantages. They have much wind resistance, and they begin to waterlog after a few casts and especially after a catch is made. Nevertheless, deerhair bugs, if you can find any, are extremely effective.

The secret of successfully casting any bug for largemouths lies quite obviously in the weight of the line. As most readers know, fly lines presently are designated not as they once were, i.e., HCH, GBF, etc. They are now standardized by weight in grains, with some leeway in range. The first thirty feet of line, the "working" standard, is used for the weight. A light line (not suitable for bass-bug fishing) that has the first thirty feet weighing 80 grains (with a leeway range between 74 and 86) is designated as a No. 2

line. Lines run from 1 through 12, progressively heavier. The old double-taper HCH, with which I have cast to many a bass with light bugs, becomes a No. 6. Before the number, letters are used to tell the type of line: DT for double-taper; WF for weight-forward; ST for single taper; L for level. Following the number comes a letter telling whether floating or sinking: F for floating; S for sinking; plus combinations such as F/S for fast sinking.

Some bass fly-rodders are happy with the old level line—a line the same diameter and weight throughout its length. I have used them many times. An advantage is that a length of monofil can simply be cut for a leader. However, the weight-forward line is the best for casting heavy bugs. Some lines are made with what are called special "bug tapers." These are weight-forward lines (a heavy section up near the front end, then tapered down, such as the old nomenclature GBF, HCF, etc., but with a short (twenty-five-foot) "head" which helps turn a heavy bug over neatly, even in wind, and cuts down on the need for lengthy false casting in order to work line out.

Although each rod requires for best efficiency and casting ease a line of specified weight, one can step up to a size heavier if needed, slow down the casting rhythm a bit, and learn to work it well. Most bass fishermen, myself included, prefer the weight-forward lines for bass fishing, particularly for bugs. However, there is a new type of line now available, called the Vari-weight, currently in two sizes, that has distinct advantages. This is basically a double-taper line—each end tapered so the line is reversible. But, in the Variweight each end is of a different weight. The lines that will balance any rods suitable for bass bugging can be pretty well covered with Nos. 6, 7, 8, 9. As noted, there are two different Variweight lines presently marketed. One has a No. 5½ end and a No. 7½ end—in-between weights so that either end is *close* to two different weights, so close in fact that one cannot detect the difference in practice, when the line is matched to the rod. This line therefore will serve well with any rod taking a No. 5, 6, 7, or 8 line. The other has a No. 7½ end and a No. 9½ end and will fit rods requiring 7, 8, 9, and 10 lines. Thus, these two lines can, by reversal when necessary, match any bass rod. Frankly, I believe almost any average bug fisherman can do nicely with the smaller size, the Nos. 5½-7½, using a rod of modest length and weight but good power.

A great many fishermen use level leaders—just a cut length of monofil about the length of the rod—even with tapered lines. However, a properly tapered leader is better. The tippet has to be sturdy in order to handle the bug. For bugs of only modest size a 1X is standard. Larger bugs require heavier leaders. If you can't get the bug to fall gently and with leader straight, probably you have a leader that is either too wispy or else it is too long. But if the bug hits the water straight out but too hard, then try a lighter leader tip, or else a leader a bit longer.

Probably the average or newcomer bass-bug fisherman should not, to begin at least, take wholly to heart my rather opinionated slant on rod lengths and weights. I like the lighter ones, as I've said, and have learned to use them, with bugs of modest size. A fair standard for beginners would be to go for a good glass-to-glass rod (ferrule-less) in probably eight or eight-and-one-half-feet and five ounces. Remember that today's glass rods are far lighter in weight, compared to their power, than those of even a few years ago. Such a rod, properly fitted with a line, will handle well all but the largest, heaviest bugs. For those you may have to go a step higher. But the casting will not be as pleasant. Remember that in all bug casting the casting rhythm is *slower*. The heavy bug pulls back against the air and the line takes longer to straighten on the backcast.

Here is one other little gimmick regarding rods. Bugging is really difficult in the drowned timber of many of our impoundments. But it can be sporty indeed, even though you may have a good many hang-ups, and lose some fish. I have gone to a six-and-one-half-foot fly rod for this work. The rods in this length that I have are exceedingly powerful, with large power-type butt and fairly stiff action. Certainly this is not the perfect bass-bugging rod; it is special-purpose. But the short length, in timber, is just great. I sometimes snip back the end of a weight-forward line a bit to give me an opportunity to make very short casts with pinpoint accuracy. While timber fishing is not the most pleasant fly fishing because one can't "let himself go," it is still very effective and great sport.

I've purposely said nothing so far about reels. There's little to say. I use single-action reels entirely because they balance so much better with any rod. But some bass anglers like automatics. I have no quarrel. Either is just a storage place for the line.

FISHING THE BASS BUG

Because this is a specialized method and more bass fishermen are coming each year at least to try it sporadically, I believe it is important to know the rudiments of fishing a bass bug. In Chapter 4 we noted that deep fishing gets most of the bass, and the biggest bass, and this naturally is away from the shoreline. But in bug fishing the opposite is true because you can only appeal to bass that are in shallow water, from a foot to six feet deep. Thus shoreline, coves, rock ledges, and similar structures are the destination of the bug. Occasionally bass cruising over deep water but operating near the surface will strike a bug. However, the majority will come out of the shallows and near cover.

Cast always, as we've seen in Chapter 6, to the shady side of any object. Actually the best bugging times are in low light, which means early and late and on overcast days. This is because bass are most likely to be in shallows at such times, and also because one drawback of the fly outfit is that fly lines throw a heavy shadow. Bass are often frightened not by the plop of the lure, but by the line flying out over them and leaving a shadow below. Thus the best action ordinarily evolves when the line is least likely to be a fright factor. In any case, begin with short casts near the boat, or if you are wading a shoreline—an excellent manner of bugging—near yourself. Work the water out from you as you go, refusing to be tempted to make a long cast to the far stump or log or rock until you have worked the water in between.

Most bug fishermen work the lure too fast. I confess I am so inclined, and inclined also to work it too noisily. When you drop the bug, then pop it, and no strike is forthcoming, the temptation is to try to "wake 'em up." But the fact is, much of the time a quietly fished bug does best. I can recall numerous instances of seeing a bass race up to a popping bug and lie with its nose only inches away. If you let the bug lie too long, such a bass will leave, and if you pop it raucously the bass may be frightened and leave. A gentle bobble, however, often elicits an instant strike.

Of course one must judge when a noisy action is needed. Occasionally you have to really send out a call. And occasionally, too, a bug swiftly worked across a good hole will get strike after strike. Most of the time, however, if you will make a modest cast and spend as many seconds fishing out your cast, with minimum racket, as its length in feet—thirty seconds to a thirty-foot cast—you will find you'll catch the most bass.

Not all surface bugs are "poppers." Today these are by far the most popular, and it just may be that they are the most productive. Some have hair or feathers around the hook, which runs through a cork or plastic body. Others wear a rubber skirt. These at times are tremendously effective. Still other bugs—many in fact—nowadays are equipped with legs made of rubber. These quiver and bend on each movement of the bug and I have found that some of the most productive bugs are so equipped. Probably there are reasons why some are better than others. I recall an old brown cork number I once had, without a dished-in face to make it pop—a homely, simple, and cheap lure—that outcaught any of my others. I never knew why. However, even though the poppers are so popular and productive, is a good idea to try others. The bullet-headed bug—with a cone-shaped head—is designed to come through bits of floating weeds and debris without picking up a lot of it. It is a fairly quiet lure.

A few years ago I did a lot of experimentation with deerhair bass bugs, some of which had a closely-clipped body and big deerhair wings. These latter were actually made for big brown trout, and for fishing for them at night on streams in northern Michigan. That's where the ones I used originated. When used for trout, I habitually cast them *downstream* and across, let the bug swing around and made it "creep" upstream across a pool, by weaving in my fly line with my left hand. This technique was stunningly effective. So when I tried using the same big flies for bass, and on lakes, I did likewise—just made a cast, let the lure lie inert a few seconds and then crawled it in at a steady pace so that it left a wake but made no sound. The idea proved to be a productive one.

Regardless of the type of surface bass bugs you use, and especially if you tie your own, it is a good idea to consider the upturned hook. These are close to weedless, although getting the hook into the fish is difficult. When fishing any bug in lily pads or pencil-type reeds, keep in mind that you must gently steer the bug around and through tiny openings. A bug that runs under a pad leaf will all too often hit the stem and hang, and you will have to mess up the water to get free. Reeds are as bad. A bug hooked into a reed will pull up along it and skin it but seldom come free. A trick I use is to cast right into reeds, then fish the lure very gently and slowly, guiding it. If it touches a stem, be very careful to jiggle around. If it appears to hang, make a very precise, quick roll cast to flip the bug free and then do an instant pickup all in one movement.

When fishing any of the surface bass "flies," keep your tip low after the cast, and *pointed at the lure*. Never have slack on the water. When you twitch a bug, or pull a bullet-headed bug along, instantly lower the tip and take in the slack. The moment the bass hits you must be ready. Raise the rod tip firmly and immediately and you'll have your fish hooked. Bear in mind, too, when a bass hits a lure and is hooked there is a momentary—

usually very brief—time lag as the fish is confounded and before it explodes into action. Get used to taking advantage of this instant. Don't slack off. Keep the head of the bass up. That way it will not be likely to dive into cover.

UNDERWATER BASS FLIES

Submerged flies that run at modest depth are often very productive with largemouths. As we said, the bugs work best prior to, during, and just after spawning, sometimes in fall when bass return to shallows, and in shallow waters much of the year, especially in the South. But there are times when bass will not touch a surface lure, yet will readily take one only a few feet down.

Most of the underwater flies used for bass were not originally tied just for bass. They are replicas of trout and salmon flies. The spinner-fly combination is famed for catching bass, but as I've said earlier it is difficult and certainly not enjoyable to cast with a fly rod. It is far more efficiently used with a spinning rod. The various streamers and bucktails all do well for bass because they represent minnows upon which bass feed. The muddler in large size, fished wet and just below surface, is an excellent bet. So are silvery marabous that pulsate as they are retrieved.

I dislike saying that sunken flies cannot be as effective used for bass as the surface bugs because some fly fishermen are determined to the contrary. It is true that the sinking fly lines now in common use can take a fly deep. But from a practical standpoint they cannot take it deep enough quickly enough, and get the fly through bottom cover, as well as casting tackle can work a heavier lure in a similar situation. It is possible to fish a sinking line, cast and count seconds, letting the fly go down twenty feet or more. Few anglers will do this, however, because it is so much easier to use other fishing methods.

Even in trout fishing, I have often used a fast-sinking fly line and added a split shot up the leader ahead of a wet fly, to get it down on the bottom in swift current. But casting such a contraption is annoying, and the line and leader are inclined to drop quickly on the backcast, then belt the angler in the noggin on the forward cast. It seems to me that for unlimited enjoyment in fly-rodding for bass one should use the tackle as it is intended and within its limitations.

Personally I like the *sinking-tip* fly lines better for sunken flies than I do the sinking lines. With these specialized lines, the body of the line floats, but a certain number of feet at the tip sink, taking the fly down. Sunken flies can be handled well down four to six feet with these lines. That is about the practical average for underwater fly fishing for largemouths. I'm speaking of lake and pond fishing. Streams, which will be touched on in a discussion of the smallmouth in the next chapter, are entirely different propositions. Seldom does one need to go deeper than that in a stream.

One of the problems with largemouths and the wholly sinking line is that the line itself becomes somewhat awkward, in still water, when deeply submerged. Strikes are difficult to manage, and debris seemingly is always in the way. Further, the times of year when sunken flies take largemouths well are not much greater than the periods for surface bugs. When the bass hole up deep, in cover, it is just not very practical to try to cast a fly to them.

Fly-rodders should be aware of the new weedless sunken flies. I believe the name "Keel Fly" is a copyrighted brand name, or the name of a patented brand. These are the best types of the submerged streamers and bucktails usable for largemouths. The principle is based on a hook that rides with point upturned, and a shank that is bent sharply down from the eye and then runs straight or nearly so back to the beginning of the bend. Material tied into the head streams back to cover the upturned hook point. These flies are as nearly snagless and weedless as sunken flies can be made. There are numerous patterns and many are effective on largemouths.

CHAPTER THIRTEEN

Fishing for Smallmouth Bass

A DIFFERENT FISH INDEED

Only a small percentage of the total of U.S. bass anglers are acquainted with the smallmouth. Many have never caught one, many have never seen one. A few have casual acquaintance, and a few others, lucky anglers, "grew up" with this fish and, living within one of its major bailiwicks, have been catching it all their lives.

One of the latter, a close friend, told me after he had made a bass fishing trip into the mid-South and Florida, where he became initiated into large-mouth fishing: "I can understand now just how great the difference is between smallmouth and largemouth. A fellow who had never caught a smallmouth but had been brought up on largemouths might find his first smallmouth trip mighty puzzling and maybe unsuccessful. But if he were an expert at smallmouths, he'd find the largemouth, by comparison, much easier to attach to a hook."

That states the case about as precisely as it can be stated. It reminds me of my years in Michigan when I used to hunt ruffed grouse and pheasants. If I did my pheasant hunting first, I found them tricky birds. But if I spent a week on the deep-woods ruffed grouse first and then went after pheasants, I wondered how the heck I could miss one. It is true that in some waters where both bass happen to be able to sustain themselves, an angler may

173

be about as likely to catch one as another. Or at least *because* he catches both he feels that there is not much difference. But if he will analyze his catches he will find that with the smallmouths he fished very specific places, and usually "finer" than for the largemouths. It has been said by one well-known writer that there are more likenesses between these two basses than there are differences. True. But to understand the smallmouth properly it is the *differences* that count most.

I am convinced that smallmouth bass are more wary by far than their relatives. They are also less greedy. To repeat what was stated in the first chapter of this book regarding the smallmouth, this species seems in better "control" than the largemouth. It has the quality of restraint. It might even be termed conservative. Fundamentally it is a product of its environment, and that environment typically is somewhat different from the surroundings in which the largemouth thrives. While the two basses do overlap, the smallmouth is by no means as tolerant of less than optimum conditions. For example, it cannot live in most waters of the South, whereas the largemouth does well in most waters of the North.

In basic character the smallmouth may perhaps best be described as a stream fish: a fish of fairly swift, cold streams with rocky and gravel bottoms. Yet of course it dwells in dozens of lakes and in fact grows larger in suitable lakes than in streams. But if you think of it as a fish of clear, cold, swift streams, you will set it apart in personality easily from the largemouth, which cannot tolerate such a habitat, and is found, when in streams, invariably in slow, warm flowages and even in these it never colonizes as well as in lakes.

By comparison the number of waters inhabited by smallmouths is small. It thrives in Maine, where it was introduced. Certain lakes and streams across southern Canada as far as Manitoba offer beautiful smallmouth habitat. Northern Michigan and portions of the Great Lakes, Wisconsin, Minnesota—these places are the heartland for U.S. smallmouths. In certain clear, deep, rocky, cold lakes of the mid-South—Tennessee and Kentucky—smallmouths have long been famous. The Ozark streams are renowned smallmouth habitat, and the fish does fairly well in some of the lakes to which these streams are tributary, but not as well as in the streams themselves. Numerous eastern streams have long been famed for smallmouth fishing—for example, the Delaware, the Potomac, the Susquehanna, Virginia's James. And nowadays the Snake River in the West, particularly in stretches along southeastern Washington above and below where the Grande Ronde joins has become, through transplanted fish, one of the all-time great smallmouth waters.

Thus smallmouth havens of note are scattered and must be ferreted out and selected. But all have much in common—clarity of the water, temperature lower than that preferred by the largemouth, rocks and gravel rather than weed beds and softer bottoms; in other words a habitat from infertile to only modestly fertile, ofter rather sparse in variety of forage species. The smallmouth usually grows more slowly than its relative. In its colder, less-fertile waters it may be less than ten inches long at three or even four years of age. It does not attain as great size at maximum as the largemouth. In dozens of good smallmouth streams fish of one-half to one pound weight make up the bulk of the catch, fish of two pounds are noteworthy, and a three-pounder has to be shown to everyone.

To be sure, certain waters grow them larger. The record, from Dale Hollow Lake in Tennessee, is eleven pounds fifteen ounces, but fish even approaching that are exceedingly rare, and have so far come almost entirely from a few impoundments along the Tennessee River, in northern Alabama and Tennessee. Some of these turn up annually—six, seven, eight pounds. But from Maine to Manitoba to Washington to the Ozarks and Alabama, a smallmouth of four or five pounds is a fine specimen indeed.

The smallmouth is always a more active fish than the largemouth. That is, when feeding it might be described as sprightly. It almost always jumps when hooked. While we like to imagine the largemouth does likewise, the fact is that only a fraction of hooked largemouths actually clear the water. I have seen a two-pound smallmouth go up six times in a row, well above the water. They are active during spawning, too, groups of them often jittering about on gravel beds seeking proper places. And, indicating their proclivity for streams, if suitable tributaries are present to lakes where smallmouths live, many will make spawning runs into these, even into small streams. They will refuse to spawn unless they find clean sand or gravel. I have watched largemouths clean away mud and silt to find a spawning place on soft clay or even among roots of vegetation. That will discourage the smallmouth.

While it is true that smallmouths can be caught at times on any lure that will catch any bass, they are not eager to take large lures. And overall they incline toward a narrower selection. I presume this is because forage species are more limited in variety in most of their habitats. The crayfish is a staple. Aquatic nymphs make up a substantial portion of their diet.

Minnows of course are important. In a few impoundments where small-mouths are found, there are shad. But this forage species plays little part, throughout the range, in feeding these bass. Freshwater lampreys and salamanders are among their foods. Small frogs are also a top bait. But the smallmouth is not renowned for eating mice or small birds or "anything that moves," as is the largemouth.

A great many smallmouths are taken by surface lures, but this might lead a novice to believe they are predominantly surface feeders. This is not true. Smallmouths are more inclined to feed beneath the surface. Only during certain periods do they avidly feed on top, and when they do this it is indeed a joy to the fisherman. Their innate wariness is due without doubt partially to the clarity of their habitats. Catching a five-pound small-mouth is about as hard as catching brown trout of the same weight. Such a fish has had plenty of experience. It is probably at least seven years old and it may be ten!

All smallmouths should be thought of as poised and well disciplined. There is no mad rush to grab a lure just because it wiggles. It is calmly appraised beforehand. The fish seems to "think" in a manner as uncluttered and clean as its habitat, and it is always shy and conservative. It can also be exasperatingly moody and selective. I well recall one of the finest small-mouth weeks I ever experienced, in the northern end of Lake Michigan one June when the bass were simply swarming inshore. Where I waded to fish there were coarse gravel bars that fell off without pattern into deep holes. In some of these big boulders lay. One morning I caught fish just casting rather indiscriminately, using light spin tackle and a nightcrawler without adornment. The next day I could not catch a fish unless I laid the crawler on a deep boulder and left it there!

On that same trip—well before plastic worms had come on the scene—I experimented with lures. With the light so far as I could determine exactly the same on two days in a row, I caught fish the first day on a gold spinner with a bare treble hook. The next day the fish shunned it totally—but as soon as I added a piece of nightcrawler they couldn't wait. Yet, on another day, if I fished a crawler hooked through the head, the fish would bite off three-fourths of the crawler and never touch the hook. I tried pushing the crawler clear up the leader and leaving the hook in the tail, wholly unorthodox. This I fished very slowly—and I caught every fish that dared try it. The smallmouth reminds me constantly of trout in its wariness and conservatism and selectivity—and unpredictability.

TACKLE FOR SMALLMOUTHS

There is more leeway in tackle for smallmouths because of their cleaner habitats. What you use depends entirely upon where and how you are fishing. Much more fly-fishing is done for this fish, most of it on streams. Spinning is also popular on streams as well as lakes. In clear water lines or leaders must be finer, and there is also more opportunity to let a fish run and to play it. On the other hand, if you are going to fish for big smallmouths in deep water, you have to use tackle suited to this purpose.

For example, when D. L. Hayes from Litchfield, Kentucky, caught what is still the world record smallmouth in 1955—that monster just one ounce short of twelve pounds—he was trolling a well-known deep-running plug called a Bomber. This lure, and facsimiles, has long been popular at Dale Hollow Lake in Tennessee, where that big fish was caught. Several local anglers have made smallmouth history there by deep trolling, or else by letting a plug sink to the bottom and then reeling furiously. Deep operation of lures requires sturdy tackle, and in this case the requirements are identical to the worming rods and casting reels already described as so popular among largemouth fishermen.

Undoubtedly there are more truly large smallmouths in the Tennessee-Kentucky-Virginia-Alabama area than anywhere else in the U.S. These are chiefly lake fish, although some good ones come out of rivers such as the Clinch. Dozens of fish from six to eight pounds have come from Dale Hollow and Center Hill in Tennessee. Norris Lake, an older impoundment, has big ones too, and so does a not so well known reservoir, Woods, near Tullahoma. Watuga and South Holston are another pair with big bass. Wheeler in north Alabama is another example. These are lakes where stout, powerful tackle is needed, exactly as for largemouths, and where the deep-running plugs and spoons, as well as plastic worms, have long been racking up the heavy catches. In spring especially natives use live salamanders, locally called "spring lizards," which are deadly on smallmouths here and elsewhere. The soft plastic replicas do as well, too.

In the lakes of Maine and elsewhere in New England, there is not as much chance of hooking extralarge bass. Specimens of two to four pounds are considered substantial. Many of the lakes are smaller, the bass hit best in water of medium depth, and there is not as much emphasis on extremely deep fishing. Common tackle here is an ordinary casting rig not as powerful as the worming-rod outfits. Many also use medium-weight spin tackle successfully. In some lakes there is good top-water fishing, with plugs, during and immediately after spawning. But much depends on how clear the water is and how deep the fish lie. Spoons and spinners, and spinner and fly combinations, often with the spinner weighted to get it down quickly, take fish regularly.

There has always been a great deal of bait fishing for smallmouth bass in the Great Lakes region. The live crayfish, hooked in the tail, the night-crawler, minnows, or big hellgrammites are the baits I've seen used most and used myself most successfully. I have fished a variety of waters through-out Michigan, from Lake St. Clair where wonderful smallmouth fishing was available, to small lakes of the North, many of the beautiful streams of the Upper Peninsula, the spring gatherings of smallmouths inshore in upper Lake Michigan and Lake Huron, the streams and lakes of Wisconsin and Minnesota. Never have I found this bass especially eager to strike surface lures anywhere in this region.

On one occasion I used a large deerhair fly—mentioned in the preceding chapter—that had been tied for night use after outsize brown trout. I cast it along lily pads at the edge of a rocky northern lake, made it crawl slowly across the surface, and toward evening simply decimated the fish. Conversely, when thousands of smallmouths were gathered inshore along upper Lake Michigan prior to spawning, I have cast my arm lame with surface lures—even when the bass were shallow—without any result what-ever. Yet in the same place, with a spinner I once took twenty-six small-mouths, all around two pounds I'd guess, in twenty-six consecutive casts! One spring on the Canadian side of Lake St. Clair while producing a TV film, several of us fished smallmouth beds and could not catch a fish on surface. This was because in the clear water the beds were too deep. When we used underwater lures, we were very successful.

In most of my Great Lakes Region smallmouth fishing I have used medium casting or spinning tackle on the lakes much of the time, but have been personally partial to fly-rodding the streams. Streamer flies, bucktails, varied marabous,and large nymphs were far and away the most telling lures. The big Woolly Worm and the Muddler, tied for large trout in the West, seldom failed to catch fish and are used elsewhere successfully, too. When I say "large" or "big," I do not mean enormous outsize flies for under-water use. Most stream smallmouths will feed on minnows of one and one-half to two inches in length. Streamers, etc., should match these. Large nymphs are common, and so the fly patterns can be of realistic, but not overdrawn, size. Many old smallmouths are wary of lures that do not imitate their natural food. The clear water allows them a sharp view and good judgment. Obviously, leaders have to be as fine as for trout in comparable waters.

The thing always to keep in mind about lures where smallmouths are concerned—especially in streams—is that these habitats are severe and sparse in *variety* of food. A smallmouth becomes exactly like a trout in the same type of habitat. There are only a certain few foods that make up the preponderance of its diet. Thus, lures that imitate these foods are more likely to take fish than are lures strange to the local life chain. The largemouth has such a wide-spectrum diet that any moving object may attract it; not so the smallmouth. I recall an article written by the world-famous fly-fisherman and fishing editor of *Outdoor Life* magazine, Joe Brooks, in which he told of fishing the Snake and using with great success a black marabou fly. It was locally tied to represent a small sand eel plentiful in the river and an important diet item for the smallmouths.

While I favor sunken lures for smallmouths, they certainly will take surface bugs and lures. Bug fishermen should by all means fish their lures quietly. Often the deerhair types or the bullet-headed "quiet" bugs outdo the poppers because there is always the inclination on the part of the fisherman to pop the bug noisily. Again, smallmouths like realism, not phony animation. I have used deerhair bugs of varied types, from frog simulations (great!) to moth copies, in both lakes and streams. Natural movements are best. In streams it is not easy to keep deerhair bugs dry, but pressing them in tissue after a few casts or after a fish is taken will help, after which a few false casts dries them thoroughly.

Standard popping bugs are difficult to work in flowing water. The bugs with concave faces dig in, are too noisy, and are inclined to go under when you try to lift them. Other types, such as with a convex V-shaped head, a slanted face, or a rounded head are better. They are quieter, and can be more efficiently handled in riffles or swift glides.

I have noted bucktails for underwater use. The bucktail trailer for a spinner—neither one large—is a standard stringer-filler. Colors in all flies should be conservative. In the bucktail and spinner combinations, brown, black, white, and yellow can be interchanged until you find the ones that seem best. Streamers in black, grays, browns, and yellows with white or red intermingled are commonly most effective. But one aspect of fly-fishing we have not touched is dry-flying, exactly as for trout. Patterns can be a bit larger than for most trout fishing—dries tied for big trout when they are not too selective as to size. Numbers 8 and 6 are good, although on occasion you'll have to drop down to No. 10. Realistic trout patterns are fine. The fluffy, high-floating types, such as the bivisibles in their full range of conservative colors, float well and present a lifelike appearance. If the fish refuse the flies dry, but you see them coming up for a look, change to a similar color and size, but wet.

WHERE AND WHEN

Because smallmouth surroundings differ so much as a rule from largemouth habitats, it may be confusing to beginners in smallmouth fishing to read the water and know where to find them. Actually it is quite simple. When you strip away much of the weed growth (not all, of course), remove the masses of drowned timber and submerged brush so common to the largemouth impoundments, there are only certain cover items left. And since smallmouth waters usually have hard or rocky bottoms and shorelines, anything from fair-sized stones to sunken boulders to rock ledges and caves will be utilized by the bass. This is true both in lakes and in streams.

A great many smallmouth lakes in the Northeast, the Great Lakes region, and southern Canada contain crisscross jams of logs, or fallen trees along shore. Even though the lake may have a rocky shoreline the timber debris serves as added and superb cover. I recall a wonderful lake in northern Wisconsin that contains both smallmouth bass and muskellunge, as well as walleyes. Typically the lakeshore is bordered with balsam and cedar intermingled with white birch. Over the years portions of the shoreline that are steep or abrupt have had leaning trees succumb to natural pressures and finally fall into the water. Once submerged, wood keeps well. Among and below this jackstraw rim of blowdowns both muskies and bass lie. In fall especially I have mopped up by casting to such areas—and I've lost a lot of good bass, too!

Another lake that comes to mind is one in Michigan's Upper Peninsula. At one time there was a lumbering operation here and thousands of logs were floated across the lake. Scores of them, sunk and lost a hundred years ago, are still embedded below water along shore. The wood is as perfect in many of them today as it was when they were cut. In fact, salvage operations were popular some years ago in such lakes and more so in the streams where many a log boom had gone down. At any rate, the criss-cross of sunken logs is a smallmouth paradise.

Thus in any smallmouth water you really can locate the cover spots more easily than in the more lush and varied habitats of the largemouth. Reeds grow in most instances in rather infertile soils in sand or fine gravel. If rocks or logs are absent, clumps of reeds will be gathering places for the bass, at least when they are in shallow water. As one goes deeper, in lakes it is a good idea to probe for gravel bars down in fifteen or twenty feet of water. If there happens to be weed beds on two sides of a cove, look for deep bars in the center or near the shoreline end but away from the weeds. Rocky shorelines that fall away steeply will have bass lying along the drop-off edges. If there is a rock slide running down to the water, undoubtedly it continues. This is a perfect spot for smallmouths, but you have to find the proper depth.

Numerous smallmouth lakes typical of the north country contain small, rocky islands. These are among the most perfect of places around which to locate bass. They are like small underwater pyramids that draw forage, and bass, from the surrounding water. But don't overlook the "island" that doesn't quite show above water, the mid-lake reef. A circle or line of floating weed growth may be a giveaway for such a spot. Or when cruising in a boat, keep watch for the suddenly shallow spots out in a lake. These usually are areas that rise up from bottom but not far enough to break the water. Their slanted sides are excellent places, offering both cover and food for the bass. Inshore shoals are just as good, when bass are feeding. Those that slant down so that there is five or six or ten feet of water before the final drop are best.

Lake *points* are among the best of all gathering places for these bass. A rocky point that thrusts far out has much good water on both sides. A gravel point may be just as good. Water which drops away on either side, and often straight off the point, will offer both resting and feeding areas, but possibly at different depths. Check stony points to see if crayfish are plentiful. If they are you will discover bass habitually feeding, at proper hours, at the depths where the crustaceans are most heavily colonized. Keep the lure right on the bottom and let it bump along. All of these structures are the obvious spots. When the bass are very deep, of course you have to either guess at the contours or use a sounder.

In streams the fallen tree, the submerged log thrusting into a bank, the sunken boulder will point out havens for smallmouths, just as in lake waters. But stream currents obviously influence the fish and must be properly "read." If you are an experienced trout fisherman, do not be misled by looking for smallmouths in the swift, deep runs where trout often lie. The bass will select less turbulent and commonly rather quiet spots just on the edge of heavy currents. At the head of many a pool you will note a swath of bits of debris and usually, if the pool is the culmination of an especially swift pouring, a patch of froth. This is obviously a spot where all the forage pushed down by the current will first settle and be concentrated, and it is likely to be a hangout for a covey of bass. Sometimes, however, depending on what they're taking, they may fool you and be eagerly feeding on the riffle above a deep hole, or in another down below it. When they lie in the middle of a deep hole, on the bottom, covered by enough water so they are fairly well hidden, they probably won't be in a mood to strike. They are resting. Yet a feeding spree may start at any time.

If a stream has stretches of grassy bank that is even slightly undercut, these will hold fish. But the deeper spots will most often hold them. On a bend a surefire spot is where a stream gouges out a six-foot deep hole that cuts under a grassy bank. In streams that have numerous large boulders, smallmouths, exactly like trout, will lie *behind* the boulder, that is, in the slick on the downstream side. Food washes in here, and from here, resting easily and protected from current, bass can dart out to grab passing morsels. A straight rock bluff that turns a stream on a bend will have bass lying, usually deep, along the rock face, but below where the force of the current is broken.

Only under special conditions will you find smallmouths in sunny places. Fish the spots where a tree or trees shade a proper piece of cover, or fish the shadows behind a big boulder. Deep water may serve as shade. If there is a gravel bar ten feet deep in the stream, it may be difficult to fish but it will be a good place. Of course you should be extremely conscious of water temperature. (See Chapter 8 for a discussion of favorite temperatures.) In a stream it may not differ drastically from spot to spot, but it may tell you when to try the sunny, shallow riffles. If there is a good hatch on, often the riffles will be loaded with bass, occasionally even when the temperature is a bit high or low. The riffle feeding sessions are the exception regarding smallmouths feeding out in the sun. These periods may not last long. All told, stream cover is fairly obvious. But never overlook a small rock or a small "bassy-looking" pocket. It may be the home of a big brute that wants to be overlooked!

The "when" of smallmouth fishing may be more complicated than for largemouths. On many smallmouth streams, and some lakes of the North, the season is not open all year round but is timed to open after the bass have spawned. This eliminates a period when the fish can be caught most easily, and often on the surface, in bedding areas, or at least in fairly shallow water. Depending upon latitude, spawning will take place either in late May, or else up to mid-June. If you fish where it is legal to take smallmouths during and just prior to spawning, then seek shoreside areas of clean gravel or sand, preferably interspersed with boulders or reed beds for some sort of cover. The spawning areas will be in protected bays or coves, where wave action is least likely to disturb the eggs. If nests are no more than three feet deep, surface action may be good while the males are making nests and after the spawn has been deposited. If nests are deeper, four to eight feet, undoubtedly you will have to fish a sinking lure such as a spinner and fly, or a spoon or a plug, to get results.

Immediately after spawning the fish feed heavily. This is true in both lakes and streams. But they will now be less inclined to strike on top. Spoons, small plugs, spinner and fly, and streamers fished well down all should take fish, and this heavy feeding will be in water of modest depth rather often and will continue for two or three weeks. In stream fishing, as for example in the Ozarks, the water may be high and commonly a bit roily in June. This makes fishing easier. The riffles may be aswarm with feeding fish, and wet flies and streamers will do well.

As soon as this postspawning activity eases off there will be a general dispersal of the fish. The lake fisherman will have a tougher time than the stream angler. The fish will be scattered and traveling back toward deeper water in lakes and regrouping in summer haunts. It takes work to find them and they may be feeding less heavily now. In a stream, however, it is easy to track down the bass, but in early summer it may not be easy to get them to strike.

Contrary to the opinion of earlier days, summer fishing can be *better* than ever—if one will patiently locate the fish and give them what they want. In lakes the depth sounder can ferret out the bottom structures which is, as we have already noted in Chapter 9, where they'll be. If the fish do not have really deep cover to get into, then you will discover that their feeding is mostly done early and late, when light is slanted or low. As summer continues, if water temperature is high, feeding may be almost entirely at dusk and dawn or at night.

During July and August the streams require exceedingly careful, fine fishing. The water is low and clear. But this can also be one of the most productive of all times on the streams. In fact, some excellent top-water fly-fishing is on tap in midsummer. Hair bugs that float, cork and plastic bugs, and large trout-fly patterns fished dry will all get results. But the fine leader and the careful fisherman who keeps hidden and dresses drably will be the most successful, for the stream fish are terribly skittish now, due to the low water and its clarity. Early and late fishing will usually be best. Dusk and on to as late as you can see will account for a substantial number of the largest bass. After dark, fishing top water, strike at the splash.

Don't give up on sunken flies in summer, either. Streamers and spinner-and-fly combinations are both effective. The streamer is one of the easiest and quietest of lures for a so-so fly-fisherman to manipulate. Good-sized nymphs, cast upstream and allowed to tumble back through the pools, or dropped alongside undercut banks, are more difficult for most anglers to fish properly, but are telling lures when expertly handled. During August the streamer in varied types and patterns has proved on numerous streams the most effective of all lures.

In streams during the hottest weather the bass will be forced to gang up in the deep holes. Don't be fooled by hordes of big fish in such a pool, for most smallmouth streams also contain species such as suckers, and the bass and rough fish may have to share the pools. When these bass schools, or forced gatherings, are in evidence, the fishing can be very good if you are delicate about approach. If you spook one fish, you've spooked them all. But they may allow a closer approach now because they have nowhere else to go.

When early fall comes, smallmouths may reappear in shallow to moderate depths in the lakes. Bait fishing is especially effective now. But the preference for types of lures is difficult to establish. I have had fine top water fishing in September, and just as good results using streamers, bucktails, spinners, and spoons. On the whole, it is important to watch for a movement of fish inshore at this time. Old log jams and sunken boulders will again appeal to the fish. Shallower gravel bars and shoal waters where minnows school up should not be bypassed.

The season may close on many northern or Ozark smallmouth streams and lakes in early or midfall. But it does not close on some of the big lakes of the mid-South and Southeast. Here, though most fishing is done in moderate weather, there are old hands who fish right on through the

winter and haul in some fantastic catches. One of the Tennessee lakes had
for some seasons a "Frozen Fisherman" contest. Many of the anglers fished
in the bitterest weather imaginable, and curiously some of them fished on
cold winter nights, even during snowstorms. They knew where to find the
bass, in deep water, and during these bad-weather periods a good many
big ones were taken, and still are. The jig-and-eel, the plastic worm, and
particularly the bucktail jig are good lures to use when the fish are deep,
either in winter or summer.

There is one word that applies to the smallmouth with much heavier
emphasis than it does to the largemouth: unpredictable. Just when you
think you have them doped, they decide differently. Thus it takes an angler
willing to experiment and be ever alert to new ideas to take smallmouths
consistently.

I remember a hole in a big stream in northern Michigan where I tied up
my boat during a float trip and cast a big dry fly to a feeding fish. The bass
kept coming upstream through the hole, gulping an insect from the surface
every couple of feet. I laid the fly a yard ahead of the last gulp and instantly took a two-pounder. Other fish also began feeding the same way. But I
could not get one to hit.

I switched to a Muddler pattern, cast far across, let it sink a few inches,
then began the retrieve as the current took it. I saw a wake. Never drop
back when a smallmouth starts; if anything, increase the speed. I did, and
I instantly had the fish. Again I could not catch another. Finally I changed
to a big streamer and again took a bass. In all I caught six from the hole,
in the period of an hour, every one on a different lure. Why? Only the bass
knew. Had they been largemouths, I'll bet all would have favored the same
lure. The smallmouth is indeed an individualist. It is also an exciting challenge, and in its battle one of the most dramatic of all American game
fishes.

SMALLMOUTH RELATIVES

In Chapter 1 we remarked that the spotted bass is in habits, temperament,
and in selected habitats about like a cross between largemouth and smallmouth. In a great many waters inhabited by this bass there is really no
method of fishing exclusively for it, because it mingles with the largemouth.
For example, a few months before this was written I took an exceptional

specimen on the edge of the Ozarks while fishing for largemouths. The
stream habitats of spotted bass are never, or seldom, as swift as those of
the smallmouth, and over much of its northernmost range the larger pools
where current is slow will be the places which spotted bass most frequent.
In the southern range, however, commonly they are taken in more active
water. In the Texas Colorado I have caught them in swift spots among
submerged boulders, and I did mention in the opening chapter that in quite
swift, clear streams in Alabama I had caught them, of modest size, over
gravel runs.

A hint as to fishing for spotted bass can be gained from studies done by
fisheries personnel in Texas. While testing forage requirements of Texas
largemouths, Florida largemouths, and spotted bass, each in segregated
ponds stocked with sunfish in identical ratio, it was found that the Texas
and Florida varieties mopped up all their sunfish forage in short order.
But the spotted bass spent most of their time ferreting out crayfish that
were hiding in bottom gravel and rocks in their pond, and ate only half
their sunfish ration.

By and large this is a bottom and below-surface feeder, predominantly.
Lurewise this means one should use submerged artificials or baits fished on
or near bottom. We also noted earlier that spotted bass are often found
in much deeper water than are either largemouths or smallmouths. This is
another clue, for lake fishing. My experience on streams seems to indicate
that streamers, spinners, small spoons, and underwater plugs do the best
job. I think of this fishing as very similar to fishing for smallmouths. Late
in the season, or during fall's cool weather, look for concentrations of
spotted bass in lower stream reaches, in the big, even murky, pools. In
spring they'll more likely be moving up into headwaters or small tributaries.

Aside from the stream fishing, about the only time one must make
special efforts to meet the needs and whims of spotted bass is when fishing
specifically for them in one of their strongholds, such as the famed Lewis
Smith Lake in Alabama. Even here, the locals claim spotted bass are of all
varieties the most erratic and difficult to catch consistently. In such a lake
the water is so deep that the bass often "disappear" during summer, going
down as much as one hundred feet, showing up occasionally—as at night
—to feed at higher levels but unpredictably—or so it seems at this point
in the specific and concentrated experience of fishermen after them. Spring
is one of the best times in such lakes, for it gives the angler a better chance
of reaching the fish in water of modest depth.

These fish are renowned for their schooling. That, too, adds difficulties. One morning a tributary stream mouth along a lake shore may be swarming with them, and the next day there won't be a fish. But below a huge rock bluff where water drops down the stairsteps below for many feet they may be ganged up. Depth sounders are most helpful in a classic spotted-bass habitat such as Lewis Smith Lake. Often large schools, or at least their likely lairs, can be pinpointed, but they may be deep. Around this lake the varied spinners such as the safety-pin types, the deep-diving plugs, and the plastic worms are the most successful lures. All told, the fishing is much like that for largemouths in deep water, crossed with habitat and techniques used for smallmouths in a place like Dale Hollow in Tennessee—at least for summer fishing.

At Lewis Smith Lake, or any comparable spotted-bass lake, look for high ridges or cliffs that run out to a point and slant steeply down, with rubble and shale disappearing underwater. Bear in mind that such places will have ample forage such as crayfish and minnows, and will draw these bass to feed along the steep slant. When a spotted bass takes a lure, it usually hits with a hard strike, like a smallmouth, and keeps going toward deep water. It is not the leaper the smallmouth is, but it is a most stubborn, hard fighter.

One tolerance of spotted bass that all anglers experienced with them have noticed is that they'll put up with exceedingly murky water. In spring when streams tributary to a lake dump in much silt, spotted bass don't seem to avoid the areas. In fact, some of the best fishing comes at such times. I remember the milky flow of one stream I fished in Alabama. In some stretches it was downright muddy but most of the way it was reminiscent of glacial streams I've seen in the high-country West when fishing trout in early spring.

The fall fishing may be in clear water or the water may be roily from storms. Some of the larger spotted-bass streams offer excellent sport. I recall a magazine piece written by Charlie Elliott, southern field editor for *Outdoor Life* magazine and a very dear friend. He told of fishing the lower portion of the White River in Arkansas, in September. That month is of course still hot weather, but the lower White nowadays is no gin-clear trout stream at any season. The veteran spotted-bass anglers with whom Charlie went enlightened him as to their method of using twelve-foot (or longer) telescopic fiberglass poles with a four-foot length of stout nylon tied to the end, and with a white-hackled jig for a lure. They floated the river, keeping close to shore and dancing the jig in figure-eight configurations in small holes in debris or around the ends of logs or stumps. And they simply mopped up. Although readers may not wish to use exactly this method, it is certainly a hot tip on a general approach for such waters.

Many of the Arkansas and Oklahoma spotted-bass addicts prefer late May and early June, except in periods of high water. The fellows who showed Charlie how it's done by their interesting approach claimed wintertime (November-December) is one of the very hottest seasons. In fishing the Texas spotted-bass streams, and in Alabama, I discovered that almost every fish that would hit was close to the bank. Charlie Elliott's story about the White River confirmed this. Conversely, I have caught scads of smallmouths in streams, right out in the middle at the head or foot of a pool or on a long riffle.

Actually the spotted bass needs a lot more study by fishermen and by biologists. It deserves more specific attention than it gets, and it may be that certain waters, even stocked, would offer real bonanzas with it, if we knew more about it. Likewise there is not much that can be said about the how-to of fishing the other full-fledged bass species. The Guadalupe bass of Texas, very restricted in range, is only an incidental in any fisherman's catch and undoubtedly seldom recognized when caught. The Suwannee bass is so obscure in Florida that it is hardly recognized as a U.S. sport fish species and probably is too small to be of much importance anyway.

The redeye bass really deserves serious attention. Much is still to be learned about it, which seems incredible in our age of scientific and sporting progress. It is basically a stream fish of the Southeast, a sprightly fighter and a fish that feeds heavily on surface insects. I predict that one day a dedicated fly-fisherman will spend some time in, say, Georgia, possibly on the Flint River, which I have fished, and come up with some wondrous tales of big redeyes. A specialist who might desire such a project should make up his mind first to catch and identify this fish, then fish specifically for it, foregoing the temptation of the largemouths. A redeye of four to six pounds—and who knows, there may be larger ones—taken on a dry fly will be an experience some fortunate and persistent angler can tell about for the rest of his life.

CHAPTER FOURTEEN

Varied Methods and Approaches

TROLLING

Time was when trolling for bass was one of the accepted and most popular of fishing methods. It is still practiced to some extent but is definitely out of style nowadays, what with so much new knowledge of better ways. To troll successfully one must choose the water with care. Obviously it is not possible to troll a lure into the deep brush and the snags and many of the hiding places bass like most. It is feasible to troll along the edges of weed beds, along the edges of rock faces, or over ledges or points.

I recall visiting with and watching an expert native fisherman on Dale Hollow Lake in Tennessee who trolls across and along the points, using a deep-running plug. He did his trolling swiftly because he had to in order to force the lure deep and make it bump the bottom. This man was amazingly successful. His was a specialized method, dependent upon his intimate knowledge of the points where he fished. He knew that bass often lay at the ends of the points, or along the slopes on one side or the other.

However, as we have said at several places in this book, one should always keep in mind that bass are not long-distance chasers. I have actually watched a big muskellunge follow a lure for fifty yards or more, and then not make any attempt to strike it. But a bass is predominantly a lurker. You can observe how one will race ten or fifteen feet to a surface lure, but

189

except when bass are roaming in schools seeking schools of forage, they do little wide-scope roaming, and then seldom chase after a lure very far regardless of its speed. Thus, pinpoint presentation is by far the most important part of handling the lure, once you know where the bass is or may be. By "pinpoint" I don't necessarily mean dropping it right on top of the fish, but it must be near enough for the fish to become easily aware of by one or another of the senses. And if the lure gets away too far or too swiftly, the fish will simply give up the chase.

This is why trolling can never be as successful as casting. It is simply not possible except under specialized conditions of habitat to get the lure to the bass as efficiently. I have fished many days in shallow water where I'd drop a bug exactly into tiny palm-sized pockets in weeds or among lily pads. Or I'd drop the bug atop a log or a pad or even on shore and pull it off, fishing to individual fish—or at least to spots that I judged should contain a fish. The Tennessee angler trolling deep and swiftly of course got his lure near every bass that struck, too. But this was one of the few situations—fishing deep on the gravel or shale points—where he could avoid hang-ups. And his assumption was that by covering a lot of water swiftly—since he already knew the hangouts of the bass—he was certain to pass the lure near a number of fish. This is a bit of a shotgun method, but it will work.

In Florida I recall a slow stream I used to fish often, where trolling could be made unusually successful. Along each side of this swamp stream the water hyacinths and "lettuce" formed massive floating beds. There might be six feet or more of water under them. As all Deep South bass fishermen know, hordes of fish laze back under these shady roofs. By trolling gently right along the edge, which on this stream ran for some miles, a lure running below surface was unimpeded and could be seen easily by any bass lurking under the vegetation. I trolled slowly and with a fairly long line, although I doubt that the small motor bothered the fish any. I caught a good many bass. But I must confess that to me trolling is not very exciting. I like the action of the casting, and besides, trolling covers too much fishless water.

In lakes where trolling is feasible, that is, where cover is such that you can get the lure near the bass, there is a method practically unknown to bass men that can be very effective. As we've seen (in Chapter 8), on any given day the fish will lie, most of them, at the same depth, assuming that water temperature is fairly even over the lake, or the portion of it one is fishing. For the method I'll describe, which I learned some years ago not from a bass fisherman but from a kokanee expert in Montana, you need a stiff rod, preferably a regular saltwater boat rod, and reel to match, and a lead-core line. These lines can be purchased with color coding. That is, every so many feet—commonly five or ten—the line is a different color.

The lure is rigged with no sinker, but with a monofil leader tied to the heavy line. When trolling is begun, a speed is decided upon and must be kept constant. The rod, placed in a holder if possible, is set so that the tip is a known and constant distance above the surface. Let's say you have found that the temperature is proper at the ten-foot depth. When you begin learning the method, orient yourself by measuring the ten-foot depth over open bottom. Then troll at a given constant speed, and feel when the lure is bumping.

Instantly observe what color on the line is at the surface, and how much of that color extends above surface. You know that, with rod tip at the same height, boat moving at the same speed, when that color shows a certain amount above the surface your lure, far out behind, is at ten feet. By pulling up until the next color shows, you can raise the lure. By letting down a full color segment, you will lower it—not as much of course as the segment is long. But after a bit of practice you will learn how far out to let the lure, and how much difference a whole color segment or a portion of one makes. For those who love trolling and have water where it can be done with success, this is an exact method for placing a lure at any time at a known depth.

SNEAKING UP ON BASS

Although most of the bass fishing of today is on large impoundments, and much of it is either deep fishing or fishing long casts, there are times on all bass waters where a sneaky approach will outdo the usual. On my own lake we tried some experiments one time with me sitting on a high bluff watching bass in the clear water below, while a friend in a small boat did the fishing. By hand signals I could show him where the bass were. He let the boat drift in, and sitting down low on a seat made gentle casts. He spooked few fish and he caught several. Then we tried another spot, same operation, except the fisherman stood up. He spooked every bass.

Thus when short casts are to be made and bass are in shallow water, the crafty approach is called for. Most of today's modern bass boats have high seats, like barstools, from which the casting is done. Or the anglers stand to cast. This is fine for long casts and also for deep fishing. Contrary to the "safety" thinking of many, standing up in one of today's excellent boats, which might be termed "solid casting platforms," is not at all dangerous. In fact, some boats have a foredeck purposely arranged to allow the caster to stand on it. In a small craft on rough water an inept angler could fall in. But on small ponds, or while using regulation modern bass boats on big water, the high-seated or the stand-up caster is in little if any danger. If he feels he is, then a life jacket is called for and, as everyone knows, laws today require them on most waters.

At any rate, the big sneak is needed only when bass are very shallow, when the water is clear and especially when it is placid, and when the casts are to be short. At such times, the lower the fisherman's silhouette, the better. The boat should drift, or be moved gently with the small electric motor. The angler should make as little commotion with his casting as possible, just flip the lure out without a lot of arm waving. Even his mode of dress is important.

For example, we did other experiments using white shirts in one and camouflage clothing in another. Although as we've already noted (in Chapter 7) bass can see colors, the color of a man's clothing won't spook the bass but its *intensity* may call attention. A white or light-colored shirt is very obvious. Believe it or not, in the experiments we tried, when I wore full camo clothing right down to headnet and gloves, I spooked fewer fish at close range. A drifting boat may not in itself frighten fish, but overly obvious movement of the fisherman will. Full camo makes him only a kind of shapeless "blob." If he keeps low in the boat and keeps his arm movements low when casting, he is not likely to disturb the fish.

We tried camouflage not only in a boat but while making real stalks on fish that could be seen in clear water. When I moved very slowly, hunched or crouched, along a bank, the bass did not seem to know what I was. I even got into the water very slowly one time and got within a few feet of a good fish before it became disturbed enough to flee. I'm not suggesting that camo should be worn all the time. But it is a fact that manufacturers of modern fishing clothing have begun offering camo shirts, fishing vests, etc., for anglers. At the least, drab clothing should be worn when fishing short casts in the shallows.

Although dark glasses of any kind annoy me unutterably (I'm an exception to the rule), I readily admit that wearing Polaroids can be immensely helpful for shallow work. It is so much easier to see the fish, almost regardless of sun angle. Once you have spotted a bass, you can stalk it more easily because you know exactly where it is and how much it can see.

When making a sneak on bass, be ever mindful of shadows. When the sun is low it may throw a boat shadow or your shadow into the water where the fish can see it. Moving "people" shadows spook fish almost without fail. So will a rod shadow when water is clear, and so will the shadow of a lure sailing over the water, or of a line, especially a heavy fly line.

Nonetheless, a great advantage to an angler is to fish so that the sun is either behind him or at least quartering. There are two reasons. When you have to face the sun it is most uncomfortable, and you cannot see well where you are casting. But more than that, by placing the sun in the eyes of the bass, you have it at a disadvantage. To be sure, light rays are bent by refraction as they enter water, and thus dissipated to some extent. But in clear, shallow water that is smooth a fish facing the sun cannot see you anywhere near as well as it can if the sun is in your face or quartering across you from the front.

In low sun, early and late in the day, try to select the shallow short-cast spots so that the sun slants quartering from behind over your shoulder. This way you can avoid throwing your shadow or a boat shadow into the visual field of the bass, an dyou also have the fish looking at least partially toward the light. Another old trick is to keep the sun behind you but keep your craft and you in the shadow of a bluff or shoreside trees. The bass will almost always be in shadows looking out. If you are fishing to them from shadow, you are that much less likely to spook them.

In my opinion a fisherman in shallows—and elsewhere, for that matter —who will stop his boat and fish the area within reach is less likely to frighten fish than one who keeps always on the move. If you look around in tackle stores you will find some little gadgets that probably will be called "brush anchors" or some such name. These are spring-type metal clamps, tied to a short length of stout nylon cord or small rope, that can be fastened to brush to hold a boat. Ease into a shadowy spot, clamp the boat snug with these "anchors" from two places, cover the water carefully, and then move on.

This assumes, naturally, that there is brush or timber to hook up to. In so many of the big impoundments there is timber everywhere. And incidentally, a caution we've overlooked so far in speaking of drowned timber is to take no chances with it during storms. Get out of it! On a lake like the famed Sam Rayburn or Toledo Bend, for example, forests, literally, of huge trees thrust from the surface. In a wind storm blowdowns can kill you. In an electrical storm any tall tree may be struck. Flee the timber if a storm is coming.

BANK SNEAKS, WADING, AND FLOATS

What a bass undoubtedly sees first when a boat fisherman bears down toward it is the hulk of the boat bottom. As it nears, the bass then may see the angler. In a choppy surface, boat outlines (and everything else) are broken and this assists in covering the angler. In any shallow-water situation a fisherman can get by with shorter casts in a chop than he can on a flat surface. The rule is to cast long when it's flat—if this is possible. But there are numerous situations where it may not be, in close nooks and crannies that are certain to be bass-filled but perhaps impossible to get a bass boat into. In fact, in many wonderful expanses of standing timber the big bass boats never allow one to fish some of the most intriguing spots of all. One can't get to them. This is where the bank sneak, or some sort of float, can be used.

Of course bank fishing on a stream or a pond or even at a large lake may sometimes be necessary. And at those times the fish may well be in shallow, calm water where they are terrifically spooky. Some classic "stalking" situations can arise at such times. For example, I recall fishing old strip-mine pits in southeastern Kansas, where some really sensational bass fishing is available. But I soon learned that in these clear waters with steep banks thrusting up from each pond, the approach is most important. A local angler much envied for his success by other locals allowed me to watch how he did it. He dressed in full camouflage, even to headnet and gloves, slunk slowly along the water's edge, and then hunkered low, making casts from a squatting position.

Indeed, stepping softly to avoid vibrations, and keeping in shadows and making oneself inconspicuous is mandatory when it is necessary to fish from shore, at least when the fishing is short range and in shallow water. Wading can actually be a better practice, where it is possible. I grew up wading streams, fishing for trout, and when I fished for other species it was natural to wade. Much of my early adult bass fishing was done by wading shoreline waters of lakes. Some are of course too soft-bottomed, and some are too deep. But many a good spot can be selected, and this is an unusually successful manner of fishing.

For one thing, if you can get into fairly deep wading water, up to the hips or waist, the remainder of you is so low to the surface that you are difficult for fish to see. It is also surprising how a wader who moves very carefully, and slowly, placing each boot in slow motion, doesn't seem to disturb fish. I have stood very still, in shaded water, casting for bass and panfish, and had several of each cavorting right around my boots. Probably this is because the fish don't see the "whole fisherman." Wading is also a great lesson in fishing a piece of water with complete concentration. One time in a northern lake I got into a position, fishing for smallmouths, where I could go no farther. I was forced to stand still, but the surrounding area looked good and I decided to fish every bit of it. I caught ten bass right from that spot. Had I been able to move on, I'd have fished less carefully and probably have caught less.

There is in fact a great deal of enjoyment in wade-fishing. Many anglers follow this method in wadable streams, but few seem to realize how deadly it can be along lakeshores. Certainly the fishing is confined to fairly shallow waters, except where there are sharp drop-offs that can be reached. To add an extension, a surprising number of southern and southwestern bass fishermen use tube floats. Most readers will know what these are—a big inflated inner tube that has a canvas cover and a seat in the middle, with leg holes, and with as a rule a pair of suspenders that go over the shoulders. A number of these floats are commercially made. Some have a tackle pocket and a place to tie up a stringer.

The seat should be low enough so the upper part of the body doesn't overbalance the tube float. One firm in Oklahoma, I recall, even builds fins that are fastened to one's wader legs—chest-high waders are worn. These are a great help in moving around over the water when it is too deep to touch bottom. But with the suspenders one can wade along in a shallow water, the tube hanging from the shoulder harness, then keep right on going out where the boot feet don't touch.

These floats allow one to get into all sorts of places a boat cannot go. In the beginning they were utilized mostly by pond fishermen, in the thousands of ranch tanks throughout the southern half of the U.S. But later astute bassers began to carry a tube float and harness along in a boat. As

I write I visualize a piece of water that reaches back into a narrow cove, too deep to wade, and so dense with drowned trees that a boat can't get into it. Often there is exciting evidence of bass feeding back in the timber. A friend with whom I fished this water a lot a few years ago would invariably carry his tube in the boat. When we got to this spot he'd have me put him ashore—the safest way to get launched. He'd then move along the deep edge and finally into the trees, making short casts and maneuvering easily. Invariably he came out with a heavy stringer of bass.

There are many uses for these floats. Nowadays there are also others that are seeing a lot of use here and there. There is a foam-plastic float built in my state that is capable of carrying several hundred pounds. You sit on it and put your feet and legs to the knees through a cut-out area up front. There is a small livewell built into each side of this float. These can be used for bait or to keep the catch, or tackle can be put into them. There are depressions on the deck into which rods can be laid. Some anglers use swim fins to paddle these floats. Others use a small wooden paddle or their feet.

The one I have is of fair size, roughly four by six feet. It even has a plank stanchion at rear on which a small motor—three horse or less—can be mounted. The use of these floats is one of the new looks in modern bass fishing. A number of anglers carry such floats along, fish reachable water from their boat, then transfer to the float for close-in work in places that look especially good but are difficult to reach in a large craft.

NIGHT FISHING

In several places in this book fishing at night has been mentioned casually. Night fishing is a sport in its own right, wholly different in atmosphere and "feel" from daytime fishing. Where bass are concerned it has a very definite place and use. I do not believe in night fishing for bass during winter months, except possibly in Florida. There is no real need for it. And during all seasons when bass are lying deep and feeding deep they can be caught in daytime just as easily. But in a good many waters during the hottest weather the fish may stay deep and feed little during daylight hours, yet move surfaceward or inshore to feed when darkness comes, cruising the shallows.

This is common with smallmouths that have gravel bars available on which crayfish are abundant. It is also common throughout the South where some very big trophy bass cruise at dusk and after full dark in shallow places. Some anglers wade at night, where that is feasible. Most use a boat. It is mandatory to have calm water, or at least it is easier and more pleasant to fish at night on calm water. Some night-fishing enthusiasts use underwater plugs and plastic worms. Certainly these work well. I have mentioned earlier how some experts fish in winter at night in the cold of the mid-South. But in my opinion this isn't really necessary. Night fishing is made to order for surface lures. These offer the most sport because you must fish by "sound" and strike at the splash, and it is a warm-weather endeavor.

Probably the most important part of any night-fishing technique is knowing the water intimately. It is best to select one bay, or one point—an expanse of modest size—and come to know every foot of it. By selecting such a block of water known to contain bass and known to offer good feeding conditions for them, one can be oriented constantly and not have to blunder about.

During the best of the night-fishing months (summer) some light will linger until very late. The sharp night fisherman won't use a flashlight at all unless he absolutely has to. A light shone upon shallows will frighten fish, and it will also slow up one's night vision. By staying in near-dark for a couple of hours, it is surprising what one can see. The boat should be drifted or paddled noiselessly. Casts should not be indiscriminate, but pinpoint to places and small areas known by previous study to be productive. A lure, whether surface or underwater, should be worked very slowly. There is no rush in this game, and you don't have to coax a fish. It will either take or not. Some of the shyest bass become real suckers at night. On waters that are especially clear, summer evenings give one a chance to catch those big fish that seem uncatchable during daylight.

Some years ago I had what I consider the most efficient schooling in night fishing that it is possible to acquire. It was not for bass, but for big brown trout. But the little tricks of this trade apply equally as well to bass fishing, and I later applied them. The trout fishing was with a fly rod. In my estimation this is the perfect tool for night bass fishing, for one vital reason. Backlashes with casting tackle seem to come more often at night, probably because the caster is not used to fishing blind. And such troubles are abominable when a light has to be used to untangle the mess. Fly lines are not likely to get tangled and are easily straightened out without a light if they do.

What several of us worked out on the brown trout was a methodical technique for knowing what we were doing without, so to speak, having even to have our eyes open. No fish on earth is more difficult than a big brown. But, oh, can they be gullible after dark! So we would spend summer evenings sitting by what appeared to me a good hole on a stream, just listening. If an outsize brown lived in the hole, it would almost certainly give itself away eventually with some wild feeding splashes after dark. Browns are notorious for this.

Once we'd established that a bruiser was resident, we then went to the pool by daylight and studied it carefully. We selected where we would stand to cast. If we were going to fish a big bushy dry fly upstream, we knew that when a fish took it would run downstream toward us. Were there any snags below the standing spot? We finally got into the hole, in daylight, and "cast it out," thoroughly. By so doing we learned exactly how far was the maximum cast. If there were good spots within shorter distance, we memorized those, too.

I used to tie a wisp of wool yarn onto my fly line very snugly at the spots which would be coming *into my left hand*—which handled the line, of course—at the varying cast distances. It is also easy for a fly fisherman to memorize precisely the *load* that is put upon his rod at any given cast length. You can feel it and you know with surprising accuracy how far out the lure is. It is much easier to do this with fly equipment than with casting or spinning rod.

Now when the night of the big trial came, we'd wait until full dark and preferably until we heard the big trout splash. Then with utmost caution we'd ease into the pool, to the standing spot. Casting and fishing by feel and sound, I have taken many a big brown that was simply uncatchable by daylight. Exactly the same techniques can be used for bass at night, whether it is on a smallmouth stream or on a lake or pond. It can be done from a boat or by wading. The whole secret is in knowing the water, every foot of it, knowing where obstructions are, knowing where you are every minute, and how far you can cast and which spots are likely to be best.

The trouble with night fishing is that it can become hypnotic. Again I see little point in fishing plastic worms on the bottom at night. After dark, fishing at its best is mostly a "dog days" operation. At least that is when it becomes most necessary, even though it certainly can be successful at any time of year.

WACKY INNOVATIONS AND OTHERS

Although we have examined in this book the modern look of bass fishing, I cannot help having a kind thought for the past, and I do believe we can come to understand much that is new by examining history. Out of the history of bass fishing there are a number of wacky approaches that have locally been absolute killers. And there are some very solid, if unusual, methods exceedingly difficult to criticize, from which anyone can learn.

I personally have vast respect for the angler who, in a difficult situation, solves the problem heroically. For instance, I vividly remember my introduction to bass fishing on Reelfoot Lake in western Tennessee. As mentioned, this lake was formed by an earthquake in 1811 that changed the course of the Mississippi River. It is a sprawling, shallow body of water studded with cypress trees, with enormous stumps below water, and with a covering most of the time of great bonnets and other vegetation that one not used to it would think impossible to fish "through."

Invited for a few days there at the cottage of a rather wealthy man from Nashville, I showed up with my fly rod, an utterly worthless tool, I was to discover, for that time of year and for bass, on Reelfoot. Even the boats, born to the lake, were wonderful oddments. The oars were hinged so that when you pulled they actually shoved the boat in the opposite direction, so you could see where you were going and avoid the obstacles. They used small inboard motors and there was a steel plate beneath that enclosed the propeller. Thus we rode over the top of many a stump.

The tackle used by the natives—and my guide—was a short, steel rod stiff as a piece of oil-country sucker rod. The reel was a single-action almost as large as a dinner plate. The lure was a weedless spoon with a rubber skirt pulled on the hook, but reversed. This was cast without any regard whatever for the impossible vegetation. Some of those bonnets were two feet across. The lure was allowed to sink a bit and was reeled in simple fashion so that it dodged stems, hit stems, crawled over pads, fell into pockets. And whammo! Every now and then a bass would bust it so water flew and the bonnets were rent. The angler laid back as if handling a recalcitrant mule and literally hauled the bass to and into the boat.

I have often wondered if this specialized approach could not be applied somewhere else, perhaps with modifications, and become useful. And then there was the baby nipple experience. A good many years ago I spent a summer at Buckeye Lake, Ohio. At that time I was in a far different business, in fact I was writing music for a name band and doing six coast-to-coast broadcasts each week from a pavilion there, the longest remote at that time in the U.S. Radio, obviously, since then there was no television.

Fishing even at that time was my first love. And that spring the locals around Buckeye demonstrated to me how to obliterate bass. In those days there was no special stigma in using a cane pole. These people had them. I went with these mentors to a drugstore in a nearby small town.

"Cliff," one of them said to the clerk, "you got a batch of white rubber nipples for baby bottles? Maybe a dozen?"

Cliff guffawed, "You don't mean to tell me!"

"Aw, shut up!"

Cliff had the nipples. We went to the lake. Into the bottle end of a nipple the eye end of a treble hook was inserted. The eye was forced upward and thrust through the upper, or nipple, end and the treble hooks were brought up outside and around the lower, bottle-capping end. The hook eye was now tied to a length of ordinary braided fishing line—the old salt-and-pepper type—roughly the same length as the long cane pole, to which of course the line was tied.

Now one man paddled the boat carefully along shore, selecting sunken logs and stumps and other cover. The pole man reached out and let the nipple down above bassy-appearing lairs. The fish were in the shallows at this season. As the bottom of the nipple touched water a deft motion of the pole made it suck the surface and it was danced with this suction noise. Suddenly a big bass smashed it and engulfed it. During that first morning these gentlemen simply loaded their stringers with big bass.

I tried to copy the method and believe me I discovered it is an art. Probably we don't need to use this sort of approach today, but I hope recording it here is meaningful. I think the fundamental moral is that there is always something to be learned about any subject and bass fishing is no exception. There are times when application of the same general principles used in some of these old-time wacky approaches may furnish a modern angler with a brilliant flash of insight. Imagination is the greatest fishing lure.

When I was a kid—and I sort of shudder nowadays to recall this—an older lad who was a real woodsie showed me how to make a surefire bait of a small frog in the once-lovely but now man-ruined Flint River in Michigan. He caught the frog, selected a hollow grass stem, thrust it into the frog's rectum, and blew the creature up. The frog could not expel the air. When hooked through the lip and tossed onto a pool in the river, it floated, and tried to swim ashore. That action brought it to the attention of a bass, which instantly struck. I don't suppose that young fellow thought of this as a cruel trick. He was simply doing his best to catch a fish, and if the cruelty can be overlooked, it must be admitted it was clever.

We have mentioned bait only occasionally throughout this book because the fact is that modern lures and methods have made bait for the most part unnecessary. Nonetheless, bass baits, of which there are dozens, are still as deadly as ever. I don't think much time needs to be spent on the subject here. But I must mention that an old man, long gone to his fishing reward, who taught me some of my first fishing tricks, showed me how to hook a crawdad through the tail, cast it out on a horrible old ratchety outfit I had, and let the sinker pull it to bottom. He wanted me to drop the bait not among the rocks on bottom but in a clear place *near* the rocks, a distance not too discouraging to the unfortunate crawdad. Then it would vainly try to get to the cover of the rocks. And that motion, noticed by a smallmouth, beckoned it to the hook.

Nightcrawlers, spring lizards (salamanders), hellgrammites, and minnows still serve mightily to bring bass to the boat. The catalpa worm, the larva of a butterfly and common in parts of the Midwest, is a nastily juicy item to handle, especially when turned *wrong side out*. Ohioans discovered many years ago that this is one of the most deadly of bluegill baits, and when two or three are pulled like the sleeve of a coat wrongside out and strung on a hook they are formidable as a bait for bass. Apparently the innards, floating off juicily, send out an irresistible scent call.

Skittering, and a host of other names by which noisily hauling a lure across the surface has been called, has for years been a vicious decimator of southern bass. Mostly this is accomplished by country gentlemen using long cane poles. I knew one who would first lash the surface with pole tip, to "wake 'em up." Then with a lure on his line, some sort of metal spoon as a rule, he'd "figure-eight" the surface and wind the lure dancing among the bushes. Don't knock it! Casters can perhaps use this theme sometime, with modulations, to save a lost day.

And so it is that ingenuity, in the last analysis, modern or otherwise, is the most admirable trait a bass angler can exhibit. We should be, in our age, as well informed and filled with up-to-date lore as we can be. But we should still not overlook the past. I could not end this book in a more fitting manner than to tell you that every time you decide (along with me) that you have discovered precisely and mathematically how to catch every bass in the lake, or every big bass you need to win a tournament or to feed your ego—you should sit for a moment in your boat and take stock. Will it work?

Maybe. But the most lovely aspect of bass fishing is that maybe it won't. Otherwise, why go? Let me tell you—if someone demanded today that I go out and catch a trophy bass, gave me my choice of places and methods, but put a premium on time, do you know how I would, without even a moment's thought, decide to try? In order to make my point, let me take you back in time and relate a story from out of possibly one of the most dramatic and inspiring bass-fishing periods of my lifetime, and that takes in at this point very close to half a century since as a kid I caught my first one.

I was in Florida and I was fishing with a young Negro guide named George Mobley. I think George thought that I would be trying to tell him what to do, but he soon discovered that he was wrong. We got along famously and after he had let me fish my way—several times—and I had caught bass aplenty of so-so proportions, George said to me:

"Would you like to catch a big one?"

I was astonished. "I already have," I said. "Isn't eight pounds big?"

George laughed. He said, "Let's go out this evenin', after supper. We'll fish the dusk and we'll catch us a big 'un."

So we went. I had tackle stacked six deep. Now I must interrupt to explain that previously George had taught me how to use a casting rod, with a bobber about four feet up the line, and a minnow with no sinker on the hook below. He had shown me how to hurl this out along the edge of floating hyacinth beds. The minnow would swim around and attract a bass lurking back under. The bass would grab the minnow and run and George would tell me when to snug up and when to belt the bass. And as I've said we had taken fish to eight pounds.

And so this evening when I met George at the dock we zoomed up the lake to a quiet cove and he dug into the live well. What he hauled forth was a fish that at first I thought should go on the stringer. It was a Florida shiner at least a foot long. These Florida minnows—yes, they're of that family—smell horrible to a human. George caught them by baiting a spot with bread and using a cast net.

"Why in the name of the Almighty," I said, "are we using this brute for bait? It'd choke a bass."

"Just take the rod," he replied, "and get it out there, any old way."

He had selected a small pocket among hyacinth beds and already I could see in the dusk a wake or two of cruising fish. I hurled out the foot-long bait fish. It swam around. Circle after circle. Suddenly there was a wake coursing toward it.

"Pull in!" George commanded. "That there's a grinnel." This was a local term for a bowfin.

But before I could move the huge bait, another wake sailed in. The huge, smelly shiner was literally engulfed.

George was instantly overwhelmed with excitement. "Let 'im run! Let 'im run!" he counseled.

I let him run. And presently George barked, "Slam 'im."

When this wild slice of excitement was over, full dusk had closed into darkness around us—and we had in the boat a bass of better than thirteen pounds!

It is difficult to argue with that variety of success. It can still be accomplished today. Bass fishing in that respect has not changed. Yet I cannot renounce the new knowledge because it has proven for some years now so fantastically successful. In closing, I would say, go modern—but look also at history. Be tolerant. I am positive today's methods hold the most promise for the majority. But Dr. Henshall also caught many bass. Put yesterday and today together. This is how the ultimate in expertness evolves. The bass fisherman who is unwilling to learn from the past probably won't learn much from the present, and the dead end of that is stagnation. This is too lively a sport to deserve such a future!

Index